Online Teaching and Learning

DATE DUE

PRACTICAL GUIDES FOR LIBRARIANS

ⓖ About the Series

This innovative series written and edited for librarians by librarians provides authoritative, practical information and guidance on a wide spectrum of library processes and operations.

Books in the series are focused, describing practical and innovative solutions to a problem facing today's librarian and delivering step-by-step guidance for planning, creating, implementing, managing, and evaluating a wide range of services and programs.

The books are aimed at beginning and intermediate librarians needing basic instruction/guidance in a specific subject and at experienced librarians who need to gain knowledge in a new area or guidance in implementing a new program/service.

ⓖ About the Series Editor

The **Practical Guides for Librarians** series was conceived by and is edited by M. Sandra Wood, MLS, MBA, AHIP, FMLA, Librarian Emerita, Penn State University Libraries.

M. Sandra Wood was a librarian at the George T. Harrell Library, The Milton S. Hershey Medical Center, College of Medicine, Pennsylvania State University, Hershey, PA, for over 35 years, specializing in reference, educational, and database services. Ms. Wood worked for several years as a Development Editor for Neal-Schuman Publishers.

Ms. Wood received a MLS from Indiana University and a MBA from the University of Maryland. She is a Fellow of the Medical Library Association and served as a member of MLA's Board of Directors from 1991 to 1995. Ms. Wood is founding and current editor of *Medical Reference Services Quarterly*, now in its 35th volume. She also was founding editor of the *Journal of Consumer Health on the Internet* and the *Journal of Electronic Resources in Medical Libraries* and served as editor/co-editor of both journals through 2011.

Titles in the Series

1. *How to Teach: A Practical Guide for Librarians* by Beverley E. Crane

2. *Implementing an Inclusive Staffing Model for Today's Reference Services: A Practical Guide for Librarians* by Julia K. Nims, Paula Storm, and Robert Stevens

3. *Managing Digital Audiovisual Resources: A Practical Guide for Librarians* by Matthew C. Mariner

4. *Outsourcing Technology: A Practical Guide for Librarians* by Robin Hastings

5. *Making the Library Accessible for All: A Practical Guide for Librarians* by Jane Vincent

Online Teaching and Learning

A Practical Guide for Librarians

Beverley E. Crane

PRACTICAL GUIDES FOR LIBRARIANS, NO. 29

ROWMAN & LITTLEFIELD
Lanham • Boulder • New York • London

Published by Rowman & Littlefield
A wholly owned subsidiary of The Rowman & Littlefield Publishing Group, Inc.
4501 Forbes Boulevard, Suite 200, Lanham, Maryland 20706
www.rowman.com

Unit A, Whitacre Mews, 26-34 Stannary Street, London SE11 4AB

British Library Cataloguing in Publication Information Available

Library of Congress Cataloging-in-Publication Data Available

ISBN 978-1-4422-6716-9 (pbk. : alk. paper)
ISBN 978-1-4422-6717-6 (electronic)

♾™ The paper used in this publication meets the minimum requirements of American National Standard for Information Sciences—Permanence of Paper for Printed Library Materials, ANSI/NISO Z39.48-1992.

Printed in the United States of America

Contents

Figures and Tables

Figures

⊚ Tables

Preface

Online learning is becoming mainstream across the country. Online courses are being taken by more students in higher education, and certain states even require K–12 students to take at least one online course prior to graduation. Businesses are employing more online training to employees and customers, and public libraries post materials and resources on their websites.

Across the country, libraries are forging a new identity, prompted largely by libraries' expanded role as they re-establish their relevance. As a result, all libraries—academic, public, special, and K–12—are being drawn more and more into the online teaching and learning environment. Online learning, often called elearning, virtual learning, or distance education, is gaining traction in all library venues and providing new opportunities for libraries.

When librarians decide to enter the online training and learning world, they face new challenges. They need to be knowledgeable in skills such as teaching, designing, planning, creating, and assessing online courses; developing self-paced materials; promoting their offerings; adapting to new approaches to teaching through technology; and working closely with students and patrons at a distance. Thus, librarians are often faced with major tasks so that they can assimilate this way of learning that is different from face-to-face instruction.

Online Teaching and Learning: A Practical Guide for Librarians puts it all together to provide what librarians must consider as they prepare for this new challenge and opportunity. It provides a comprehensive guide to help librarians create online teaching and learning programs that incorporate library services as part of their program. It is also designed to instruct librarians on how to employ strategies necessary to build a virtual library environment and teach skills required to meet the needs of online learners. As the educational landscape changes with blended and online learning taking center stage, new and established librarians need a guide to inform them of skills they will need and show them how to create the resources for their new online audience.

This book offers ideas, step-by-step instruction, and resources for all librarians—veterans and those new to the profession. They are based on learning and instructional theory so that those who have not had this background will know why they are creating a module in a certain way, teaching students using a particular approach, or developing a specific learning object. With the pedagogy and design elements offered in part 1, and examples and step-by-step instructions described in part 2, librarians will be able to identify and enhance their roles and use their own creativity, knowledge of research, and information literacy. As a result, in part 3, they will be able to create, present, and assess their own unique personalized online instruction to meet the needs of a diverse twenty-first-century audience, no matter in which type of library they are employed.

⊚ Organization

Online Teaching and Learning: A Practical Guide for Librarians is divided into three parts, each with a particular focus.

- **Part 1** provides the theoretical framework on learning that ultimately influences practice. It includes a range of learning theories to use as the basis for content and strategies. It also focuses on design, an important aspect of creating online instruction.
- **Part 2** describes the process of creating online instruction, including design and instructional tips.
- **Part 3** puts the theory into practice. Library examples demonstrate how online teaching and learning is taking place in different types of libraries. Step-by-step detail explains how librarians can create online courses and materials on their own. Included are handouts, strategies, and exercises.

⊚ Part 1: Theory into Practice

Part 1 supplies the basis in theory that ultimately influences practice. There are numerous learning theories so the focus here will be on those that influence online learning and that are appropriate for your audience and the purpose for creating online teaching and learning.

- Chapter 1 introduces the concepts of online teaching and learning: what it is, a brief background on learning theory as it relates to online learning, characteristics of effective online teachers, instructor roles, benefits and challenges of online instruction, and differences between face-to-face and online teaching.
- Chapter 2 describes instructional design theory, its importance, and how it relates to the categories of online learning (synchronous and asynchronous).

⊚ Part 2: Creating Online Instruction

Part 2 explores how to create an online course—describing components and stepping through the process using a model on the topic of information literacy. Design and instructional tips for creating other types of online instruction are also given. Chapters 3 through 5 explain the phases in the process to consider when developing online teaching and learning.

- Chapter 3 begins with preplanning and planning the learning involved in online instruction, emphasizing audience and purpose, goals and objectives, communication, engagement, and motivation.

- Chapter 4 explains design principles and elements to consider when developing an online course. It also describes components to include in an online course.
- Chapter 5 demonstrates how to create, implement, and disseminate the instruction online. Included are considerations about content, materials, strategy, collaboration, and interaction. It also analyzes assessment and explores reflection upon the course and its outcomes. Technology and how it is integral to online learning is also covered.

⑥ Part 3: Practical Examples for Public, Academic, Special, and K–12 Libraries

Part 3 focuses on practical online teaching and learning applications appropriate for all types of libraries and learning situations. Each application showcases examples and includes a step-by-step model with features for librarians to consider when they create their own online instruction. Also provided are sample worksheets, activity handouts for learners, exercises, and links to other resources based on the topic under discussion.

Chapters 6 through 10 focus on applications that demonstrate online teaching and learning, and chapter 11 discusses what's to come.

- Chapter 6 begins with examples of librarian models of asynchronous teaching and learning. A detailed, step-by-step process describes an asynchronous virtual on-demand course that can be used in a public library. Tips for creating asynchronous self-paced materials are also given.
- Chapter 7 begins with illustrations of embedded librarianship in academic and special libraries. Discussed are the different roles a librarian can play in an embedded setting and a description of how to get started in an embedded librarian's role. A step-by-step example illustrates the librarian's role in an academic embedded course where the librarian assumes an equal partnership with faculty.
- Chapter 8 focuses on blended learning in a K–12 library environment. It also provides steps and tips showing how to teach a blended class (e.g., topic creation, delivery, assessment, reflection).
- Chapter 9 describes flipped teaching and learning, another form of blended learning. Detailed instructions include how technology fits into the learning, considerations, and tips when using this approach.
- Chapter 10 provides examples of MOOCs (massive open online courses) and suggests ways librarians can take a lead role in this latest online teaching and learning environment.
- Chapter 11 looks at the future of online teaching and learning and roles where librarians may partner with others, as well as lead this online revolution.

Designed for experienced librarians, librarians new to the profession, and library school students, *Online Teaching and Learning: A Practical Guide for Librarians* provides a comprehensive framework that encompasses all aspects of planning, designing, creating, implementing, and assessing online learning for all types of libraries, including public, academic, special, and K–12. It also provides a valuable guide for teachers, administrators, and other educators.

Acknowledgments

Thanks to educators in academic and K–12 classrooms and libraries, as well as public and special libraries, who have taken leading roles in online teaching and learning. These pioneers serve as role models for faculty, librarians, students, and trainers who have now stepped into this growing educational environment. With the latest technology available, professional development for educators is often free online so that educators—veterans and those new to the profession—have opportunities to learn from the best worldwide. Their efforts and the programs and resources they have and will create continue to help others as they pursue online teaching and learning. Thanks to those who permitted sharing of examples of the work they have accomplished in this book. Their ideas will be helpful as you begin your own online journey so that you, too, can share your newly gained expertise with others.

Thanks again to Sandy Wood, my editor at Rowman & Littlefield, a talented librarian and wonderful professional editor—now through technology, an online friend. As always, patient and helpful, she has kept me on track and provided valuable suggestions and advice.

THEORY INTO PRACTICE

TODAY, LIBRARIES ARE BEING called upon to offer different kinds of online learning to their patrons, students, and employees. For example, librarians are now requested to partner with faculty as embedded librarians taking active roles in academic courses. Special librarians are offering webinars to employees of their organizations in all parts of the world. K–12 teacher librarians are demonstrating and instructing teachers and students in technology at their schools, and public librarians are offering virtual courses, on-demand sessions, and online self-paced materials to patrons who need help on a variety of topics, such as interviewing skills, information literacy, and technology, to name a few.

These new online service requests require librarians to demonstrate competencies they have not been trained in or ever thought they might be doing when they began their library careers. In 2014, Lucy Green and Stephanie Jones conducted a survey of librarians "to uncover their attitudes toward online learning and teaching. While 80 percent had experienced online environments as learners, they did not have instructional experience, and 60 percent of the respondents said they had no formal preparation to teach" (2014: E14). Thus, librarians are often faced with a steep learning curve to embody this way of learning that is different from face-to-face instruction, which they may or may not have delivered.

The shift to online learning brings with it benefits that you will explore throughout this book. A listing of ten benefits from an article by Tom Vander Ark (2015) points out ways digital learning can change teaching and learning, both formally and informally, for educators, students, and library patrons:

- **Personalized learning.** Digital learning provides opportunities for students to learn at their own pace and the ability to customize it to the needs of each student.
- **Expanded learning opportunities.** The ability to learn in a worldwide community opens the doors of a classroom offering authentic, diverse learning opportunities, including MOOCs (massive open online courses) taught to thousands by instructors at renowned universities.

- **High-engagement learning.** Using games and other technologies to facilitate learning brings with it learners motivated as active participants in their own learning experiences.
- **Competency-based learning.** Learners demonstrate mastery of what they know with individualized progress models to learn at their own pace.
- **Assessment for learning.** Continuous feedback and data collected from assessment within technological systems enables students to track their progress to focus on areas needing improvement.
- **Collaborative learning.** Social learning systems enable educators to create and manage groups, and technologies such as Google Docs make collaborative authoring easy whether at a local library or one across the world.
- **Quality learning products.** Using digital tools, students can participate in project-based learning and share them with public audiences through presentations, publications, and portfolios.
- **Open educational resources.** More equitable access to free materials and content can save money and make sharing possible.
- **Relevant and regularly updated content.** Learners can benefit from constantly updated content in scientific and medical changes; current, real-time news; business opportunities; and more.
- **Learning for educators.** Through online learning, educators have more opportunities for personalized learning at free online conferences and with professional learning communities (PLCs) where they can ask questions and share with a global community.

Advantages like these have influenced the growth of online teaching and learning. Examples of libraries that have implemented online teaching and learning will be explored throughout the rest of this book to give you ideas for implementing these types of learning situations and materials at your own libraries.

Part 1 provides the basis in theory of teaching and learning that ultimately influences practice. Chapter 1 includes a definition, importance in today's society, benefits and challenges, and categories and types of online learning with examples to illustrate each. Chapter 2 delves into aspects of instructional design, an important component of creating online learning.

References

Green, Lucy, and Stephanie Jones. 2014. "Instructional Partners in Digital Library Learning Spaces." *Knowledge Quest* 42, no. 4 (March/April): E11–E17.

Vander Ark, Tom. 2015. "The Shift to Digital Learning: 10 Benefits." Getting Smart. November 6. http://gettingsmart.com/2015/11/the-shift-to-digital-learning-10-benefits/.

Refresher on Learning Theory

IF YOU ARE TO BE AN INTEGRAL PART OF TEACHING AND LEARNING at your library or as a teacher, you must know the fundamentals and principles of how both adults and children learn. So, what is learning theory? What are the different theories postulated by educators and psychologists on how adults and children learn, and why are they important to online teaching and learning? Chapter 1 introduces the concepts of online teaching and learning, offers a brief background on learning theory as it relates to online learning, identifies characteristics of effective online instructors and the roles they assume, points out benefits and challenges of online instruction, and discusses differences between face-to-face and online teaching.

What Is Learning?

Learning is the process of "acquiring new or modifying existing knowledge, behaviors, skills, values, or preferences and may involve synthesizing different types of information"

(Schacter, Gilbert, and Wegner, 2011: 264). It occurs throughout your lifetime. From learning to walk and talk as a child to how to get along with friends to playing the piano, kicking a soccer ball, or using an iPad, you are increasing your knowledge and skills every day. Your learning builds on your experiences and changes as you grow and mature.

A definition on *Wikipedia* (2016) states that learning theories are "conceptual frameworks describing how information is absorbed, processed, and retained during learning. Cognitive, emotional, and environmental influences, as well as prior experience, all play a part in how understanding, or a world view, is acquired or changed and knowledge and skills retained." Review a comprehensive list of learning theories and their definitions at http://www.learning-theories.com/.

Information on how children and adults learn comes from researchers who study these practices, such as B. F. Skinner, Jean Piaget, Jerome Bruner, David Kolb, Carl Rogers, and Malcolm Knowles. Each expert looks at learning from a different perspective, and ideas from one researcher build on the work of the others. The briefs that follow outline theories based on behaviorism, cognitivism, constructivism, and humanism. These and definitions of different types of online or elearning you will look at later provide a basis to contemplate as you begin your online teaching and learning journey.

ⓖ General Learning Theories

To create successful learning experiences, it is necessary to define how learning takes place. Pedagogy, or how children learn, differs from andragogy, how adults learn, in important ways. Research on learning over the years has also brought about significant changes in how educators teach. Table 1.1 summarizes important differences among some major theories in areas of knowledge, learners, learning, and the teacher's role. Note the continuum moves from authoritative, directive behavior by the instructor and passive response from the learner in behaviorist methodology to a more facilitative approach by the teacher who focuses on a more personal involvement by the learner in a humanistic approach.

Table 1.1. Theories of Learning

	BEHAVIORIST: SKINNER	COGNITIVIST: PIAGET	CONSTRUCTIONIST: BRUNER	EXPERIENTIALIST: KOLB	HUMANIST: ROGERS
Knowledge	Stimulus—response—reinforcement	Active from real world	Active based on current/past experiences	Based on reflection	Relevant to real-world events
Learners	Passive recipients	Construct knowledge	Construct knowledge based on past experiences	Reflect on what see, hear, touch	Personally involved in learning process
Learning	Programmatic repeated acts	Builds on prior knowledge	Focus on real-world problems	Achieved by doing	Self-initiated
Teacher's Role	Authoritative, directive	Coach, mediator, facilitator	Coach, mediator, facilitator	Facilitator providing opportunities for experimentation	Coach, facilitator providing nonthreatening environment

Learning Differences between Children and Adults

The terms "pedagogy," a child-centered teaching approach, and "andragogy," an adult-centered way of teaching, focus on helping children and adults learn. Educational research prior to 1950 concentrated on children's learning, and little was known about how adults learn. However, specific characteristics affect adult motivation, as well as their learning ability, and these traits are different from those of children. Knowing them when creating elearning is vital to engage and motivate adults.

Malcolm Knowles developed an educational theory specifically related to the ways adults learn. He noted that adults bring their prior experiences, values, and expectations to their learning. According to Knowles (1984), characteristics of adult learners include the following:

- Adults are mainly self-motivated and self-directed and learn better through experience, preferring active participation. They like to take responsibility for decisions, so it is important for them to have control over their learning. Self-assessment, a peer relationship, and subtle support from the instructor, as well as diverse learning options, are important practices in the course.
- Adults are focused often by necessity not just on learning but on additional tasks, such as family and work. They want to know why they should learn something and whether it can be applied to their immediate future, for example, if the subject relates to their work or personal life. They are practical and results oriented and want information that applies to their professional needs, improving their skills for work. As a result, too, they need some flexibility to accommodate personal obligations.
- Learning experiences, activities, and assessments must be meaningful and engaging to motivate adults who appreciate how-to learning and problem solving that is learner centered. They like to discover things for themselves, with instructors facilitating and providing guidance when necessary.

It is important to apply these adult learning principles to the design, implementation, and evaluation of their online courses, lessons, activities, and materials.

Feedback from adults enables design to be based on learner needs (Pappas, 2013).

- Adults will be more motivated if they are part of creating the curriculum. Remember adult learning is often voluntary, so attending a course to improve job skills or achieve professional growth is the motivation behind learning.
- Experience enables adults to explore the subject matter through projects and exercises. They can learn to solve problems through trial and error and to master skills, a more meaningful approach.
- Real-world applications should be the focus of the subject matter. For example, how are principles of a course going to apply to situations they will face every day? This will increase engagement. Providing the "why" for what they are learning and linking new concepts to ones they already know will make them feel more comfortable exploring new ideas.
- Elearning courses should to be problem centered, focused on "doing," as in simulations rather than memorizing. Use personal experience as a resource; encourage discussion and sharing to create a learning community so learners can interact.

Figure 1.1. Characteristics of Adult Learners. *Created by author online. Adapted from Pappas, 2013*

Adults have high expectations and demand immediate results, so the course must meet their individual needs as well as addressing learning challenges. These adult learning principles when applied to activities in a course offer benefits of improved comprehension and knowledge retention (see figure 1.1).

Another area to consider is learning style and multiple intelligences theory, defined as individuals' characteristic methods of responding to and processing learning events as they experience them (Watrous-McCabe, 2005). Learners can be categorized into three types of learners who learn best by:

- Watching and seeing = visual
- Hearing = auditory
- Doing by touching things = kinesthetic/tactile

This learning style theory emphasizes preferred modes of learning. Although you may have a most comfortable way of learning, it does not mean you cannot function effectively in other modes.

Howard Gardner researched learning modalities in the form of multiple intelligences. Figure 1.2 describes Gardner's nine intelligences (Watrous-McCabe, 2005).

Another definition to understand is that of twenty-first-century skills. This theory is important when creating your online learning, addressing specific audiences, and preparing patrons and students for the twenty-first century. There are numerous visual depictions of twenty-first-century skills. Some focus on the four Cs—communication, collaboration, critical thinking, and creativity; others emphasize technology. See an example of the four Cs needed in today's society in figure 1.3.

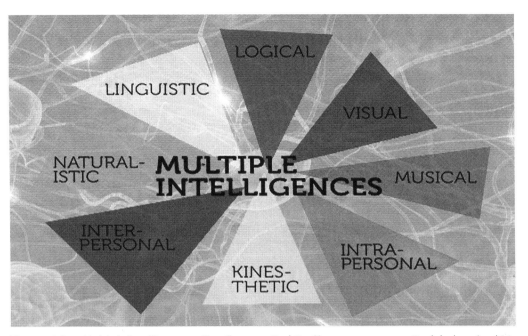

Figure 1.2. Multiple Intelligences. *One Community. http://www.onecommunityglobal.org/multi-in telligences. Used with permission, Creative Commons*

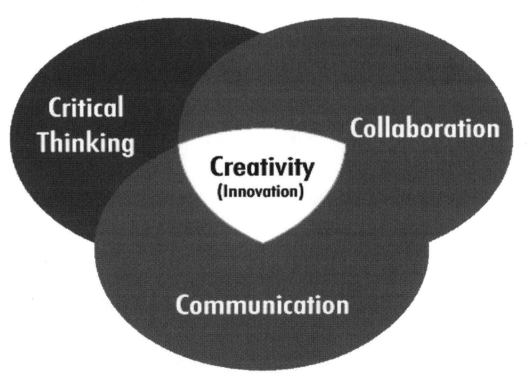

Figure 1.3. The 4Cs. *Techie Teacher Tricks. https://techieteacherstricks.com/2013/06/30/the-4-cs-crit ical-thinking. Used with permission, Creative Commons*

Today, there are many aspects to elearning as it has become more widespread in libraries and other organizations at all school levels and in businesses. Simply put, electronic learning or elearning is the "delivery of a learning, training, or an educational program by electronic means." It can be part or all of an educational curriculum whether it's in a school, part of business training, or a full distance learning course (eLearningNC.gov, 2016).

Synchronous versus Asynchronous Learning

Elearning is divided into two categories: synchronous and asynchronous teaching and learning. Online instruction can include one type or the other or a combination of both as in blended and flipped learning.

- **Synchronous instruction** occurs online in real time and is constrained by time and place. It must be completed within a specific time and schedule. Features include whiteboards, discussion forums, virtual classrooms, and scheduled online examinations. An instructor is involved to provide collaborative learning techniques to promote social interaction and problem solving and to motivate students so they do not feel isolated. These courses usually have higher attendance rates, and often students can participate through text, chat, audio, video, or social media. Students can interact with one another so it is easier to build community among learners, as well as with the instructor.
- **Asynchronous learning and teaching** occurs when interaction between instructor and students is not limited by time and place. This type of instruction can be carried on offline and is more convenient and flexible. Students can complete their learning at their own pace in their own time by using the Internet. Common features include self-paced courses, materials, and other online resources.

Many elearning courses are attended by students from around the world. Often materials are managed by learning management systems (LMSs) that can administer elearning courses and online exams, analyze student data, and/or use content management systems (CMSs) to store training materials. Some systems are hosted in the cloud and are often used by special libraries; others are installed on internal networks and maintained by an academic institution or an organization, such as a public library. An infographic at https://www.mindflash.com/wp-content/uploads/2012/03/what-is-e-learning1.png describes synchronous and asynchronous learning visually.

Blended and Flipped Learning

- Teaching and learning include different types of online learning, such as blended learning and flipped learning discussed later in this book. **Blended learning** is a fast-increasing form of online learning. The Clayton Christensen Institute, a leader on research about blended learning, defines it as "a formal education program in which the student learns in part through online learning, and partly in a supervised brick-and-mortar location away from home" (2015). Students have some control over time, place, and/or pace. Instructors create numerous active learning opportunities so that students can engage with the content.

- **Flipped learning** is a popular form of blended learning. The flipped rotation method is designed to be learner centered. In this model, activities, a class, or an entire course can be flipped to increase student engagement and improve learning. Students receive the core lesson as homework outside the school through online learning using technology. During class time students apply what they learned through videos, readings, and more, in their assignments and projects with the teacher's support as facilitator. Learning can be more personalized in this model, and instructors can provide one-on-one attention to students. More on blended and flipped learning in chapters 8 and 9.

⑥ Why Participate in Online Learning?

Is online learning the future of education? It certainly is not going away and is increasing in popularity and numbers of students. In today's fast-paced world, it is necessary to find alternatives to traditional face-to-face instruction in a brick-and-mortar environment. Online learning offers benefits to library patrons and students alike, and librarians are ideally placed to take the lead in online instruction. Numerous advantages make online instruction an important alternative for more and more of the population:

- **Flexibility of time and place.** Instruction, content, and resources are available 24/7 in any geographic location. For example, college students who work full-time can still start or continue their education because they can work at their own pace with content available at their convenience. State libraries can offer instruction to patrons in geographic areas remote to a local public library. Public libraries can offer instruction about job interviews, technology, or résumé writing so that patrons can access webinars, videos, or online resources at their convenience.
- **Accessibility.** Disabled students, the elderly, and those with special needs can learn through online classes from the comfort of their homes. They can log in after a doctor's appointment, take an enrichment course, or review a lecture multiple times. All these uses and more are benefits of participating in elearning.
- **Pacing.** Students prefer online learning because it allows them to work faster or slower, and repeat information they need to reinforce the content.
- **Variety of programs and courses.** From online four-year universities to enrichment programs via elearning, numerous options are available for students. Whether it is physics, economics, education, or language learning, you can study these subjects in four-year online universities or enrichment courses via elearning and obtain career certificates or doctorate degrees. In addition, learners can easily update their professional skills later in their careers online, as well as participate in online training offered by future employers.
- **Lower total costs.** Tuition costs may not be lower, but associated costs can be less expensive. For example, there are no commuting costs; textbooks can often be free online through open educational resources (OER). Free massive open online courses (MOOCs) offer opportunities from the best colleges and can even fulfill general education requirements for little or no cost.
- **Improved technical skills.** Learning computer skills, such as navigating learning management systems (LMSs), creating documents, collaborating via social media,

incorporating audio and video materials into assignments, and completing online training sessions translate to many career opportunities.

- **Engagement.** Students who have difficulty speaking out in class can post to an online discussion forum. They can take their time to arrange their ideas before responding. Learning also becomes more personalized as students form a one-to-one communication with their instructors.

⊚ Challenges Facing Online Instructors

Successful traditional face-to-face instruction does not always translate to effective online teaching. Whether disadvantages outweigh benefits depends on your teaching and learning environment and your learners. When contemplating virtual learning, there are challenges to consider:

- The amount of time to develop and maintain an elearning course can be considerable. Instructors must rethink and reengineer courses to adapt them to online delivery.
- Administrators and faculty who are uncomfortable with change can often disrupt the chance for successful implementation of online instruction.
- An assessment issue that bears watching is online cheating and implementing curriculum methodology and technology to limit it.
- Major commitments of time and training may be necessary to learn technology, such as the LMS.
- Support challenges, including lack of knowledge to design courses with technology and lack of confidence to use technology in teaching, must be considered.
- Technology issues, including inconsistent platforms, tools, and software, need to be addressed.
- There is often difficulty incorporating open-ended application questions in assessment. Peer assessment with a robust rubric can provide better feedback.
- Isolation, an often commented upon disadvantage, must be overcome through the possibility of discussion forums, courses in groups, and learning hubs.
- A curriculum that reflects dialogue among students, group interaction, and participation has to be developed for an online medium.

⊚ Readiness for Online Teaching and Learning

Online courses of different types are available at the college level and are even being mandated in many states as graduation requirements for K–12 students. Businesses are taking advantage of training their customers and employees online, and public libraries offer online instruction to patrons on a variety of topics. However, as you just learned, elearning and face-to-face learning have their benefits and challenges. What are some of the traits necessary to succeed as an online learner or instructor?

Traits of Your Online Audience

As the instructor when you begin designing online instruction, consider your audience. It is a good idea to make them aware of the following traits, important for success in an online learning environment. Online learners should be:

- Self-motivated to maintain a routine and have the discipline to complete coursework on time
- Able to work independently without constant surveillance of the instructor
- Organized and able to set up a routine with a study schedule they can stick to
- Technologically ready by having the required equipment—computer, Internet, books, and materials, and have online access to classes. They should also have an understanding of the virtual setup, such as an LMS.
- Able to commit enough time to complete all assignments, readings, projects, discussions, videos
- Familiar with online communication, including e-mail, social media, discussion forums, and perhaps Skype or Google Hangouts, to name some, to interact with the instructor and classmates

A questionnaire created at http://www.unc.edu/tlim/ser/ by Vicki Williams at Penn State University may help online users assess their readiness to learn online.

Traits of Effective Online Instructors

Not only does it take special skills and traits to succeed in online classes, it also requires certain talents to become a successful online teacher. Online instructors must consider the following:

- **Accessibility.** Since students and teacher do not see each other every day, the instructor must set frequent, predictable office hours, send and answer e-mails promptly, answer student questions by phone, offer content clarification, and provide timely feedback about assignments and assessments.
- **Adaptability.** An online instructor must be able to handle the unexpected. That might mean managing technology, including taking advantage of the LMS system to make sure students are actively involved in the class through appropriate numbers of logins, answering content-related questions, and adjusting content and strategies when necessary to personalize student learning, to name some.
- **Technology skills.** Often librarians are skilled in technology and have the ability to communicate their expertise to their patrons, students, and faculty. It is very important to understand the learning management system (LMS) that will be used to gather and organize student data into spreadsheets or create and save formative and summative assessments. Experience as an online learner also allows the instructor to demystify the technology for the students.
- **Encouraging attitude and patience.** The best online teachers know how to encourage their students from a distance. When, how, and how often the instructor responds to students determines the effectiveness of the instructor who needs patience to know the most appropriate way to deal with each student.

Online teachers and librarians must be concerned as to whether their students are getting the validation from them and other students so they do not feel isolated in cyberspace. Educators also need to feel that connection with their students. Students' eager looks, intense stares, or the smiles when students understand a concept or read a poem in front of the class let the educator know that he or she has taught a good lesson, touched students, and made a difference in their lives. An e-mail connection may not provide this same validation to the teacher. Online educators must find other ways to obtain the sense of purpose they obtain from face-to-face connections. Online teaching requires more emotional security and greater self-confidence on the part of both the instructor and student.

Differences between Online and Face-to-Face Learning

Educators often think they can teach the courses they taught in a face-to-face classroom in the same way in an online environment. This is a false assumption. Throughout this book, you will be identifying, analyzing, comparing, and contrasting traditional courses and those you will teach online. Knowing the differences will enable you to create courses to teach and motivate an online audience. Some of the following components have been mentioned. Table 1.2., "Online versus Face-to-Face Learning," synthesizes the information.

Table 1.2. Online versus Face-to-Face Learning

DIFFERENCES	ONLINE	FACE-TO-FACE
Flexibility	Molds with students' schedule; no specific time requirement	Students have more time in their schedules to attend class
Discipline	Students need ability to self-motivate and ability to set deadlines and prioritize	Students need discipline to complete work
Social Interaction	Students feel comfortable interacting via social media	Students need direct interaction with instructor
Planning	For instructor, heavier workload prior to first day of class because all components of course must be completed	Content, strategies, and assignments can be changed during course
Technology	Vital part of course	May or may not be used

When librarians decide to enter the online training and learning world, they face new challenges. They need to be knowledgeable in skills such as teaching, designing, planning, creating, and assessing online courses; developing self-paced materials; promoting their offerings; adapting to new approaches to teaching through technology; and working closely with students and patrons at a distance. Thus, librarians are often faced with a steep learning curve to embody this way of teaching and learning that is different from face-to-face instruction.

Key Points

Understanding differences in learning theories, how children and adults learn, and identifying characteristics of effective instruction provide the theoretical basis for creating effective online instruction. This chapter has provided background on which to base further discussion of online teaching and learning in the chapters that follow.

- General educational learning theories range from behaviorism, focused on programmatic repeated acts, to more active learning, a cognitivist approach building on prior knowledge, to constructionist learning based on current and past experiences, experientialism achieved by doing, and a humanist approach where the learner is personally involved in the learning process.
- Identifying different characteristics between how children learn (pedagogy) and adult learning (andragogy) provides the basis for effective online instruction.
- Learning styles—visual, auditory, and kinesthetic/tactile—and multiple intelligences should also be considered when creating a program of online instruction.
- Not only does it take special skills and traits to succeed in online classes, it also requires certain talents to become a successful online teacher.
- Educators who are best in their fields are ones who can facilitate learning.
- According to adult learning theory, the best learning environments are those that are collaborative and utilize a problem-based, active approach.
- As with a traditional class, benefits and challenges must be considered before deciding to create online training.
- Considering differences between traditional face-to-face learning and elearning is important to create effective online training. They are not the same.

With the groundwork laid, you now have the tools necessary to learn the basics of designing elearning in chapter 2. See table 1.3 for more sites on teaching and learning.

Table 1.3. Additional Resources for Chapter 1

DESCRIPTION	URLS
Infographic on Knowles's adult learning theory	http://elearninginfographics.com/adult-learning-theory-andragogy-infographic/
Mind map of learning models	http://www.nwlink.com/~donclark/learning/pedagogies/ped.html
Clickable learning framework to see more information	http://www.nwlink.com/~donclark/learning/learning.html
Proficiencies of instruction librarians	http://acrlog.org/2015/11/24/update-on-the-standards-for-proficiencies-for-instruction-librarians-and-coordinators
Multiple intelligences and elearning	http://elearningindustry.com/multiple-intelligences-in-elearning-the-theory-and-its-impact
Framework for twenty-first-century learning	http://www.p21.org/about-us/p21-framework

◎ Exercises

Completing the following exercises will reinforce what you learned about theoretical aspects of teaching and learning.

1. Which of the learning theories discussed in this chapter do you feel most comfortable with? Which is most like your own? Explain why.
2. Identify at least three training needs in your library that can be achieved through synchronous and asynchronous learning.
3. What would you say is your dominant learning style? Name several strategies or activities that help you learn better based on your style.
4. Review multiple intelligences and describe an activity you might use for each intelligence.
5. List traits of an online instructor you think are most like you. Then answer the following:
   a. Which ones do you think you need to improve to be successful at online teaching?
   b. Create a plan that will enhance traits necessary for an online instructor.

◎ References

Clayton Christensen Institute. 2015. "What Is Blended Learning?" http://www.christenseninstitute.org/blended-learning/.

elearningNC.gov. 2016. "What Is Elearning?" Accessed March 10. http://www.elearningnc.gov/about_elearning/what_is_elearning/.

Knowles, Malcolm. 1984. *The Adult Learner: A Neglected Species*. 3rd ed. Houston, TX: Gulf.

Pappas, Christopher. 2013. "8 Important Characteristics of Adult Learning." elearning Industry. May 8. http://elearningindustry.com/8-important-characteristics-of-adult-learners.

Schacter, Daniel L., Daniel T. Gilbert, and Daniel M. Wegner. 2011. *Psychology*. 2nd ed. New York: Worth.

Watrous-McCabe, Jan. 2005. "Applying Multiple Intelligence Theory to Adult Online Instructional Design." *Learning Solutions Magazine*. July 25. http://www.learningsolutionsmag.com/articles/258/applying-multiple-intelligence-theory-to-adult-online-instructional-design.

Wikipedia. 2016. "Learning Theory (Education)." *Wikipedia*. Accessed March 10. https://en.wikipedia.org/wiki/Learning_theory_(education).

◎ Further Reading

The Center for Teaching and Learning. 2016. "The Intelligences, in Howard Gardner's Words: A Quick Overview of the Idea of Multiple Intelligences." UNC Charlotte. http://teaching.uncc.edu/learning-resources/articles-books/best-practice/education-philosophy/multiple-intelligences.

Gagné, R. 1985. *The Conditions of Learning*. 4th ed. New York: Holt, Rinehart & Winston.

GSI Teaching & Resource Center. 2016. *Overview of Learning Theories*. Berkeley Graduate Division, Berkeley University of California. Accessed March 10. http://gsi.berkeley.edu/gsi-guide-contents/learning-theory-research/learning-overview/.

Pappas, Christopher. 2015a. "5 Differences of Pedagogy vs. Andragogy in Elearning." elearning Industry. November 13. http://elearningindustry.com/pedagogy-vs-andragogy-in-elearning-can-you-tell-the-difference.

———. 2015b. "Multiple Intelligences in eLearning." eLearning Industry. May 15. http://elearningindustry.com/multiple-intelligences-in-elearning-the-theory-and-its-impact.

Smith, M. K. 2002. "Malcolm Knowles, Informal Adult Education, Self-Direction and Andragogy." *Encyclopedia of Informal Education.* http://www.infed.org/thinkers/et-knowl.htm.

CHAPTER 2

Instructional Design for Online Teaching and Learning

AS DISCUSSED IN CHAPTER 1, educators who have taught face-to-face classroom courses often think putting their content in a video or having students read it from the computer screen makes an effective online course. This does not work! Looking at the importance of instructional design when creating an online course is the focus of chapter 2. Instructional design principles and how they relate to learning theory, skills needed to create online learning, best practices to consider, and a general outline of the steps to create an elearning course will be covered.

What Is Instructional Design?

Chapter 1 discussed different learning theories, identifying advantages for using them with specific learners. Knowledge of learning theories is important because it enables you, the designer of learning, to look at instruction from different points of view to see many possibilities and ways of visualizing objectives, assessment and content, and strategies for

▲ **17**

implementing the subject. Theories offer opportunities for designers to see what works and how to implement it. For example, some learning requires prescriptive solutions to solve problems whereas another type may be best suited to the learner controlling the learning environment (Schwier, 1995). In this chapter you will focus more fully on designing instruction.

By one definition, instructional design is "a process for creating effective and efficient learning processes" (Reiser and Dempsey, 2007). Others think of it as a "framework for developing modules or lessons that increase and enhance the possibility of learning, make the acquisition of knowledge and skill more efficient, effective, and appealing, and encourage the engagement of learners so that they learn faster and gain deeper levels of understanding" (Merrill et al., 1996: 5). Whatever the definition, instructional design can enhance learning.

To incorporate instructional design into courses, librarians and educators must ask themselves these questions: (1) what assumptions of a particular theory are relevant to instructional design, and (2) how should the course be structured to facilitate learning? Besides content considerations, another variable is the level of the learners. Novice learners, for example, may need a more structured approach since they lack prior knowledge about the subject and are not familiar with the content. As learners become more knowledgeable about the topic or perhaps have more life skills, they can take more control of their own learning, even creating some of it. Thus, understanding learning theories is not about selecting one and following it rigorously to create your course, but rather knowing what aspects of different theories will bring the desired outcomes for different types of learners.

Two examples—from a behaviorist and constructivist perspective—illustrate how courses are designed based on different approaches:

- When designing from a behaviorist or cognitivist perspective, for example, the designer analyzes the situation and sets a goal. Individual tasks are broken down, and learning objectives are developed. Evaluation consists of determining whether criteria for the objectives have been met. In this approach, the designer decides what is important for the learner to know and attempts to transfer that knowledge to the learner using specific strategies. The learning is created by the designer with little or no intervention or input from learners. Although this approach may allow for some branching and change, the learner is still confined to the designer's "world."
- To design from a constructivist approach, on the other hand, requires the designer to produce a product taking a much more facilitative than prescriptive approach. The content may not be prespecified by the instructor; direction may be determined by the learner, and assessment is much more subjective because it does not depend on specific quantitative criteria. Standardized tests to show mastery of the learning are not the norm in constructive design; rather, evaluation is based on notes, early drafts, final products or presentations, and journals.

Instructional design provides the framework that guides the structure of a course or other instructional activity. Although the structure of the course focuses the topic, the learner can still control active learning. Whichever approach is used, however, if a course is not well designed, a student may not know where to start, how the objectives and outcomes align, or where to find resources, and may spend more time on the technology than on the learning.

ⓖ Instructional Design Principles

It is important to understand the principles of instructional design so you can apply them when designing your own online courses. The following theories are well known and lend themselves to online learning. To form the base for your own designs, review the following three instructional design theories—ADDIE, Robert Gagné's nine events of instruction, and Bloom's Taxonomy of twenty-first-century learning. You can review other resources on instructional design principles in table 2.1.

Table 2.1. Instructional Design Principles

DESCRIPTION	URLS
An instructional design model	http://www.nwlink.com/~donclark/hrd/learning/id/id_model.html
A framework for designing learning models	http://www.nwlink.com/~donclark/hrd/learning_environment_framework.html
Design methodologies based on ADDIE	http://www.nwlink.com/~donclark/design/designmodels.html
Backward ADDIE model	http://www.nwlink.com/~donclark/hrd/ADDIE/ADDIE_backwards_planning_model.html
Instructional design based on ADDIE	http://teachinglearningresources.pbworks.com/w/page/19919537/ADDIE
Design process based on the backwards planning model	http://www.nwlink.com/~donclark/hrd/sat3.html
Rethinking Gagné's nine steps for adults working with a special librarian (PowerPoint)	http://www.slideshare.net/donclark/rethinking-gagnes-nine-steps-of-instructional-design
Gagné's nine-step model (PowerPoint)	http://www.slideshare.net/CPappasOnline/robert-gagnes-instruction-design-model-the-nine-events-of-instructions
Gagné's conditions of learning (PowerPoint)	http://www.slideshare.net/cristineyabes1/gagne-conditions-of-learningbse-2-mapeh
Robert Gagné's nine events of instruction (infographic)	https://www.pinterest.com/pin/279786195572438874/
Robert Gagné's nine events of instruction by Nicole Legault	http://nlegault.ca/2011/09/05/infographic-the-addie-model-a-visual-representation/

ADDIE: A Framework for Designing a Learning Model

The acronym ADDIE by definition is a systematic approach to course design that encompasses analysis, design, development, implementation, and evaluation. Each of the phases is often considered when designing an online course. Formative evaluations are used throughout, and a summative evaluation is included at the end of the process. Note that analysis, design, and development (Phases 1–3) are designed prior to the beginning of an online course before students are integrally involved. Review the specifics of each phase:

- Analysis

  During analysis, identify the learners' needs, existing knowledge, and other relevant characteristics. Define the goals and objectives. Consider the learning environment, any constraints, delivery options, and the timeline for the course.

- Design

  In this phase, it is important to determine the best ways to accomplish the specified objectives—what you want your learners to achieve. You will want to influence values, attitudes, and feelings as well as knowledge, reflective thinking, and skills. Review various strategies, such as discussion boards, group projects, readings, lecture, technology, and others, to determine the most appropriate delivery method(s). Consider kinds of technology to use and where.

- Development

  In Phase 3, create the content and learning materials, including the syllabus, student handouts, presentation materials, visuals, and other reference resources.

- Implementation

  During implementation, the course is put into action. Materials are delivered or distributed to the students. After delivery, its effectiveness is evaluated.

- Evaluation

  The evaluation phase contains both formative and summative assessment. Although you need an end-of-course assessment, you should also consider evaluation throughout so you can continue to improve the course. Consider Donald Kirkpatrick's (1959) four levels of evaluation:

  - *Students' reaction to the course*: Includes satisfaction of learners, how actively they are involved, how they have contributed to the learning experience, and whether they have the opportunity to apply what they've learned to the satisfaction of those affected by the results of the learning
  - *Learning*: Attitudes, skills, and knowledge, as well as confidence and commitment learners should have acquired
  - *Behavior changes*: Demonstration that they can apply what they learned on the job, in life activities, and so forth
  - *Results or outcomes from the learning*: Review the ADDIE model of a library workshop at https://kevinthelibrarian.files.wordpress.com/2012/07/addie-pro totype1.pdf that shows how to introduce MEDLINE, a database that provides authoritative medical information, to medical residents. One complaint about using ADDIE is its lack of flexibility in that it is too prescriptive. However, it does provide a basic structure that librarians can adapt as they plan online instruction for their own audience. See figure 2.1.

Gagné's Nine Events of Instruction

Robert Gagné, a cognitive psychologist, developed a systematic approach to instructional design that focuses on the outcomes from instruction. His nine-step process or events of instruction address conditions he thought were important for learning. They include five categories: verbal information, intellectual skills, motor skills, attitudes, and cognitive strategies. Although some steps may not be needed in a certain instructional event, Gag-

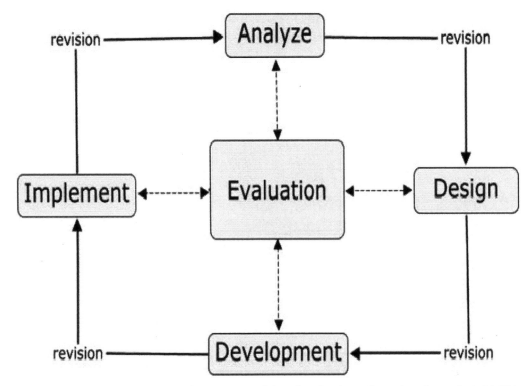

Figure 2.1. ADDIE Instructional Design Model. *Wikipedia. https://en.wikipedia.org/wiki/ADDIE_Model. Used with permission, Creative Commons*

né's steps provide a checklist of key design steps to take into account as you plan your instruction.

Gagné's instructional design model can help in developing curricular content, enhancing interactivity, and creating assessment. For example, medical librarians play a significant role in teaching information retrieval skills in medicine, and knowing learning theory and curricular design and instruction is a priority of the Medical Library Association (MLA) (Giustini, 2009). In a library workshop, librarians can follow different steps of Gagné's model outlined next to help improve instruction, engage users, and use assessment to teach about medical information.

1. **Gain attention.** Identify problems or scenarios that appeal to learners and stimulate their interest. In online learning, grabbing the viewers' attention is especially important so they immediately become involved in the learning process. Some devices you might try include: demonstrations, presenting a problem to solve, or telling a story. Especially important to adult learners is identifying how the subject relates to their needs.

   For example, to gain attention, a librarian might start off with a question: "When you need to find specific information about a medical topic, where do you go first?" Most students respond with "Google." The librarian then piques their interest by explaining that instead of retrieving thousands of results, they can gather a concise number of responses from authoritative sources by using a discipline-specific database like MEDLINE. Users are now ready to listen.

2. **Describe the objectives.** Let learners know what they will accomplish and how they can use the knowledge they gain. This allows viewers to organize their

thoughts on what they will learn and relate it to their own situation—their job, education, or interest. Transforming the objective into a language that relates to the learners is more motivating to them.

3. **Stimulate recall of prior knowledge.** Emphasize related information they already know and scaffold the information so they can build on their earlier knowledge and skills. For instance, use graphics such as mind maps to visualize knowledge. Technology can help here.

4. **Present the material.** Present material sequentially and in small chunks to avoid information overload. Offer feedback on individual tasks. Incorporate a variety of materials, including visuals, sound, and simulations sequenced to Bloom's Taxonomy of levels of difficulty.

5. **Provide learner guidance.** Use examples, analogies, and case studies so retention is greater. Demonstrate or model the behavior you want so students can act upon the behavior or use the skill required. Also, provide ways for users to obtain feedback through discussion forums, the instructor, or additional resources.

   For example, offer support to users as they try their own searches in MEDLINE and then bring the discussion back to the whole group to describe challenges each person faced when using library resources. Users will also welcome appropriate feedback.

6. **Elicit performance.** Provide ways students can practice the new skills, behavior, or knowledge to reinforce their understanding.

7. **Provide feedback.** Explain specifically and immediately when something is wrong or right and guide learners to correct a wrong response. Use tests, quizzes, or comments as appropriate.

8. **Assess performance.** Evaluate learners on what they have learned and provide general progress information. This is often available in an LMS, to be discussed in more detail in chapter 5.

9. **Enhance retention and transfer.** Provide additional practice in similar situations, offer supplemental materials, and review the lesson. Making your examples applicable to your learners will help enhance their retention of the material and provide a better avenue for applying the new skills to real-world situations. See figure 2.2 for an illustration of Gagné's process.

Bloom's Taxonomy

Benjamin Bloom, an educational psychologist, designed a pyramid from lower-order thinking skills such as remembering and understanding, to applying and analyzing, to the highest-order skills of evaluating and creating. By categorizing these six levels of thinking, you can identify appropriate activities that correspond to Bloom's levels of learning to achieve the desired level of mastery. Certain activities are useful for each level, such as creating lists for remembering, comparing and contrasting to analyze, and constructing and designing to create. Educators, including Andrew Churches (2008) and Lorin Anderson and David Krathwohl (2001), revised Bloom's Taxonomy to create Bloom's Digital Taxonomy that focuses on using Web 2.0 technologies to facilitate learning. Bloom's Digital Taxonomy focuses on collaboration and creativity as being essential twenty-first-century skills. It will help you map your learning objectives to delivery technologies. Review an in-depth update of Bloom's Taxonomy at http://edorigami. wikispaces.com/Bloom%27s+Digital+Taxonomy (see figure 2.3).

Figure 2.2. Gagné's Events of Instruction. *Adapted from Infographic and Slideshare Presentation.*
http://elearningindustry.com/9-events-of-instruction-infographic-slideshare-presentation

Librarians can benefit from familiarizing themselves with learning theories and selecting instructional design models (IDMs) that will suit the needs of their users. These models can help new librarians develop and organize teaching content or provide new methods for experienced instructional librarians to modify their approach.

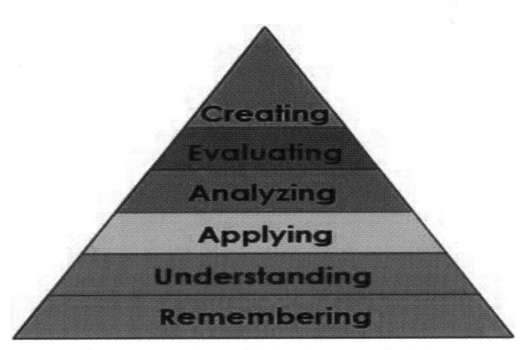

Figure 2.3. Bloom's Taxonomy of Thinking Skills. *Used with permission, Creative Commons*

⊚ What Makes a Good Online Course?

To be effective, online learning courses, including their activities and resources, should be well integrated, whether it is in a course that is totally online or one that is blended or flipped and contains both face-to-face classes and online portions. The course should be clearly aligned with assessments and course learning outcomes. It must be presented with clear explanations of your expectations. You must tell your students what you expect from them in terms of participation online and be prepared to support them to engage with the online community.

You'll be able to learn appropriate technologies, introduce them in your classes, and use them to good effect in teaching and learning if you have a sound knowledge of educational principles, select the right tool for your own teaching content, and understand whether a particular technology is best to achieve learning goals. Before introducing technology, consider the time and effort it will take for you to gain proficiency in using technologies, revise your course design (some courses require substantial revision to be effective), and manage teacher and student workload.

Instructor Design Skills

The effective instruction librarian who plans to create online learning has important traits that ensure the success of both synchronous and asynchronous learning. The teaching and learning may be in totally virtual courses, models of embedded librarianship in academic libraries to create an integrated library presence across subject areas in the institution, the flipped classroom model in K–12 and public libraries, specifically surrounding technology, or blended learning that combines both online and traditional brick-and-mortar classroom learning. Subsequent chapters describe these different types of online learning.

Content or curriculum knowledge. A part of the total knowledge for an instruction librarian includes information literacy integration skills. The librarian takes the lead and describes the role of information literacy, especially in academia. As embedded librarians, they collaborate with faculty to integrate information literacy competencies and skills into library instruction, assignments, and course content. Increasingly, they are also planning together and implementing the instruction in subject curricula and also implementing faculty training.

Assessment and evaluation skills. The librarian, independently or in collaboration with faculty, designs effective assessments of student learning and uses the data collected to guide personal teaching and professional development.

Presentation skills. As discussed in chapter 1, librarians typically do not take courses in library school related to delivery of training. The following tips will give librarians a head start as they begin to deliver instruction. The instructor must consider personal presentation, technology to use, and the content itself.
- Keep the class lively and students engaged with voice contrast, and eye contact with the camera. Practice and refine content to become familiar with and confident during the presentation.
- Present content in a variety of ways—oral, visual, written, through presentation software. Clarifying terminology that may be new or confusing, avoiding jargon,

and using vocabulary appropriate to student level is important for clear student understanding.

- Use diverse technology to intersperse different activities throughout the lesson. These might include visuals (photos, charts, graphs), polls, Q&A, and other Web 2.0 tools or features of an LMS. Make sure to make smooth transitions between technological tools.

Subject expertise. Effective instruction librarians must keep current with theories, methods, and topics in subject areas where embedded, and incorporate relevant ideas when planning instruction. Another area of expertise is to identify core primary and secondary sources in a subject and describe and promote these resources through instruction.

Teaching skills. Teaching librarians, whether in academic institutions, K–12 schools, or public libraries, need to create learner-centered environments through active, collaborative, and other learning activities. They must understand learning styles and modify teaching methods to address these differences, as well as differences caused by language abilities, developmental skills, age groups, and other diverse needs of learners. As librarians work with faculty, they need to participate in student-teacher exchanges by encouraging questions and asking engaging questions that promote critical thinking. As partners, faculty and librarians can encourage interactive discussion to link library and course content. Of course, reflection on practice and acquiring new knowledge of teaching methods and learning theories will improve teaching skills. This enables teaching librarians to share their teaching skills and knowledge with other library staff.

Moreover, using today's sophisticated technology, librarians can create asynchronous training for library patrons. For example, LibGuide tutorials, videos, infographics, and other search aids explain concepts, such as fair use, information about learning management systems (LMSs) like Moodle, and other Web 2.0 tools, such as making the most of YouTube, creating Pinterest boards, and using social media.

A well-planned lesson, practice in presentation, confidence with technological tools, and reflecting and refining the total message encourages librarians to take risks, try new approaches and technology, and share experiences and resources.

Often when starting out with online instruction, educators think that the courses they have been using in face-to-face teaching can be ported into online teaching with little or no change. This is the first mistake and cannot be repeated too often. There are many differences in elearning that educators must address as they begin working in the virtual environment. The next part of this chapter will focus on many of these differences and how to address them in your synchronous and asynchronous training.

Best Practices for Librarians Involved in Online Courses

With the increase in virtual schools, online classes, and blended learning courses, educators today need to compile strategies, tips, and guidelines to use when teaching or creating instruction that is different from that in face-to-face classrooms. These suggestions will help you get started:

- **Develop a strong online presence.** Whether you use technology, such as discussion boards, an LMS, and/or social media (e.g., Facebook, Google Hangouts,

ZoomIn), you will want to keep in touch with your students multiple times weekly or even every day so students do not feel isolated. Creating discussion questions and relevant subject content encourages students to think critically and collaborate with their classmates, too.

- **Encourage feedback from students to other students.** Interactivity requires more than one post per student. Students also need substantive feedback from the instructor and encouragement to respond to each other's comments and ask questions that forward the discussion.
- **Check for questions frequently and provide timely feedback.** Instructors should monitor their courses daily and respond quickly to student posts, questions, and submitted work. Again, this eliminates the feeling of isolation and lets instructors know who and how much learners are involved in the course.
- **Model respectful behavior for students.** Teachers should be mindful of tone in their responses and be helpful and supportive. Address students by name, and sign your posts.
- **Help students develop time management and organizational skills.** Make sure students know what is expected of them and when assignments are due. A syllabus and assignment due dates should be given at the beginning of an online course. It is helpful to be consistent, for example, by having a weekly checklist and rubrics that the teacher monitors.
- **Provide a manageable course load.** Break the course down into manageable modules and try to provide a consistent amount of work throughout the course. In this way students can absorb the knowledge as you build upon what they are learning.
- **Present material in different ways.** Engage students by addressing different learning styles, considering both synchronous and asynchronous activities, including collaboration, reflection, interactive brainstorming, and sharing.
- **Include different types of resources.** The course might build toward a final project where tasks revolve around completing the project. Navigation directions to outside resources, including websites, should be clearly stated; annotations about resources provide an advance organizer.

Educators who will be involved in online instruction, whether planning, creating, or teaching it, need to have the benefit of training for these tasks. Different types of professional development opportunities—learning from peers already participating in online teaching; initiatives and programs that have been successfully implemented in other schools or libraries; tech-focused conferences, many of which are free; and taking online courses—all provide novice online teachers with strategies and tips that will make them feel more at ease as they begin their online adventure. You will see these types of resources as you proceed through each chapter of this book. The textbox contains tips for creating your elearning content.

Steps for Designing an Elearning Course

Many educational institutions, instructional design companies, and individuals explain how they have created online learning courses. The following sequence of steps, a composite of the suggestions of others, offers guidelines to help you formulate your online course. The chapters in part 3 describe examples and provide suggestions for pre-plan-

TIPS FOR CREATING ELEARNING CONTENT

Tips	Strategies
• Be concise and keep content relevant to measurable learning objectives that ultimately benefit the learner. • Engage your audience so that they want to consume your content.	• Bloom's Taxonomy can guide you to reach educational goals (see figure 2.3., "Bloom's Taxonomy of Thinking Skills"). • Telling a story, using different technologies, games, visuals, humor, all make your content more exciting for the learner. Also, using examples relevant to the audience makes the content more engaging. For instance, educational case studies or real-life examples from the library make the content more interesting to your students or patrons.
• Keep verbiage concise and succinct.	• Omit jargon and language that is too technical. Using bulleted lists, visuals to explain complex material, and audio to meet different learning styles makes content more readable and understandable.
• Proofread carefully; these mistakes will reflect negatively on your course and organization.	• Watch for unclear organization, grammatical and spelling errors, and incorrect facts.

ning, planning and design, implementation, and assessment of an online course that you are creating from scratch. You should also consider these steps if you are transforming face-to-face instruction to elearning.

Earlier discussion points out that creating online instruction is all about the learning and the learner. The technology required to present content, implement strategies, and complete the rest of the work that goes into creating a course is secondary to the learning users will take away from the instruction. Many of the following steps will be familiar and ones you probably already consider if you are currently teaching courses; however, they will not be the same as those you have used in your face-to-face classroom.

So, let's get started with general steps based on some tried-and-true research from Arthur Chickering and Zelda Gamson (1987). Although this research was done in 1987, the "Seven Principles for Good Practice in Undergraduate Education" is still a most often cited source. It focuses on interaction, both faculty to faculty and student to student, encourages active learning and facilitating time on task. Instructors must provide rich, quick feedback as well as communicating their high expectations for learners. Finally, a respect for diverse learning is important. These qualities should also be incorporated into the learning you create. You will learn more about each step in chapters in part 2.

Step 1: Preplan before Starting the Actual Course

How long it takes to preplan is a function of where you are starting (new design or redesign) and your other obligations. If you are using the ADDIE model, this step is part of A for analyze phase to analyze the need, audience, goals, topic, and task. Gather all the resources from previous courses you have taught, content and instructional materials you have researched or picked up from colleagues, such as syllabi, notes, textbooks, lectures, handouts, quizzes, exams, online resources, assignments/papers/projects, journal articles, and any other pertinent material. Organize them in a format in files.

Step 2: Design Your Course

Conduct an instructional analysis, identifying the component parts of learning modules (objectives, instructional strategies, outcomes, materials, delivery system, assessment, flowchart). Plan how you will align objectives with outcomes, and select strategies to achieve both. Determine materials to achieve results and also engage learners. Create a design for the entire course—what each module will contain, strategies, such as media, lecture, and small-group work. Creating a flowchart may help clarify each module of the course.

Step 3: Develop the Course

Identify and compile the content necessary to meet the objectives. Select a course management (CMS) or learning management system (LMS) and develop documentation to help you explain it to your students. Decide on other media and how it will be used and by whom (students or instructor). Create necessary documentation and explanatory material.

Step 4: Implement the Course

In an online course, all content, methods, materials, and resources must be created prior to implementing instruction. Facilitating the interaction between students and teacher, providing feedback, keeping regular contact with students—these are just some of the responsibilities during the progress of the course.

Step 5: Evaluate the Success of the Course

Both formative and summative evaluations will determine students' learning, the success of the methodology, and effectiveness of the entire course. Summative evaluation provides data to assess the overall effectiveness of the course. Formative evaluation is quite important to identify revisions necessary to instruction.

Step 6: Refine the Course

When the course and all assessments are completed, review the results and refine the course, if necessary. See table 2.2 for more resources on topics covered in chapter 2.

Whether you are planning a synchronous or asynchronous online course or materials, one designed to be used on traditional or mobile technology, or developed for an adult or younger audience, the steps and tips in this chapter will provide a guide that you can

Table 2.2. Additional Resources for Chapter 2

DESCRIPTION	URLS
Instructional design models and theories table	https://elearningindustry.com/instructional-design-models-and-theories
Infographic based on the Gagné instructional design model	http://elearningindustry.com/9-events-of-instruction-infographic-slideshare-presentation
Steps to create an online course from Blackboard	http://www.cgs.pitt.edu/sites/default/files/Doc6-GetStarted_10EasySteps.pdf
Dick and Carey instructional design model	http://www.instructionaldesign.org/models/dick_carey_model.html
Kirkpatrick level of evaluation visual models	http://tiny.cc/iwpofy
"Seven Principles for Good Practice in Undergraduate Education"	http://teaching.uncc.edu/learning-resources/articles-books/best-practice/education-philosophy/seven-principles

modify and adapt to meet the needs of your particular audience as you progress further through this book.

Key Points

Theory related to instructional design is an important part of creating online courses and both synchronous and asynchronous materials. This chapter has discussed the basics you need to begin designing your instruction from components to consider to different philosophies to use in creating, implementing, and assessing your training.

- Instructional design consists of a set of principles for creating learning in the form of educational and training materials.
- Instructional design models, such as ADDIE, Gagné's nine events of instruction, and Bloom's Taxonomy of thinking skills, provide frameworks to create online instruction for diverse audiences.
- Designing instruction includes accurately assessing that learners can perform behaviors as a result of the learning.
- Whether a course is created by several persons or just one, diverse qualities are required that include content expertise, presentation ability, design and teaching skill, and others.
- Steps to preplan, design, develop, implement, and evaluate a course provide a structure to use when creating your own course of instruction.

You now have the theoretical learning and design tools on which to base the online synchronous and asynchronous instruction you will be reviewing in chapters that follow. Chapter 3 in part 2 delves into the preplanning and planning phases of creating your online course.

⊚ Exercises

As you complete the following exercises, think about what you learned in this chapter and how the content will help you design online instruction.

1. Thinking about the definition of instruction design, list ways you think you can apply design as you create your course.
2. Select the group (children or adults) that best applies to your library patrons. Analyze traits that are important as you create a lesson for them.
3. Identify a particular type of instruction needed by your own library (e.g., information literacy such as evaluating databases, using a technology tool). Demonstrate how you would use each step of the ADDIE instructional design model in a learning event for your library users.
4. Gagné's events of instruction serve as a guide to help you create a course of study for your learners. Briefly map out two strategies incorporating the nine events for both children and adults.
5. Create a learning activity for each phase of Bloom's Taxonomy (e.g., evaluate an online source).
6. Incorporating principles of instructional design, select a learning need at your library, and create an outline of the course, including steps discussed earlier.

⊚ References

Anderson, Lorin W., and David R. Krathwohl, eds. 2001. *A Taxonomy for Learning, Teaching and Assessing: A Revision of Bloom's Taxonomy of Educational Objectives (Complete Edition)*. New York: Longman.

Chickering, Arthur W., and Zelda F. Gamson. 1987. "Seven Principles for Good Practice in Undergraduate Education." The Center for Teaching and Learning. UNC Charlotte. http://teaching.uncc.edu/learning-resources/articles-books/best-practice/education-philosophy/seven-principles.

Churches, Andrew. 2008. "Bloom's Taxonomy Blooms Digitally." Tech & Learning. April 1. http://www.techlearning.com/news/0002/bloom39s-taxonomy-blooms-digitally/65603.

Giustini, D. 2009. "Utilizing Learning Theories in the Digital Age: An Introduction for Health Librarians." *Journal of the Canadian Health Libraries Association* 29, no. 3: 109–15. https://ejournals.library.ualberta.ca/index.php/jchla/article/view/22811.

Kirkpatrick, Donald L. 1959. "Kirkpatrick's Four Level Training Evaluation Model." MindTools. October 5. https://www.mindtools.com/pages/article/kirkpatrick.htm.

Merrill, M. David, Leston Drake, Mark J. Lacy, and Jean Pratt. 1996. "Reclaiming Instructional Design." *Educational Technology* 36, no. 5: 5–7.

Reiser, R. A., and J. V. Dempsey. 2007. *Trends and Issues in Instructional Design*. 2nd ed. Upper Saddle River, NJ: Pearson Education.

Schwier, Richard. 1995. "Issues in Emerging Interactive Technologies." *Instructional Technology*. 2nd ed., 119–27. Englewood, CO: Libraries Unlimited.

ⓖ Further Reading

Brooke, Elizabeth. 2015. "Blending Learning: A Basic Overview of Typical Implementation Models and Four Keys to Success." Lexia Learning. March 5. http://lexialearning.com/re sources/white-papers/blended-learning-four-keys.

Gagné, R. 1985. *The Conditions of Learning and the Theory of Instruction.* 4th ed. New York: Holt, Rinehart & Winston.

Horn, Michael B., and Heather Staker. 2011. "The Rise of K–12 Blended Learning." January. Innosight Institute Inc. http://www.innosightinstitute.org/innosight/wp-content/up loads/2011/01/The-Rise-of-K-12-Blended-Learning.pdf.

Pappas, Christopher. 2013. "Nine Events of Instruction." Infographic and Slideshare Presentation. eLearning Industry. January 13. http://elearningindustry.com/9-events-of-instruction-info graphic-slideshare-presentation.

Powell, Allison, Beth Rabbitt, and Kathryn Kennedy. 2014. *iNACOL, Blended Learning Teacher Competency Framework. iNACOL,* October. The International Association for K–12 Online Learning. In Partnership with The Learning Accelerator. http://www.inacol.org/resource/ inacol-blended-learning-teacher-competency-framework.

Whybrow, Li. 2015. "9 eLearning Ideas to Think Differently about Your eLearning." eLearning Industry. September 29. https://elearningindustry.com/elearning-ideas-learn-how-to-think-differently-about-elearning.

Part II

CREATING ONLINE INSTRUCTION

A MAJOR CHALLENGE TODAY FOR LIBRARIES and online librarians is to provide library services and resources that equal those that are available on campuses of academic institutions for the traditional student, for employees at companies with widespread offices, at public libraries for the elderly and homebound patrons who can no longer visit their local library, and for K–12 students who have diverse needs and may need more personalized learning (Cassner and Adams, 2012). As far back as 2003, research by John Shank and Nancy Dewald (2003: 38) notes that librarians must become involved in online education at the course level or they "risk being bypassed by [CMS] technology and losing relevance to students and faculty." Karen Ramsay and Jim Kinnie (2006: 34) reiterate this concern that libraries must "reinvent themselves" and "reach outward to become an integral part" of twenty-first-century learning.

In addition to providing new online services, many libraries must also figure out how to change the minds of librarians from focusing only on print resources to using online resources that better meet the needs of the learner. Librarians need to update their skills with the new technologies so they can use them to teach in online educational settings. Librarians need to basically become subject-matter experts so that they can meet the growing demands and needs of the online user. For example, although corporate libraries have decreased in number, the librarian's value has increased as companies try to enhance skills of their employees with new technology tools while at the same time cutting costs—especially travel. Finally, an important role of the library is to create quality resources, tutorials, and increased online instruction to meet the unique needs of twenty-first-century learners so they can access the information they need in their own time and pace at any location.

Personalized learning is becoming ever important and lends itself well to online learning. Content can be tailored to individuals and can be self-paced—all made possible with today's technology. Examples, such as instruction on information literacy, exploring databases, and learning more about technology, to name some topics, help students develop critical thinking and research skills, and increase student and patron awareness of and comfort with library resources and services. All lend themselves to instruction that librarians are well equipped to conduct.

Using a model on the topic of information literacy, part 2 explores how to create a sample online course, including stepping through the process and describing components. Design and instructional tips for creating other types of online instruction will also be given.

- Chapter 3 describes the preplanning and planning stages of online instruction, emphasizing audience and purpose, engagement and motivation.
- Chapter 4 shows how to design all components of online instruction. Included are considerations about design elements and technology and how it is integral to online learning.
- Chapter 5 analyzes implementation (LMS, Web 2.0, social media) and assessment, and reflects upon the course and its outcomes.

References

Cassner, Mary, and Kate Adams. 2012. "Continuing Education for Distance Librarians." *Journal of Library & Information Services in Distance Learning* 6, no. 2: 117–28.

Ramsay, Karen M., and Jim Kinnie. 2006. "The Embedded Librarian." *Library Journal* 131, no. 6 (April 1): 34–35.

Shank, John D., and Nancy H. Dewald. 2003. "Establishing Our Presence in Courseware: Adding Library Services to the Virtual Classroom." *Information Technology and Libraries* 22, no. 1 (March. 22): 38–43.

CHAPTER 3

Preplanning and Planning Online Instruction

IN THIS CHAPTER

▷ Conducting a task analysis to determine the type of instruction to create

▷ Analyzing the audience for your online instruction

▷ Describing the differences between goals and objectives

▷ Writing general goals and specific objectives

▷ Identifying pitfalls that may occur in preplanning and planning phases of an online course

---

DO YOU CURRENTLY CONDUCT ONLINE training at your library? Will you offer an online course at the library in the future? Demand for online instruction is growing rapidly. Research universities have been offering individual courses at the undergraduate and graduate levels for quite a while. Now major research institutions are creating online graduate programs to take the place of traditional ones. New online instruction often solves schedule conflicts and enables students to take popular courses where space limits enrollments. Community colleges and even high schools are following suit and expanding their offerings online. Finally, the growing population of post-college learners creates a market for courses delivered online because rapid economic and technological changes create a need for lifelong learning, more people have two or more careers in a lifetime, and workers and employers need just-in-time learning. As a result, you could be asked to develop, teach, or collaborate in creating part or all of an online course or other asynchronous material at your library.

If you have not done this before, the prospect can be quite daunting. What do you need to know to assume this responsibility? Online course development can be perceived as a three-part process: preplanning and planning; design and development; and implementation, assessment, review, and reflection. Chapter 3 describes the first of the three parts: the preplanning and planning phases. You will analyze needs the online instruction should fill to determine what type of training should take place, the learners who will be instructed, general goals and specific objectives that will direct course outcomes, and how to create them. Then, based on total planning, you will look at designing the course in chapter 4.

⊙ Preplanning: Analyze Needs and Audience

Preplanning, especially when creating an online course, makes up a significantly large part of the process. As you decide whether training is needed, consider these questions: Is there a need to conduct training? Can the problem be corrected with instruction? What are the competencies and behaviors that need changing?

If you decide that an online course meets the need, there are certain key decisions about a course to be made at the outset. What are the reasons for creating an online course? Do these reasons justify the amount of work and funds involved to put together a course? If the answer is yes, how should it be designed and packaged? Chapter 2 provided a general outline for an online course. This chapter outlines the initial steps in the process and explains considerations to complete each step.

Needs Analysis

Conducting a needs analysis is vital to determine whether to embark on producing an online course. In the ADDIE model discussed in chapter 2, analysis consists of a needs and audience assessment prior to actually planning instruction. To make training worth the investment, you must make sure your training program actually meets the needs of your audience. So, the first step for any effective online training program is an elearning needs analysis. This analysis should consider whether training is needed and if so, the type to develop. The answer here must take into account the learners' needs, including their prior knowledge and relevant characteristics, and the learning environment, such as obstacles, delivery options, and the timeline for a course.

There are many ways to impart knowledge, enhance or teach new skills, and change behaviors or attitudes. The amount of time it takes to create a new course or adapt a current one to an online framework, money needed for resources and technology, and personnel who know how to create elearning instruction can be an extensive drain on resources of an organization, business, or academic institution. Therefore, you do not want to start developing a course before making sure it will be suitable to your audience and meet the purpose for which you are designing it. As a part of your needs analysis, you must determine whether training needs exist and what they are. It could be that a non-training option is the solution to your problem or maybe no change at all is best.

To gather this data, consider answers to the following questions—why, who, how, what, and when. For example, you might ask:

- Why do you think training is necessary? Check customer feedback, performance statistics, and employee observations, to name some data to collect.
- Who would benefit from the training—patrons, students, employees, other librarians? Familiarize yourself with your audience, their job functions, abilities, prior

knowledge, and interests. Also, find out if the audience is located in one specific area.

- What is the problem the training will solve and what are potential ways to solve it? Do your learners need a new skill, knowledge, a change in behavior?
- What competencies and behaviors can be changed to close the gaps between what the learner knows and what you expect the resulting knowledge, skills, behaviors, or attitudes to be?
- When and how much time would training take? Will it fit schedules of employees, students, or patrons? Can it be completed in a realistic time frame?
- Is the problem correctable through training, specifically an online course?
- What form will the training take? Should it be synchronous, an instructor-led online course, or asynchronous, such as an on-demand course or online materials?
- How will you deliver training (e.g., learning management system [LMS], social media, an online system at your organization) and what materials will you need?
- How will you measure the success of the course?
- How will online instruction help, or are there better ways to address the issue? Are there options that will make use of current resources that will meet the need so that a new course is not necessary?

Answers to all these questions should be considered in the preplanning phase. Analysis should also consider the learning environment, the interest and engagement of learners, and any constraints for the course. When you've gathered the necessary data, analyze it, and consider solutions. Rely on the data to point you toward solutions to the problem—whether the solution is an online course, an on-demand course, asynchronous material, or some other option. A task analysis can be conducted after the needs assessment and the problem you want to address is identified.

Audience Analysis

A major consideration in any instruction is the group you will instruct—patrons, students, adults, children, employees, learners with special needs. Your audience is the main focus of your online course. When creating a course, you need to know who you are training, what they already know, and how to communicate with them. As a result of your audience analysis, you should be able to communicate in a way that is most effective to your learners to achieve the desired outcome.

To analyze the audience, ask questions about them. Questions can be divided into categories, including audience demographics, existing knowledge, education, and experience. A key factor is what the primary goal of your elearning audience is. What do they want/need to take away from the instruction? What are their expectations? How will they access the course—using a mobile device, with software/hardware limitations, with limited Internet access? Are there geographic differences? And, what are their learning preferences—visual, auditory, kinesthetic—that might be best served with videos, scenarios, podcasts, case studies, collaborative activities? Considering these issues will enable you to determine the content and method(s) of presenting it effectively. Knowing your audience helps ensure a course that accommodates your learners. Use the Audience Analysis Q&A Handout as a template with sample questions for your own audience analysis. Consider modifying the questions to fit your learners.

Audience Analysis Q&A

Audience Analysis	
Demographics	**Answer Data**
Age	
Gender	
Educational background	
Cultural background, race, ethnicity	
Knowledge and Experience	**Answer Data**
Level of work experience	
Reading grade level	
Level of knowledge about subject	
Motivation level	
Technical Considerations	**Answer Data**
Hardware/software to use	
Technical expertise	
Resources available to help with problems	
Expectations	**Answer Data**
Level of participation expected	
Familiarity with terms, technical language, jargon	
Best writing style to ensure understanding	
Best tone, voice, attitude	
Reason for taking the course	
Expectations for learning	
Time necessary for training	
Special needs (visual, auditory, physical)	

In addition to analyzing your learners, you can also rely on observations, records, surveys, and peer comments. When you have completed both the needs and audience analyses and determined online training to be the best course of action, you are ready to begin planning the online course.

Planning: Goals, Objectives, and Outcomes

Your first priority in the planning process is to consider learning goals, objectives, and the resulting outcomes. These elements are the essence of your online course. To begin, you must decide where you are going and how you will know when you get there—thus, the reason to set specific goals and objectives. To understand their role and importance in learning and how they fit into the online course, you need to be able to explain the differences between goals and objectives and how they relate to outcomes and assessment. Then, you'll be ready to start writing your general goals and clear, concise objectives that lead to specific outcomes.

Goal, Objective, and Outcome Differences

As part of creating goals and objectives, the instructor must identify desired outcomes. If your learners achieve the objectives, they will attain the results—the outcomes you want. A description of goals and objectives will help to delineate the differences that make them important pedagogically to attaining the outcomes for your course. Knowing the differences will also help you write goals and objectives later in this chapter.

Goals

Goals are broad, the overarching aims you want to achieve in the elearning course. They help you focus on the big picture. A learning goal describes in a broad overall statement expected change that should take place as a result of your course—the learning outcomes. Different goals focus on different outcomes. For example, a performance goal can be categorized as an action that requires mastery of a specific skill so you can achieve the desired outcome. An outcome goal focuses on an end result.

Setting learning goals before beginning to develop a course lets you determine a starting and ending point and design activities, content, and assessments to achieve the outcome. The goal then serves as a guide throughout the process, providing clarity and structure to instructors as they create strategies to achieve the desired result. For example, a goal for this chapter might be: at the end of this chapter, learners should be able to differentiate among goals, objectives, and outcomes for elearning courses.

All parts of the course should link to the goals, including resources, assessments, activities, and specific objectives. No matter how excellent components of your course are, if the goals are not achieved, the course will not be successful. Goals also give you directions to help you write your learning objectives. Without the goal, for example, necessary opportunities to practice the newly learned behaviors and/or link the new skills to real-life situations may not be incorporated into the course. As a result, students' motivation for learning may not be what is required to become active participants in the learning.

Objectives describe what you want your learners to achieve after they complete the learning. They are a breakdown of the goal, they support the goal, and they are more actionable. They must be clear. If they are unclear, so is the purpose of the course. Objectives are more specific and directed than goals and describe what should change for a particular audience in a specific time frame as a result of the learning. A learning objective describes, in specific and measurable terms, particular elements that learners will have mastered upon completion of the online course. Objectives should not include information about your audience and the strategy you are following to develop them. They should only contain what your learners will gain by engaging in the online activity.

Robert F. Mager, a psychologist and expert on human performance improvement, defines a learning objective as a "description of a performance you want learners to be able to exhibit before you consider them competent" (1984). It is a specific statement of observable behavior that can be measured and contributes to achieving the goal. It tells the learner what to do or learn to attain the goal. These objectives provide realistic steps and milestones along the way that explain how to achieve measurable results. For example, an objective might be stated as follows: At the end of this section of chapter 3, the learner will be able to explain differences between a goal, objective, and outcome for an elearning course.

Mager (1984) states that the ideal objective has three parts:

1. **Performance.** A measurable action containing a verb, a "doing word." Words, such as to "know" or "understand" something, do not have that ability to be observed and measured. Therefore, you want to write an objective with such action verbs as "describe," "identify," "analyze," or "create," which is a performance you can observe. The learner must also be told how the performance will be evaluated. Review Bloom's Taxonomy in chapter 2 for lists of words that exemplify critical thinking skills and are effective in writing objectives.

   Which of the following objectives, for example, follow Mager's rules: "Be able to create an animal using Legos" or "Be able to appreciate a Beethoven sonata"? If you identified the first objective, you are correct, because you can observe the learner building an animal and see the result of his or her construction. On the other hand, how will you evaluate the appreciation the learner gains from listening to a piece of music? Keep verb choice in mind as you write your own objectives.

2. **Condition.** State the condition(s) under which the performance is to occur. For example, what does the learner need to use or not use to complete the task? Are there any conditions that must be present to perform the skill?

3. **Criterion.** The criterion of acceptable performance is how well you want the learner to perform.

Note that point 2 (condition) and point 3 (criterion) do not have to be written into the objective but should be considered as you write it. Figure 3.1 identifies the components of an objective.

In summary, objectives should be:

- Specific, indicating what exactly you are going to do, with or for whom
- Measurable, indicating how they can be measured

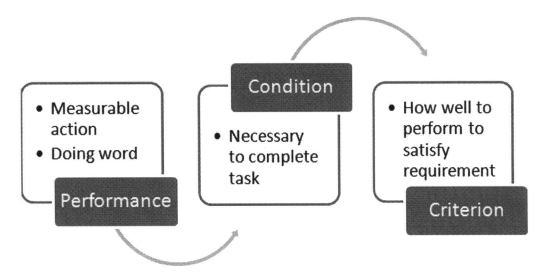

Figure 3.1. Components of an Objective. *Created by author online*

- Achievable (e.g., within a specified time frame, with money or staff available)
- Relevant, leading to desired outcomes
- Time bound, accomplished according to schedule

Objectives help you define your elearning course. The most effective way to get the desired outcome is to set performance objectives that will serve as a guide throughout the course's entire instructional design and development process. They can be written at the beginning or the end. By writing them early, you have a focus for all components of the course you are creating. They also help keep your strategies focused and define assessment so your learners know exactly what to expect. Review can then take place when all parts of the course are completed and before launching it. Objectives can be categorized as procedural, showing how to accomplish something, and as outcomes, providing a product. Note the differences between the goal and objectives in figure 3.2.

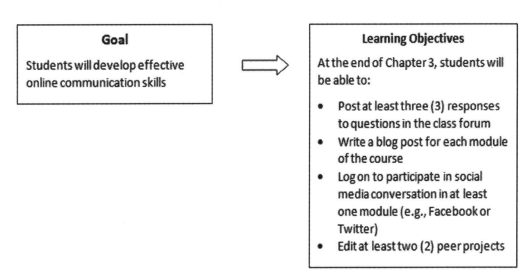

Figure 3.2. Differences between Goals and Objectives. *Created by author online*

Outcomes

Outcomes are important to the planning phase. They define what your learners should have accomplished and can measurably demonstrate—the knowledge, skills, or attitudes that the learner will know and be able to do by the end of the course. For example, can your patrons conduct an effective search for medical information in a library database? Is a student able to explain the difference between a resource that needs to be cited and one that can be used under Creative Commons? Has an attendee in your course on interviewing skills used these skills to obtain a new job?

Three components of measurable outcomes (Osters and Tiu, 2009) include: (1) student learning behaviors, (2) appropriate assessment methods, and (3) specific student performance criteria. Outcomes can be measured qualitatively or quantitatively, using measures such as statistics or percentages, to assess whether the learning outcomes have been achieved. Tools and techniques may include exams, rubrics, projects, portfolio evaluations, reflective journals, and employer surveys, to name some. The performance criteria should be expressed in measurable terms. To summarize, outcomes are measurable, achieved results or consequences and focus on what the learner has attained from the course, not what the instructor does to facilitate the learning. There can be more than one outcome related to each goal.

Writing Goals, Objectives, and Outcomes

Now that you understand the differences between goals, objectives, and outcomes, it's time to write them.

Goals

Goals are more generally stated than objectives and encompass the aim of the course. Typically, they are one or two sentences at most—for example, a goal for a course on plagiarism might be, "The goal of this elearning course is to understand what plagiarism is and to identify methods to avoid it." You might write goals for the online course and place them on the course website in advance so learners know what to expect from the course. The "Comparison of Goals" textbox shows examples of vague and more concrete goals. For example, in the first entry, you have clarified the type of writing to measure (e.g., blog posts) and that "being a good writer" means using correct grammar. You have also used measurable verbs: "write" and "use."

COMPARISON OF GOALS

Vague Goal	Concrete Goal
Understand how to write a blog post	Write effective blog posts using correct grammar
Understand beliefs of different cultures	Compare and contrast the beliefs of two African cultures
Learn about endangered species	Discuss the importance of a whale's habitat

The following tips will help you write goals that lead your learners to successfully achieve learning outcomes of the course you design.

- Identify the big ideas about the subject in question that you think students should understand after completing the course.
- Base the number of goals on the desired learning outcomes. Think about what you want students to remember about the course in five years.
- Let learners know exactly what they will achieve by completing the course before you begin its development.
- Focus on the important aspects of learning using Bloom's Taxonomy (Bloom, 1956) as a guide to higher-order thinking.
- Know your audience and create goals that are learner focused. What is the learners' level of understanding about the skill you are planning to teach? Finding out their interests, skills, and level of experience helps you identify goals to attain specific learning outcomes.
- Determine desired outcomes while developing goals. Ask learners what they plan to get out of the course. Do they need to master a specific skill, expand their knowledge about a topic? The goal and outcome go hand in hand. This knowledge will help you incorporate strategies that provide the necessary information, tools, and activities during the course.
- Show how the goals apply to actions or situations in the real world.
- Clearly communicate the course goals on the website or in the course description in advance.

See table 3.1 for sample goals and objectives you might use for an information literacy topic.

Objectives

Writing specific objectives is an important part of their success. Often they begin with: "The learner will be able to . . ." or "The student will . . ." Typically, three or four objectives are sufficient with no more than six or seven.

Table 3.1. Writing Goals and Objectives

LEARNING GOAL: GENERAL OUTCOMES	LEARNING OBJECTIVES: SPECIFICS TO ACHIEVE GOAL	BLOOM'S THINKING SKILLS
Students will be able to create search strategies to retrieve relevant articles on a topic.	Students will be able to define keywords.	Understanding
	Students will be able to use keywords in a search strategy.	Application
	Students will be able to select the appropriate Boolean operator to narrow and broaden a search.	Analysis
	Students will be able to evaluate a list of results to select five authoritative, relevant articles.	Evaluation

The following tips may help you write your learning objectives:

- Align elearning assessment with your learning objectives. Assessment is used to evaluate what your audience is learning; the more consistent with learning objectives, the more focused the course outcomes.
- Use specific and measurable verbs when writing them. Focus on Bloom's Taxonomy as you select action verbs like "apply" or "achieve," and be precise.
- Make objectives appropriate for your learners. Analyze the audience before developing objectives for the course. Are they for patrons, students, colleagues, young or old? What do they know and what is necessary for them to learn?
- Make sure objectives are supported with appropriate tools and resources.
- Ask the question: Will learners be able to perform the skill(s) they've just acquired effectively when they complete the course? To answer this question, the objectives must clearly define the desired outcomes and how they can be assessed, observed, or measured.
- Use simple language and keep them short. Those limited to one sentence will help learners focus on what is expected.
- If you have several objectives, organize them in subcategories so you don't overwhelm your learners.

See the following textbox, "Comparison of Objectives."

COMPARISON OF OBJECTIVES

Vague Objective	Specific Objective
Understand how to use technology effectively	Use word processing, spreadsheets, databases, and presentation graphics in preparing a final research project
Practice speaking skills	Present testimony in a "mock" court hearing

Finally, your objectives should be realistic and able to be achieved within the specific time span of the course. At the end of your elearning course, make sure to assess whether your objectives have been met as a result of the learning taking place in the course. The textboxes provide templates of criteria to help you outline both procedural and outcome objectives. For example, asking what learning format should be used, why the learning is being requested, who the learning will be targeted to, and how the problem can be addressed provides the basis for creating the objectives.

TEMPLATE FOR CREATING PROCEDURAL OBJECTIVES

	What?	Why?	Who?	How?	When?
Objective 1					
Objective 2					
Objective 3					

TEMPLATE FOR OUTCOME OBJECTIVES

Objectives	Number of Participants Who/Where/How Many	Change That Occurs What (How Much)	Date Needed When
Objective 1			
Objective 2			
Objective 3			

Outcomes

Outcomes should use action verbs, and should be simply stated, distinctive, and specifically aligned to the goals and objectives of the online course. As a result, you should be able to collect accurate and reliable data for each outcome. The outcomes should clearly describe and define abilities, knowledge, and attitudes learners can achieve. You will also be able to use more than one way to measure the outcomes. The following textbox, "Levels of Outcomes," shows some outcome examples.

LEVELS OF OUTCOMES

Not an Outcome	Vague Outcome	Measurable Outcome
Offer patrons opportunities to master the use of technology	Understand socioeconomic differences as they relate to planning an online course	Search library databases for medical data on diabetes
Explain to students what a learning outcome is	Write a learning outcome	Write a learning outcome that contains a condition and observable behavior based on a standard
Show employees how to write a search strategy	Search for articles on a neurological condition	Find five scholarly articles on treatment for epilepsy

⟲ Common Pitfalls

Common pitfalls can occur in all preplanning and planning phases. Here are a few problems to keep in mind as you review:

- **Pitfall:** Replicating a face-to-face course online. Changing a course from the traditional classroom to an online format does not mean putting your handouts online or lecturing as the "sage on the stage" with your online audience watching you read your lecture.
- **Reconsider:** Rethink your content. Leverage the capabilities that technology and the Internet offer to engage your learners. Substitute visuals—images, video, animated slides, photos—to make the content more interesting. Implement ways to encourage participation from your audience. Review more on this aspect in chapter 4.
- **Pitfall:** Writing too general or too specific objectives
- **Reconsider:** When you write objectives, focus on verb choice. Using words such as "understand" or "know" are too general. How will you measure general understanding of a topic? Substitute terms that are not measurable with verbs (e.g., "evaluate," "synthesize," "create") at the higher thinking skill range of Bloom's Taxonomy. Add a measurement as part of the objective, such as "Forty-five percent of parents will demonstrate increased use of verbal warnings with their children."
- **Pitfall:** Failure to design assessments when creating learning objectives
- **Reconsider:** Assessment should measure whether the objectives have been met. Considering assessment and objectives at the same time makes it easier to determine the content and activities necessary to achieve the outcomes.

⟲ Key Points

Preplanning and planning are important first steps when creating an online course. Key decisions at the outset can make or break the quality of your instruction.

- Considering the characteristics of the learners for the course—their prior knowledge, interests, skills—influence the direction your course will take, including content and strategies.
- Deciding what type of instruction is necessary to meet your training need requires a needs analysis to determine content, resources, personnel, technology, and time commitment.
- Initial steps in the planning process requires considering the goals, objectives, and outcomes of the instruction. What do you want your audience to accomplish as a result of your online course?
- Write the objective using action verbs that address Bloom's Taxonomy of thinking skills. Take into account performance, condition, and criteria for the most effective objectives with specific outcomes.

Chapter 3 has pointed out elements of preplanning and planning to consider as you contemplate instruction. Some are differences between traditional face-to-face courses and elearning. Although these two phases of the process of creating an online course are time consuming, you have just begun the journey. Chapter 4 builds on preplanning and planning analyses to move to another part of the process—that of actually designing the course. For more suggestions on preplanning and planning the online course, see table 3.2.

Table 3.2. Additional Resources for Chapter 3

DESCRIPTION	URLS
Brain facts that can influence elearning	http://elearningindustry.com/6-scientifically-proven-brain-facts-that-elearning-professionals-should-know
A model of learning objectives based on Bloom's Taxonomy	http://www.celt.iastate.edu/wp-content/uploads/2015/09/RevisedBloomsHandout-1.pdf
Lists of verbs based on Bloom's Taxonomy	http://elearningindustry.com/use-perfect-learning-objectives-to-boost-the-quality-of-your-e-learning
Clickable diagram of Bloom's Taxonomy and examples of each level	http://www.celt.iastate.edu/teaching/effective-teaching-practices/revised-blooms-taxonomy
Educator Larry Ferlazzo's lists of best websites by topic in numerous categories—very comprehensive	http://larryferlazzo.edublogs.org/about/my-best-of-series/
Websites on using Bloom in the classroom	http://larryferlazzo.edublogs.org/2009/05/25/the-best-resources-for-helping-teachers-use-blooms-taxonomy-in-the-classroom/
Examples of good/not so good learning outcomes in different subject areas	http://facultycenter.stonybrook.edu/sites/facultycenter.stonybrook.edu/files/basic-pages/90/files/examples_of_measurable_learning_outcomes_without_urls.pdf

⊚ Exercises

To reinforce principles covered in chapter 3, you will conduct some preplanning and planning activities on a particular topic.

1. Identify why each of the following objectives is effective or needs work.
   - Students will be able to evaluate articles from academic medical journals based on their authoritative content.
   - Patrons will understand the differences between a search on Google and one in a library database.
   - Students will be able to list three primary and three secondary sources for their topic.
   - Students will know how to conduct a search in Google.
   - Students will use Boolean operators (e.g., "and," "or," "not") to narrow a search in a library database to retrieve five effective articles on their topic.
   - The instructor will create a presentation illustrating how patrons can use the online library catalog.
2. For the following scenario, write at least one goal and outcome and two or three objectives.
   - **Scenario:** The local public library holds an after-school book club for teens each week. Each teen reads a non-fiction book of his or her choice during the month. They discuss their books together at each session. The librarian wants to promote a library service for teens. She wants to encourage more teens to come to the library to read and discuss non-fiction.
   - **Goals** (e.g., Teens to read and discuss non-fiction)
   - **Objectives** (e.g., Read at least one non-fiction book in one month, attend at least three of four weekly discussions)
   - **Outcomes** (e.g., Promote teen reading by increasing the number of teens in the after-school book club by ten)
3. Select a topic of interest for a course to present online in your library and apply what you learned about preplanning and planning. Consider pedagogy you learned in part 1 of this book. Ask questions that will help you create a course that is based on theory, meets the needs of an online environment, and does not just mirror a traditional class.
   a. Analyze your potential learners. Some questions to answer might include:
      ◦ Who are the learners you want to take your online course?
      ◦ What do you want them to be able to do after completing the course?
      ◦ What prior knowledge do they need to be able to begin the course?
      ◦ What is the difference between online and in-class students? How should the issue be addressed?
   b. Write goals, objectives, and outcomes for the course.
      ◦ List two goals and at least one outcome for the course.
      ◦ Write three to five objectives to attain the outcomes.

⊚ References

Bloom, Benjamin. S. 1956. *Taxonomy of Educational Objectives, Handbook I: The Cognitive Domain.* New York: David McKay.

Mager, Robert Frank. 1984. "Mager's Tips on Instructional Objectives." Adapted and excerpted from *Preparing Instructional Objectives*. 2nd ed. Belmont, CA: Lake. http://www2.gsu. edu/~mstmbs/CrsTools/Magerobj.html#Objective.

Osters, Sandi, and F. Simone Tiu. 2009. *Writing Measurable Learning Outcomes*. http://www. gavilan.edu/research/spd/Writing-Measurable-Learning-Outcomes.pdf.

⊚ Further Reading

Anderson, Lorin W., and David R. Krathwohl, eds. 2001. *A Taxonomy for Learning, Teaching, and Assessing: A Revision of Bloom's Taxonomy of Educational Objectives (Complete Edition)*. New York: Longman.

Dalto, Jeffrey. 2014. "Robert Mager's Performance-Based Learning Objectives Convergence Training." *Convergence Training* (blog). November 24. http://blog.convergencetraining.com/robert-magers-performance-based-learning-objectives.

Dick, Walter, Lou Carey, and James O. Carey. 2004. *The Systematic Design of Instruction*. 6th ed. Boston: Allyn & Bacon.

Designing the Online Course

IN THIS CHAPTER

▷ Listing and explaining design principles

▷ Describing components used in the design phase of an online course

▷ Developing an outline for each phase of the online course, starting before the course begins and through the beginning, during, and after the online course

▷ Analyzing design components of an online course

▷ Using animations and interactions to keep the viewer's attention and engage the learner

IN AN IDEAL SITUATION, the librarian would have a team to help design an online course. The team might consist of a content expert; an instructional designer and graphic artist; a technology guru who knows all about the individual technology needed, including the library systems piece, like a learning management system (LMS); and someone to test the results. And, if you are really lucky, you might have a person from the administrative side to act as project manager. All of these people would work together, sharing their expertise to create the final product—an effective, motivating online course that your audience will learn from and enjoy their time while achieving the goals and outcomes of the course. Would that you were so fortunate! What you need to consider then is what areas of expertise you, the librarian, or others in your library, can count on to build an online course. And, what you will have to do yourself.

In chapter 3 on preplanning and planning, you learned how to determine whether there was a need for an online course, the intended audience, and the goals and objectives to achieve learning outcomes. You now have the analyses necessary to focus on components of design in chapter 4. Design and development must be completed before you can test or implement the online course with or without the help of a designated team just mentioned. In chapter 4 you will analyze the components to consider in designing an online course. You will also look at design principles and elements used in the layout of a course.

⊚ Design Basics

Venturing into the online arena can be quite frightening to say the least. Will students be able to use the online learning tools? Will they become engaged in each other's progress? Will a lack of face-to-face interaction hinder learning? What strategies will you use besides lecture to present the necessary content? These are only a few of the questions you must consider.

Whether you spent years teaching face-to-face, dealing with patrons on a one-to-one basis, or are new to the instructional arena, the approach to teaching online is different. For example, the veteran who has taught information literacy techniques to students in higher education may have created a course as the semester progressed without having the entire course laid out ahead of time. This approach does not work well for an online course. Therefore, the up-front time necessary to prepare for the beginning of the course is significant.

Depending on the size of the library, numbers of employees, instructional design, and technical expertise on-site, the librarian's work may involve a multitude of diverse tasks. In chapter 2, instructional design models—ADDIE, Gagné's nine events, and Bloom's Taxonomy—were reviewed. Most traditional forms of the instructional design process involve some form of ADDIE; that is, they begin with analysis, move to design and development, then on to implementation, and finally evaluation. Parts of the other models are often incorporated as well. You and other library personnel, including the library board and administrators, may be asked to perform needs analyses to determine patron, student, or employee needs and specific types of instruction to undertake. You may work with subject-matter experts (SMEs) to create objectives to address the learning needs. You might develop a content model to accommodate your library's audience. Depending on the topic, the SME may be you who creates the content for a subject, such as information literacy, copyright compliance, or technology training. Finally, you may also be responsible for assessing the knowledge and skills learners achieved after completing the online course. You might also need to develop some post-learning activities or questions to identify retention of learning over time. Some or all of these tasks may be the responsibility of the librarian—a mighty undertaking.

Instructional design encompasses all of these tasks. It is necessary to embrace the learners first so that you can create a learning experience that brings about change in them. For each part of an online course, consider these typical instructional tasks covered in chapters 3, 4, and 5:

- Conduct a pre-assessment (i.e., needs and audience analyses) (chapter 3).
- Identify learning goals, objectives, and outcomes (chapter 3).
- Design content and activities (chapter 4).
- Select strategies (chapter 4).
- Develop course materials (chapter 4).
- Implement and deliver instruction (chapter 5).
- Design assessments (chapter 5).

- Select media (chapter 5).
- Evaluate, revise, and reflect (chapter 5).

Typical online courses include components, such as objectives, strategies, activities, additional resources, and assessments. Some or all of the specific components might contain assigned readings and writings; exercises/tasks for small groups, individuals, and the whole class; discussion forums; and resources for further study. Pre- and post-assessments are also part of an online course or each module if the course is designed in individual modules.

Once you decide what you want students to achieve, how they will interact with the material, what the assignments will be, and how you are going to pre- and post-assess their work, you have the beginnings of a design process you can then replicate for different purposes and audiences in different online formats.

⑥ Essentials of a Design Plan

The design plan, often created with the help of an instructional designer or subject-matter expert, is usually the first element you will create on the way to organizing and ultimately developing and delivering instruction. A design plan is a preliminary document that lays out the different types of information that has been collected, as well as the plan for the structure of the instruction. The plan may include elements, such as results of the learner analysis, the intended audience, the needs assessment, the instructional layout, and time frame of each module or lesson in the course.

The ADDIE model (Pappas, 2013) lets you take the information collected in the analysis phase and form a framework for your design plan. This includes organizing the content and deciding on how to sequence it, and strategies to use, as well as the learning format. Then a design plan is constructed based on the components mentioned earlier.

Each part of the design is vital to the success of an online learning course. Reviewing components and sample tasks of an online course will familiarize you with tasks to focus on as you create your own course.

Preassessment Elements

As a course instructional designer, which may be one of your roles at your organization, you may be working with subject-matter experts (SMEs) and other team members to:

- Perform needs and audience analyses to determine training needs
- Create goals, objectives, and outcomes to address learning needs
- Develop content for all sections of the online course
- Use different strategies to deliver content, including diverse activities
- Decide on technology and how to use it to optimize learning
- Create assessments to evaluate learners' knowledge and decide what post-learning should be
- Develop the framework that encompasses all components

Investing time at the beginning of the process by addressing all aspects of the online course will reduce the need for follow-up and will provide students with a more accurate set of expectations about the course. Assessing students' abilities, knowledge, behaviors, and attitudes helps to align all that they will use in the course—the content, strategies, activities, technology—with the course goals, objectives, and outcomes.

Based on the needs assessment discussed in chapter 3, the design of components of instruction described in this chapter will be for an elearning course. Therefore, the first task as you start designing the course is to focus on the pre-assessment outline—what you plan to include in this section of the course. One idea is to begin with some activities that allow the instructor and students to get to know one another to create a positive learning environment from the start. For example, you might put in some low-stakes ice-breaker-type assignments and get students communicating with the instructor and with each other right away. The task can be as simple as asking them to introduce themselves on a discussion board created for the course. This exercise enables students to be actively involved immediately. It also removes the feeling of isolation that some online learners complain about and offers some immediate feedback to the instructor on the course's audience. Such an activity helps students understand that their role in the course will be interactive and sets the tone and expectations from the start.

To facilitate the learning process, other parts to the pre-assessment outline might include:

- Course information materials that students need to be familiar with and that answer the question "What is expected from me?" They might include a welcome message, an instructor biography and contact information, syllabus, course schedule, academic honesty policy, frequently asked questions, a guide on how to complete the course, a student user guide, and technology tips, for example, learning to use a learning management system (LMS) or content management system (CMS) if they will be part of the course structure. The LMS will be discussed in chapter 5.
- A communication board for group discussion, e-mail, and phone communication, and so forth
- Orientation materials explaining parameters of the course, perhaps how to use the technology and navigate the course. Especially important is to make sure that log-on instructions are clearly written and posted where all learners for the course can access them.
- Record-keeping tools to track student progress
- Lists of content topics and supplemental resources that need to be located or developed, as well as obtaining copyright clearance for materials, if necessary

These pieces that learners will need prior to (or at the start of) the course all need to be in place before the beginning of an online class. They can also form the publicity for the course on the organization's website.

Content Development

Content is an important part of any course, and developing it must emphasize both pedagogical and technology aspects. When considering content, you must decide not only what content to include but how to organize and best present it so learners get the most out of the instruction. Your design plan should determine the learning format, how to sequence the material, and strategies to use to convey the information.

Start by organizing the course, and determine how it will be divided. For example, you might coordinate materials appropriate to the content and other course components into individual course modules. Then map out connections among individual lessons of a module. You also may want to link a quiz to content readings and videos in a particular module. Creating this organizational map will also help determine where to place and store the actual content files online. If the content files have a different organizational structure, you may want to create separate organization maps for the files.

From a learning standpoint, content should be broken into chunks to enhance student learning. Begin with an overall review of the content for your training, identifying key ideas, sub-points, places to add activities or questions, or concepts that need more explanation. For example, if you are conducting a single webinar, divide content into meaningful segments that could be logical modules or units of study if you expanded the content into a longer modular course, and supplement them with other resources and learner activities. Look for logical breaking points according to sub-topics in segments of about ten minutes or less. As you create the content, you may have to develop new materials (text, graphics, and multimedia) or locate and utilize computer-based supplemental resources, if needed. Also, decide on formative assessments. If it is a modular weekly course, try to have a couple of formative non-graded evaluations—small quizzes, assignments, or pieces of projects—as part of each lesson, if possible. Learners should also be able to interact with the content such as through videos.

Additional Online Resources

Additional resources are necessary to supplement the main course content. Course resources include a diverse array of materials that can support both the achievement of the learning objectives and provide a stimulus for deeper understanding. These resources allow learners to explore topics of particular interest to expand beyond the course's core content. Often, interacting with these materials is not assessed but rather used for enrichment to explore topics that motivate the learner. These course-related materials may be journal articles, online books, freely available multimedia, tutorials, library documents, video, audio, simulations and games, websites, samples of others' work, presentations, and stories that let learners delve deeper into the content. Every online course should provide information that extends beyond the scope of the current course and offers a path to future study. You may want to research online for additional materials to make available to students in your discipline. Obtaining copyright clearance for materials may also be necessary. Making a list of the content topics and supplemental materials that need to be created is important as you develop the content.

Open educational resources (OER) are becoming more prevalent and are often copyright-free for use in education. They offer great resources on subject-specific content for online lessons and enrichment materials at both the K–12 and post-secondary levels. Lists of OER and other copyright-free resources are available at http://gettingsmart. com/2015/10/smart-list-30-ways-to-learn-almost-anything-2/.

Place these materials on the course website under the appropriate module, and write instructions on how to find and navigate to them, download and save them. Gather images, sound files, and other multimedia and work with your technology expert to get all content into a format for the Internet. Note: At an academic institution, a learning coordinator or your instructional technology personnel may need to set up accounts on appropriate servers for your online course.

Activities

Activities and feedback are important for instruction, so it is necessary to look at tasks that will make the learning fun and relevant. Activities allow learners to reflect on and apply the content and make it personally meaningful to their lives. Especially in an online class, exercises and projects should be active, engaging, and motivating for students in order to achieve course objectives, as well as diverse enough to consider different learning styles. For example, a cooperative learning activity that includes positive interdependence and individual accountability can still be used in an online setting and promotes collaboration among learners.

Practice is vital to achieve your goals and objectives. If you want learners to perform a skill, such as creating an effective search strategy, evaluating a website, or comparing and contrasting the content of two journal articles, you might model the process with an example—selecting keywords, and showing them some resulting articles. Then give them plenty of practice using content-specific searches where they select their own keywords and find results. If you just tell students about keywords without showing them how to select and use them, and then move on without practice, you are setting them up for failure.

To create effective practice tasks, analyze the performance necessary and provide the learning environment that comes closest to the actual task you want them to be able to perform. Give them problems to solve that mirror those in real-world situations. Show them screencasts of someone conducting a search. Also, think about the difficulties you as the expert may have had performing the behavior, and build practice into the activities that deals with those obstacles. To be critical thinkers and problem solvers, learners must routinely and explicitly have structured practice opportunities to examine their own thinking. Built-in self-assessment should also be a frequent occurrence. Above all, imparting too much information prior to "doing" may cause the learners to tune out this material, whereas incorporating new concepts as part of performing a task motivates them to pay attention in order to achieve the result.

Because of the potential for lack of engagement in an online course, activities must motivate students to interact consistently during the course. Develop a comprehensive student activity/assessment plan that will allow you to achieve the stated course outcomes and provide interactivity at the same time. Combine course structure and an activity/assessment plan as part of the course schedule.

Instructional Strategies

Instructional strategies assist learners in achieving learning goals and objectives. Strategies create the environment for analysis, synthesis, evaluation, and application of online course information. Lecture and demonstration activities are familiar to most people in face-to-face learning but may not be the best approach for an online course. The online environment works well for a learner-centered activity because it provides opportunities for learners to take control of their own learning. Benefits of this active learning include the following:

- Addresses different learning needs to enhance retention
- Reinforces critical thinking and decision-making skills as learners explore the course to solve problems

- Boosts learner motivation and performance when they select their own learning direction
- Has positive effects on performance with instant feedback on their actions
- Creates a sense of community through peer interaction and online discussion

There are a number of different strategies and activities that engage learners in active rather than passive learning. With instructors assuming the role of facilitator and guide, rather than the "sage on the stage," learners can acquire, process, and make sense of the information. Here are several instructional strategies to consider incorporating into your course.

Synchronous Learning

Webinars, for example, are usually live, instructor-led sessions where attendees log in via web-conferencing software or sometimes a phone connection and learn with the instructor during a set time period (e.g., one hour). Asynchronous learning, discussed in chapter 6, is an on-demand recorded online event where learners participate in their own time and place. Both methods of training can be delivered to large numbers of people, sometimes in the thousands. Some organizations use webinars to allow participants to hear from experts who may be knowledgeable on a subject or who provide inspiration or wisdom. A librarian in a corporation might use them to train employees who reside all over the world. A narrative in a video might help learners model a process or behavior. For example, an art demonstration like a paintalong might have learners paint with the instructor as the instructor develops his or her painting and provides tips. It is important to consider learners' expectations so you select the appropriate approach for your audience, the content they want, and the goals and objectives to achieve the outcomes.

Establishing and maintaining learning communities among online learners through the use of instructional technology will help to overcome the isolation that some learners worry about in a webinar. Learning activities should encourage interaction, including involvement with other learners and the instructor during the session. Often a chat feature is available, enabling participants to submit questions and comments during the online session to both the instructor and other students. Detailed, clear instructions for course assignments or activities are also important for instruction to be effective. Other strategies, including personalized learning, project-based learning, and gamification, will be described and illustrated in some of the practical applications in part 3.

Online Forums

Discussion in online synchronous courses is vital, and forums often provide the venue to give learners a place to share ideas and explore the content. Online forums aren't just for peer-to-peer discussion. They can also provide learners with the support they need from their instructors, and keep them up to date with the latest news about the online course.

First, you want to decide on the type of online forum to use. If you plan to post articles for students to read and respond to, then a blog might work. Another option is a threaded discussion board where the instructor poses questions about the content, usually once a week, and students respond to the question and each other's comments. Students may be reluctant to join in so they be more comfortable using a social media forum (e.g.,

Facebook, LinkedIn, or Google+) where you can create a group and invite learners to become members.

In peer-based collaborative online discussions, the instructor should have at least a minimal presence as facilitator to guide the conversation by posting thought-provoking questions based on a particular module's content and then monitor the debate to make sure it relates to the topic. For example, at the beginning of each week of a course, the instructor might post one or two questions, thoughts, or ideas to initiate the discussion, as well as reinforce the course content. Note that sub-groups might form to take a thought in another interesting direction. A smaller group may also help encourage students with special interests or those who are reluctant to share in a large class.

Multimedia

Another way to make a forum more interactive is by adding multimedia like videos or online scenarios to engage the learner. Links to additional resources that are part of the course are also ideal to stimulate online conversations and motivate learners to actively participate. Forums through which instructors provide thought-provoking questions about the content promote active learning and prevent students from feeling isolated.

Technology

Although technology plays a major role in an online course, learning, not the technology, should be the primary focus. Technology tools are just that—tools to facilitate learning to be used to assist learners in achieving the learning goals and objectives of the course. Tools may include an LMS or CMS (e.g., Moodle, Edmodo, Classroom Connect), or an institutional management system. Social media (e.g., Facebook, Twitter, Google Hangouts) and Web 2.0 tools (e.g., wikis, blogs, podcasts) may also be used for discussion. More about these tools in chapter 9.

Tips to Create Successful Course Design

You've reviewed the design plan—pre-assessment, content, activities, additional resources, strategies, and technology. Here's a recap to think about as you begin your own course design:

- As a facilitator, have a plan based on learning standards and course content. Manage and monitor instruction. It may look chaotic, but it should really be organized chaos that includes student discussion and personalized instruction.
- Coach for success. Encourage high expectations measured through high-quality assessment. Assessment is the topic for chapter 5.
- Group for achievement so that everyone contributes. Design assignments that use learners' strengths to advantage and help improve their weaknesses.
- Be the change agent. Plan with a focus on standards and guide students to meet them.
- Collaborate—learners with learners, librarians with teachers, teachers with teachers.
- Connect your course to the real world. Allow learners to apply what they are learning by using relevant examples and creating problems for them to solve.

Design Checklist

Use this checklist to keep track of tasks used to create the design for your online course. http://elearningindustry.com/8-important-characteristics-baby-boomers-elearning-professionals-know

Course Content

☐ Does the content flow, and is it free of grammatical or spelling errors?
☐ Is the content current and consistent with the core curriculum?
☐ Does the content help to achieve the desired learning objectives?
☐ Is referenced content properly credited and quoted?
☐ Is the language used clear and descriptive (without being verbose)?
☐ Have you chosen text that is appropriate for your audience and not gender specific?
☐ Is your tone consistent and appropriate?
☐ Have all statistics, facts, and dates been checked and referenced?
☐ Is the information consistent (e.g., all dates listed in the same manner)?
☐ Has correct capitalization and punctuation been used throughout?
☐ Is the content available in all local languages?

Course Layout

☐ Have you used no more than four fonts throughout the course?
☐ Is the body text in the same font and the headers in a larger font?
☐ Have you included the right line spacing and paragraph length?
☐ Have you used the correct font sizes and colors?
☐ Is the body text left justified?
☐ Have you used bold/italicized words for hierarchical organization?
☐ Are sources cited properly?
☐ Are screen captures current and free of personal data?

Multimedia Elements

☐ Have you included relevant and legally owned images and video throughout?
☐ Are the images relevant, compressed, and resized for easy download?
☐ Are all the multimedia elements consistent in terms of size and quality?
☐ Is the audio synchronized to the video presentations?
☐ Have you included the right line spacing and paragraph length?
☐ Have you used the correct font sizes and colors?
☐ Is any narration clear and easy to understand?
☐ Can audio or video be controlled by the user?
☐ Are all images the right file type and consistent in quality and size?

Total Course Quality

☐ Do you have a clear syllabus in place on the website and at the beginning of the course?
☐ Is the course aesthetically uniform with branding elements included?
☐ Is color usage consistent and appropriate?
☐ Does all content fit the screen without horizontal or vertical scrolling?
☐ Is the look of screens clean and organized with white space for about half the screen?
☐ Have you avoided backgrounds/patterns that may be distracting for the learner?
☐ Can instructors easily add or modify the content within the course?

Incorporating these ideas into the planning for your course design will provide a structure and keep you on track as you proceed to lay out the course. You can find more tips at http://elearningindustry.com/tags/elearning-design-tips. The Design Checklist will help librarians create an effective elearning course for educational and business organizations.

Layout and Course Design

In a perfect world where instructional designers are available to design your online course for you, they would usually undertake this part of the course design with the aid of a subject-matter expert. However, it is useful to understand some best practices of layout and design principles necessary to create meaningful courses if you must undertake the task yourself or supervise and interact with the designer.

The quotation "A picture is worth a thousand words" has had a great influence on elearning designers (Schwertly, 2014). Many researchers have pointed out that visuals get more views than text-based information, that the brain processes visuals much faster than text, that photos and pictures are more engaging to learners, and that visual information can be comprehended faster and retained longer. As a result, incorporating graphics into elearning has become the standard to engage and motivate learners so they comprehend more easily. For example, using illustrations, such as photo images, graphics, animations, graphs, simulations, and others, can help learners see how concepts are related, grouped, and organized. Therefore, it is important to incorporate design elements that work best.

Design Elements

Visual elements are used by instructional designers to enhance learning. The following elements suggest sample uses for each type:

- Timeline: shows a sequence of events
- Flowchart: illustrates a procedure or set of ordered steps
- Diagram: explains a system
- Photograph: shows a real-world example
- Chart: represents quantity relationships visually
- Screen capture: illustrates a process

Figure 4.1 illustrates a design element in the form of a diagram.

Graphics, pictures, and multimedia elements can also enhance instruction, whatever the format.

- **Graphics** are useful for illustrating ideas or concepts. Images should be integral to the content and not a frivolous use. For instance, in a lesson on parts of the human body, if students could click hotspots on a visual to see more details about a specific organ, it would allow them to control the pace of their learning. They could also see each organ in context of the entire body at the same time. In this way it might be easier for students to remember the details without being overwhelmed and review parts more than once, if necessary, for understanding.

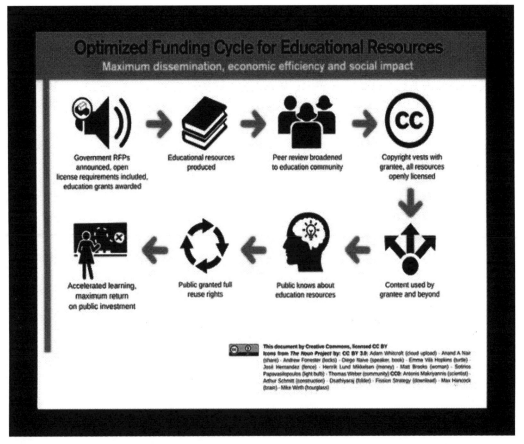

Figure 4.1. Diagram. *Used with permission, Creative Commons. http://tinyurl.com/j2jfvol*

- **Video** might be utilized when you want to showcase an expert on a topic. This could be in an online course or in a classroom setting when the person cannot be there in person. If possible, use short video clips to hold learners' attention. For example, if you were working with an elementary school science teacher, you might incorporate a video of Neil Armstrong's moon walk to make space travel real to the students.
- **Infographics** are becoming ever more popular and can help visually illustrate a process, especially one with many steps. A flowchart is an infographic that could be used to show the steps in the process of using the online catalog.
- **Animations** can show dynamic content, such as how to edit a photo with photo-editing software.

Design Principles

When you select your visuals to include in your course design, consider CRAP, the four principles of design (Wax, 2012):

- Contrast: Avoid using elements that are too similar, for example, the same size font, the same color shapes, or the same line widths. Contrast can help your learner differentiate between different text and graphic elements. It shows the learner the element that is clearly dominant or colors that are complementary.

- Repetition: Be sure to repeat certain elements throughout the learning to provide coherence. For example, if you are using orange boxes to show learner tips, repeat the use of orange boxes throughout the course; don't suddenly switch to blue boxes. In the same way, using a color, shape, or font theme throughout the learning design can help organize the content. Learners will recognize that certain elements represent certain things, such as an orange box representing tips.
- Alignment: In both text and graphic placement, be sure that every element on your screen or page has a reason for where it is placed. If text on one screen is left justified and on the next screen it is centered, this can cause confusion for the learner. Alignment can also provide a hierarchy of importance for the viewer.
- Proximity: When placing similar items on the screen, especially graphic items, group them together so that they become one unit. Proper proximity can help organize information for the student to create a cohesive unit.

It is important to make conscious decisions when creating content, whether it be text-based or graphic, to assist the learner in understanding it. Figure 4.2 illustrates each design principle.

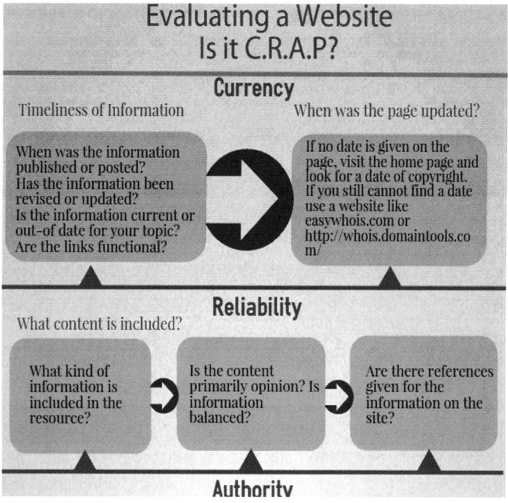

Figure 4.2. CRAP Elements. *Used with permission, Creative Commons. http://hslibguides.leanderisd. org/c.php?g=59193&p=379854*

Also important are the elements you use in the design of your elearning course. These include typography (e.g., font type and size), color, white space, layout, and visuals.

Typography

Use a limited font palette with font size that is easily legible by your learners. Different font sizes show a visual hierarchy and contrast to help organize content.

Color

Your color palette also lends emphasis and should be limited, usually to no more than two or three colors and/or shades of the same colors. Use unequal amounts of each color (e.g., 60-30-10). Complementary colors from opposite sides of the color wheel (e.g., blue/orange, yellow/violet, red/green) create a pleasing color scheme. Pick a background color that does not overwhelm other elements—especially the text font, which must be readable.

White Space

Blank space is one of the most important elements when designing a screen or page. Use bullet lists and short paragraphs if text is used to enhance readability and interest. Text should cover less than half a screen with most important elements surrounded by white space. Plenty of white space on a screen allows the reader's eye to move freely to points of interest you want to emphasize.

Layout

How content is organized affects a reader's ability to comprehend it. Having a consistent layout with headings of a similar font size and typeface and placement in the same location on a page helps the reader move logistically from point to point and enhances retention. Creating a style guide also helps keep design elements consistent throughout the course.

Visual Tools

Graphics are an important part of your design toolbox; however, always keep the learning you want users to achieve uppermost in your thoughts as you create your elearning course. Here are some images to consider:

- **Photographs.** Although learners usually enjoy photographs, select them based on their relevancy. You want them to motivate students to pay attention to the content, as well as for simplifying complex information.
- **Screencasts and captures.** These are useful to show learners how to use an application, for example, if you are explaining computer processes. The screencasts can simulate the process you want to teach them as if they were in the real environment.
- **Illustrations.** These may help the learner make sense of a complex problem.
- **Charts and graphs.** Visual maps can be used to explain complex relationships, show trends, and point out relationships between unrelated concepts and ideas.

- **Avatars.** Sometimes it is interesting to use a character or avatar to represent the instructor in the course, as well as to deliver content or explain directions. This makes the course seem less impersonal, and the avatar represents the instructor who may be missing from the online environment, especially in an asynchronous course.
- **Animated images.** These images often create more impact than a static photograph because they can convey meaning and emotion, and explain processes with less bandwidth than videos.
- **Visual notes.** Small sketches, often like a mind map, enable you to visually jot down ideas, and make connections that can then be shared with a team or small group.
- **Short videos.** Demos and tutorials made into one- to three-minute videos capture a viewer's attention and convey the ideas through sound, text, and images, helping viewers learn more effectively. Use them to explain complicated text, demonstrate how something works, or have an expert tell a story.

Design Best Practices

Although each course you design may have differences, there are always commonalities to consider. Keep in mind the following best practices:

- Structure and organize before designing. Lay out a detailed plan with clear goals, objectives, and outcomes outlined. This will help you fit each slide, piece of content, and image into the whole organization. Then review to make sure everything supports your goals and leads to the outcomes.
- Start your design when there is nothing more that can be subtracted from your content. Artists remove all of what seems to be irrelevant before they consider a painting finished. The same philosophy holds true for the designer. Subtract unnecessary clutter (e.g., words, images); remember the need for white space to focus attention and interest. Too many images or color or other design elements decrease clarity and impact.
- Design is important. Frivolous elements, despite how lovely they look, take away from making complex information clear to your audience.
- Use photographs of real people in real-life situations to demonstrate or explain content. Make images relevant, fun, and engaging so that they move the content ahead. Use these visuals to tell a story.
- Consider the position of elements using proximity and grouping, and a focal point as the most important visual element.
- Always select a picture with a high resolution for a professional look to your course.
- Take your audience into account—their culture, age, and educational, political, and professional backgrounds.

These design tips and best practices will get you started, but no course is perfect in its first iteration. A review by your colleagues, a test of a module with your audience, and your own continuous review will hone your design skills to create a better course. Also, research online courses created by other educators and librarians in public, academic, and special libraries.

◎ Animations and Interactions

Interactive online activities require learners to think, act, and try out different solutions. Animations and interactions can keep the viewer's attention and engage the learner. If learners have to physically interact with the course, it is hard to be passive. Keep these tips in mind when you create animations and interactions for an audience:

- Engage learners as soon as possible in the course. Make your point right away; otherwise, they will get distracted. Because you want learners to know what your objectives are from the start, explain how the course will benefit them in their professional or personal lives; try visuals like an infographic to illustrate what the outcomes should be.
- Minimize the use of special effects. Don't distract users from the learning.
- Keep content relevant for learners and make sure they understand why it will benefit them. Keep it short so attention is retained.
- Use interactions intentionally. Too many interactions, consistently placed, can become boring; interspersing them can help keep viewers' attention. Let learners explore content at their own pace even in a non-linear manner and let them make choices to be engaged in their learning. Interactivity between instructor and students is also an important form of interactivity.
- Include more audio and less text in animations and interactions so the learners' attention will be on the visual and audio content. Trying to view animations and read text at the same time splits viewers' attention and hinders comprehension.

When developing online training, instructional designers are often called upon to utilize both animations and interactions—tools that can help keep learners engaged in the instruction. Some popular design software for online courses includes Microsoft PowerPoint, Adobe Articulate, Adobe Captivate, and Camtasia. All of these programs allow instructional designers to animate content and create interactions. Remember, humor and entertainment as part of the course will also be more motivating to your audience.

◎ Key Points

Chapter 4 describes and illustrates components of the design phase of creating an online course.

- Well-designed elearning is effective in that it actively engages the mind, communicates a purpose, is individualized, encourages exploration, and is memorable and meaningful.
- The instructional designer of an online course usually works with a subject-matter expert (SME); performs a needs and audience analysis; creates goals, objectives, and outcomes to address learning needs; develops content; and creates assessments to evaluate learner knowledge.
- Alone or with the help of an SME, the designer creates relevant content to engage the learner and develop further interest in the subject.
- In the design phase, the instructional designer also creates any other learning materials, including open educational resources (OER).

- The online course design should offer the learner the opportunity to be an active participant, exploring content through interactivity, using questions, simulations, and graphics.
- Everything on the user interface of your course design from fonts to images to color to layout has a purpose. Elements should remain consistent across the course.

Review some of the links in table 4.1 for further ideas and resources on design.

You have now compiled your content, designed and organized your elearning course interface, and located and created additional resources. You still must address assessment as it relates to the goals, objectives, and outcomes discussed in chapter 3. Chapter 5 describes the third phase in the process: implementation, assessment, and reflection.

Table 4.1. Additional Resources for Chapter 4

DESCRIPTION	URLS
Questions to help analysis of training needs for elearning	http://elearningindustry.com/training-needs-analysis-for-elearning-2-sets-questions-ask-client
Checklist of instructional design tips for elearning	http://www.csuchico.edu/tlp/resources/rubric/instructionalDesignTips.pdf
Designing and packaging an online course	http://technologysource.org/article/creating_online_courses/
OER resources	http://gettingsmart.com/2015/10/smart-list-30-ways-to-learn-almost-anything-2/
CRAP test worksheet	https://www.csuchico.edu/lins/handouts/eval_websites.pdf
Designing an elearning course using Gagné's events of instruction	https://community.articulate.com/articles/how-to-design-your-e-learning-course-using-gagne-s-9-events-of-instruction
Facts you need to know about the power of visuals	https://blog.slideshare.net/2014/11/10/the-power-of-visuals-10-facts-you-need-to-know
Tips for developing a synchronous elearning course	http://elearningindustry.com/46-elearning-tips-for-synchronous-learning

⊚ Exercises

To reinforce and practice what you learned in chapter 4 about designing an online course, try the following exercises:

1. To clarify ADDIE, Gagné, and Bloom, compare and contrast the theories and how you would incorporate some of their features into your own online course.
2. Select content where you might normally explain it using bullet points and text; instead, use a visual explanation.
3. Apply what you learned about design in chapter 4 to your own library online course. Select a topic you would consider for an online course, and answer the questions and perform the tasks below:
   a. Who is the audience for the course?
   b. Why should you create an online course for this audience?
   c. List at least one objective and outcome and write content that you think would help your audience to achieve that objective.
   d. Develop an interactive activity that will help to achieve the objective. Try to employ one of Bloom's higher-level thinking skills as part of the activity.
   e. For a discussion forum, write a question or present an idea based on your content that you want your learners to discuss.
   f. Incorporate technology. What technology tools would you include and why (e.g., video, social media, Web 2.0 tool)?
   g. Using the structure of ADDIE, describe briefly what you would include for A = analyze, D = design in your online course.

⊚ References

Pappas, Christopher. 2013. "The ADDIE Instructional Design Model. eLearning Industry." May 8. http://www.slideshare.net/elearningindustry/the-addie-instructional-design-model-20797917?related=1.

Schwertly, Scott. 2014. "Visual Is Viral: 10 Facts You Need to Know." LinkedIn SlideShare. November 10. https://blog.slideshare.net/2014/11/10/the-power-of-visuals-10-facts-you-need-to-know.

Wax, Dustin. 2012. "Design Better with CRAP." Lifehack. July 30. http://www.lifehack.org/articles/communication/design-better-with-crap.html.

⊚ Further Reading

Anderson, Lorin W., and David R. Krathwohl, eds. 2001. *A Taxonomy for Learning, Teaching, and Assessing: A Revision of Bloom's Taxonomy of Educational Objectives (Complete Edition)*. New York: Longman.

Barr, R. B., and J. Tagg. 1995. "From Teaching to Learning: A New Paradigm for Undergraduate Education." *Change* 27, no. 6: 13–25.

Dale, E. 1969. "Cone of Experience." *Educational Media: Theory into Practice*. Columbus, OH: Charles Merrill. http://changingminds.org/explanations/learning/active_learning.htm.

Gagné, R. M., L. J. Briggs, and W. W. Wager. 1992. *Principles of Instructional Design*. 4th ed. Fort Worth, TX: Harcourt Brace Jovanovich College.

LaMotte, Allison. 2015. "How to Design Your E-learning Course Using Gagné's 9 Events of Instruction." E-Learning Heroes. July. https://community.articulate.com/articles/how-to-design-your-e-learning-course-using-gagne-s-9-events-of-instruction.

Legault, Nicole. "An Introduction to the ADDIE Model for Instructional Designers." E-Learning Heroes. https://community.articulate.com/articles/an-introduction-to-the-addie-model-for-instructional-designers.

Showers, Joyce B. 1981. "Transfer of Training: The Contributions of Coaching." *Journal of Education* 163, no. 2: 163–72. http://changingminds.org/explanations/learning/active_learning.htm.

Walter, Ekaterina, and Jessica Gioglio. 2015. *The Power of Visual Storytelling: How to Use Visuals, Videos, and Social Media to Market Your Brand.* New York: McGraw-Hill Education.

Wiggins, G., and J. McTighe. 1998. *Understanding by Design.* Alexandria, VA: Association for Supervision and Curriculum Development.

Implementing, Assessing, Reflecting on the Online Course

THE LAST PHASE OF CREATING AN ONLINE course includes implementing it for the learners, assessing the learning that has taken place, and reflecting on the course and its value. Chapter 4 reviewed aspects of designing an online course. Now that you have the components, it is time to implement the course—considering delivery methods and technology needed. As discussed in chapter 3, creating goals and objectives go hand in hand with assessment, a vital component of the course. In this chapter, you'll delve into different types of assessment and the importance of each format to determine the effectiveness of the learning. Descriptions of each kind of assessment will help you decide when to use them. The final part of chapter 5 addresses the issue of reflection on the completed online course.

◎ Implementing Your Online Course

You have designed your online course, and you are now ready to implement it—to test-drive it with your audience. Based on online learning best practices, keep in mind some tips to achieve a smooth rollout:

- Ensure predictability of the course, especially at the beginning of the course when learners are still unfamiliar with all aspects of the content, navigation, and help features. Written, detailed, consistent instructions and policies let learners know what to expect. Guide learners to use the learner management tools effectively (e.g., discussion forums, types of content, assignments, assessments).
- Up-front preparation helps students become acclimated. Your syllabus, resources, and learner support systems are vital to be able to respond to students' questions quickly and completely.
- Plan alternate delivery options in case technological issues occur. Be agile to modify activities if learners are having trouble understanding a given concept.
- Monitor your online course frequently and respond often to users' questions and concerns to alleviate aspects of distance separating you and your learners. Manage conflict between and among students.
- Communicate with your students by holding regular online office hours, encouraging dialogue by participating along with student contributions, and sharing your own examples and experiences about content.
- Point out information necessary to clarify instructions for assignments, course navigation, and assessment.
- Create an interactive online classroom culture and model your expectations for your learners.
- Decide on a delivery system for your online course and become familiar with its features and functionality.

◎ Management Systems

As part of implementing the online course, an important component is how the course will be delivered to users. Three types of commercial management systems are often used: the learning management system (LMS), the content management system (CMS), and the learning content management system (LCMS).

- A learning management system (LMS), which is a software platform (e.g., Moodle), is often used in online courses. It stores and delivers content and tracks participation in training. It incorporates all parts of the course—content, assessment, communication, resources, data collection and tracking performance, accomplishments, and connections across an entire group of learners. An LMS can also deliver different training to diverse users as needed to meet certain goals, such as business compliance training. Some organizations add a social media component like Skype or Google Hangouts, especially for the communication and discussion parts of the online course. Many academic and business organizations also use their own management system, and some use organizational systems in conjunction with commercial ones.

- Content management systems (CMSs) (e.g., WordPress, Drupal) are a collection of Internet tools used to create, store, organize, and display elearning course content, including files, images, and audio, in a central location, such as on a website. Depending on the level of permissions authorized by the organization, users can edit, add to, or just view content.
- A learning content management system (LCMS) allows users to create collaboratively content that can be published in various formats. The target audience for the LCMS is the learning content creator, whereas the LMS audience is the learner. This chapter focuses on the LMS.

When considering what system to use, ask the following questions to help you determine necessary features and functionality:

- Will all content materials be located within the LMS?
- Who will be responsible for setting up course components in the course site?
- What class management options are necessary, and how will they be set up in the course site? Will your management system contain just one course or many?
- How difficult will it be to learn to use the LMS? Will you have the support of the technology department to help?
- Will modifications be necessary?

Focusing on the LMS described next will explain how management systems work. See table 5.2 later in this chapter for links to more information on the CMS and LCMS.

⑥ Learning Management Systems

This chapter looks in detail at the learning management systems (LMSs) that can control how both the instructor and learners interact with the learning environment of the online course. The LMS, the most robust type of management system, is a digital learning environment that manages all the aspects of the learning process, including communicating learning objectives, organizing learning timelines, and letting learners know exactly what they should expect to learn and when. It is an effective way for instructors to compile, deliver, and manage their content, monitor participation, and assess performance among learners.

The LMS allows you to create a digital website where learners can:

- View uploaded learning materials, such as videos, interactive learning modules, quizzes, a syllabus, and other resources to meet the learning goals of the online course
- Access the course materials online from any location
- Track their progress so they can see what they've learned and what they still need to accomplish
- Communicate with the instructor for questions and collaborate with their peers
- Use forums to discuss content topics and work together on projects
- Receive incentives and rewards to promote learning

Examples of LMSs

There are numerous LMSs, many of which have been designed for certain industries, their learners, and needs. Not every LMS is the same. Some are quite sophisticated with a variety of features; others contain just fundamental abilities. Learning management systems continue to increase their functionality and have become an important part of many online courses. Some of the most popular are listed in table 5.1.

Table 5.1. Features of Learning Management Systems

LMS	FEATURES	AUDIENCE	ACCESS	TECH SUPPORT
Blackboard Learn	Mobile, chat, 5 videos at once, annotate whiteboard	K–12, higher ed, corporate	Cost based on number to access	Cumbersome interface
Canvas	Simple design, easy navigation	K–12, higher ed, corporate	Institution fee, free use at user level	Student Quick Guide, phone, chat, e-mail 24/7
Edmodo	Student profile, posts; teacher-moderated comments	K–12	Free access for educators/students	Limited functionality for higher ed and corporate
Google Classroom	No ads; simple to use, share, grade assignments, collaborate on documents, cloud share, connect via video, text chat; Hangouts	K–12	Free for schools with free Google Apps for Education	24/7 support, use on any device
Moodle	Clean design, easy navigation and grading, mobile access	Higher ed, corporate	Open source, free access, responsive design to mobile	Large plug-in database, online help forums, customizable
Schoology	Design focus on students, mobile, analytics	K–12, higher ed	Free for schools	Community, guides, help desk

Selecting the LMS

When selecting an LMS, you want to address institution/organization needs, as well as instructor and learner needs. You must find out if your organization already has an LMS or whether you need to research one for your learning courses. If you need one for your learning course, you must match your learning course, its requirements, and criteria, for example, data collection and course interactivity, with the best LMS that meets those needs.

Once you decide an LMS is needed, it's time to evaluate the different features and functionality offered by the various systems. Depending on the needs of the course, some features will be a must—can the LMS compile data; will students want to use the system; and how supportive will LMS vendors be?

- **Data collection.** If you collect student data, such as results from assessments or assignments, your LMS must have data tracking features and the ability to analyze data.

- **Design.** Considerations on design include: Is the design interesting and easy to navigate? Are features useful to learners (e.g., gamification or social learning)? Can the functionality of the LMS be extended, such as through plug-ins? If not, will your learning environment be limited if the need for online learning increases? Are the organization and customization of the LMS easy to learn? Do you need reporting, social networking, single sign-on, mobile support, or other qualities?
- **LMS vendors.** Look for reviews of the LMS and the company that owns it. Check with other organizations similar to yours for recommendations. Explore the vendor's support services, including maintenance that comes with your package to see if your staff has help to meet its level of expertise. Look to the future and whether what you buy today can be adapted to your organization's future requirements.

Finally, often the LMS may need to integrate with an organization's existing technology system. As you make your choice, discuss your institution's overall technology system as it relates to the LMS you may be considering. Some institutions have their own systems so that an LMS just discussed may not be necessary. Again, this is a question for your tech person. Knowing the features and requirements for your course, for example, mobile access, will help in deciding upon the best LMS for your learning needs.

The LMS you select will directly impact not only your learners but you, the instructor. Many systems have built-in assessment and tracking so the instructor and learner can chart their learning. This enables the instructor to communicate directly with learners on their progress. The LMS can also be used to provide ongoing resources even after training is completed. Review the resources in table 5.2 for more details about LMSs and CMSs and selecting them.

Table 5.2. Additional Resources on Management Systems

DESCRIPTION	URLS
Numerous articles on LMS (lists, selection tips, trends)	https://elearningindustry.com/?s=learning+management%20system
Questions to help you select your LMS	http://elearningindustry.com/9-questions-to-help-you-select-the-best-learning-management-system
Choosing the right LMS: factors and elements	http://elearningindustry.com/choosing-right-learning-management-system-factors-elements
Google Classroom LMS best practices	http://elearningindustry.com/top-10-google-classroom-best-practices
Google for Education (Google Classroom)	http://elearningindustry.com/google-classroom-review-pros-and-cons-of-using-google-classroom-in-elearning
Tips to choose the best LMS	http://elearningindustry.com/11-tips-choosing-best-learning-management-system
LMS vs. CMS vs. LCMS	https://www.opensesame.com/blog/lms-vs-lcms-vs-cmschanging-one-letter-makes-big-difference
Examples of CMSs	http://www.makeuseof.com/tag/10-popular-content-management-systems-online/

◎ Assessing the Online Course

The evaluation component is vital to any online course and should be considered in conjunction with goals, objectives, and outcomes, discussed in chapter 3. Two different forms of evaluation, formative and summative, are used in instructional design to assess whether the goals, objectives, and learning outcomes of an online course have been achieved. For example, can learners perform a specific skill, demonstrate a change in behavior or attitude, or show increased knowledge that enables them to perform their job better or solve a problem?

- **Formative assessment.** This ongoing evaluation occurs as learning is taking place and employs qualitative feedback to guide learners as instruction continues. For example, if students answer questions wrong in a quiz at the end of a topic, they can go back and review the content necessary to get the answers right. Or, a pre-assessment can check for prior knowledge to see what students know as they start a course. Check-in quizzes during or at the end of each lesson might be objective, using a few multiple-choice, true/false, or matching questions. They can also be interactive—an e-mail message from the instructor with constructive feedback to the learner.

    These assessments enable the instructor to measure the effectiveness of activities and strategies as the course progresses. They are low stakes; that is, they have a low point value or are not graded. Students can also self-assess their progress in the course and know where they may need additional help early enough to improve their performance toward achieving the objectives of the course.
- **Summative assessment.** A summative evaluation occurs at the conclusion of modules or the entire course to determine the overall effectiveness of the instruction. It is usually quantitative, such as a recorded score used as proof of learning achievement. An end-of-course assessment is often used to show completion of the online course. The summative assessment contains a larger number of questions, (e.g., multiple choice, fill in the blanks) with minimal feedback from the instructor, and scores are automatically recorded in the LMS. It also provides information about all parts of the course itself so the instructor can analyze the online course before teaching it again.

Formative Assessment

Whether in an academic institution, a public library, or a business, formative assessment is being used by educators in the teaching and learning process at all levels of instruction both face-to-face and online. In general, a good formative assessment provides teachers with information that equips them and their students and families with feedback about what each student has learned and where they need additional support. It influences online course planning, guides instruction, and facilitates student learning.

Gathering evidence of learning in real time is a general definition of formative assessment; however, many educators have different ideas about what formative assessment is. For example, one teacher in an elementary school might call the Friday vocabulary quiz or the test at the end of a unit formative assessment. Another in a university class will say it's the feedback she gets from handheld devices that record, in real time, what students have learned. Many educators will tell you that formative assessment is just about any tool or strategy that helps them find out what learners know as they're in the process of learning. Other educators note that teachers must use what they learned during the assessment process to modify instruction to meet student needs and gain insight about their students. Instructors also indicate that formative assessment lets them learn about their own practice. Based on formative assessment, instructors see what they should reteach or teach next and what strategies worked and those that didn't.

Formative assessment is something that takes place during the process of instruction and is immediately used to inform subsequent instruction. Formative assessment checks for understanding as a lesson progresses and guides the teacher's decisions about future instruction. It helps students understand what their learning goals are, figure out how far they are from those goals, and what they must do to get there (Atkin, Black, and Coffey, 2001).

Types of Formative Assessment

Numerous types of formative assessment are used to provide feedback to students so they can improve their performance. Here are a few examples: student self-assessment, performance assessment, and peer assessment.

Student Self-Assessment

As far back as 1998, research by Paul Black and Dylan William pointed out that formative assessment produced significant learning gains. One of the necessary components they listed for these increases was that students engaged in self-assessment during their learning. Today, a growing number of schools across the country are incorporating student self-assessment as one type of formative assessment. For example, Gust Elementary School in Denver, Colorado, is one of a growing number of schools across the country where student self-assessment is used. At Gust the idea is that just as teachers can teach more effectively if they check students' progress along the way, students can learn more effectively if they understand what they're working toward and where they are. The evaluation is woven into the school day.

With training, teachers can teach students how to assess their own work. For example, students writing an essay are given a model essay and an easy-to-understand rubric identifying characteristics of a well-written paper. The students then critically analyze the essay using the model and rubric. By actively judging their work and progress toward a goal, they then determine steps to take to reach the goal. This process helps students take ownership of their learning because they need to make their own decisions. In this way, student and teacher are working together as partners to improve learning. The self-regulation and self-evaluation skills students learn from this activity benefit them for a lifetime. Figure 5.1 shows an example of a formative assessment chart.

Performance Assessment

Performance assessment gives students a chance to do something that feels meaningful to them. The tasks used to assess students at the end of a unit are based in applications—for example, in math, students could engage in problems, such as where to locate a business to obtain the best profit or how to ship supplies to victims of an earthquake. The format of the project helps students feel that the tasks are meaningful. Students write letters or

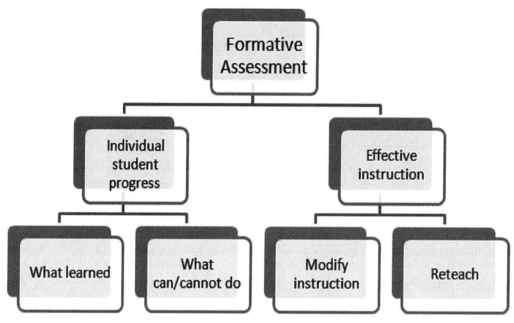

Figure 5.1. Formative Assessment Chart. *Created by author online*

plays, film videos, and create physical structures as part of different performance tasks. They recognize that these objects will be evaluated by the instructor, and that they will also show them to other students and other members of the community. Students can defend their work in front of peers, teachers, and librarians or even parents.

Peer Assessment

Having groups of colleagues assess their peers can be quite effective if used as a formative component. For example, it can be done at the end of a group assignment to identify those who failed to do their share or meet group deadlines, or who were passive members only. While identifying dysfunctional members, a final group assessment does not change what happened in that group or make the group experience one that is meaningful and effective.

One example might be for group members to respond to open and closed questions about the performance of each individual participant and how the group as a whole is functioning. Group members give each other feedback on how the group member is performing tasks. The assessment is not about personal characteristics. Assessments for group members may include: attends team meetings, communicates and responds promptly to team members, meets deadlines, completes assigned work, listens, and respectfully considers teammates' ideas and opinions.

Tips for Formative Assessment

Formative assessment can take many formats. For example, break down assignments into smaller chunks and have a couple of assessments—small quizzes, individual tasks, or pieces of assignments every week, if possible, particularly early in the course. Consider the following tips as you create your own formative assessments:

- Avoid infrequent high-stakes (e.g., graded) assessments because students who perform poorly on one may find it difficult to recover. Low-stakes assessments provide feedback and give students chances to learn how to be more effective in the course without risking a failing grade.

- Build in self-assessment as a frequent occurrence. Taking a quiz or reviewing a simulation enables learners to test their own progress and knowledge comprehension.
- Use annotation at different stages of the learning process. Include a self-grading rubric or an answer sheet, or create assessments through the LMS so learners can see mistakes and receive the correct information immediately.
- Ask students to clarify how their work measures up to learning objectives or a grading checklist or rubric. The primary goal of annotation is to improve self-regulations and reflection, and identify more easily with grading criteria so learners meet expectations.
- Let students make choices using annotations. For example, if students are writing papers, they must explain in notes why they included a specific idea or how examples support the focus. As they explain ideas or words themselves, it clarifies their intentions and they may consider other options. By annotating, students see where work is still needed, consider new options, and develop a plan for revision. Annotations help students see how they are meeting assignment goals and make plans for improvement, showing a written narrative of their progress.
- Create milestones to give online learners a chance to check their progress and ensure they are moving along the right path. Weekly checklists will help them stay up to date. You can also create a list of mandatory online assignments, projects, and exercises, as well as another for optional tasks. This process gives students more control and teaches them self-evaluative techniques that will help them later in life as well.
- Emphasize self-evaluation to reinforce course ideas. By using frequent or daily annotation, students must explain how and why their work meets course goals.
- Promote growth through annotations. For passive learners, it requires them to present themselves as experts as they make decisions. They must become their own advocates because they know what they were trying to do even if they did not succeed. They are telling their own stories of learning. Although annotation may not improve grades, it improves understanding of grading standards and places the focus on student effort.
- Plan the evaluation at the same time you create the objectives for the course. Typically, all changes will not work perfectly the first time they are implemented. Take time after a class session to reflect on course content, delivery, questions, and activities. Note what worked and what you might change the next time you teach the course. Conduct a mid-semester student evaluation that asks students how specific features helped or hindered learning.
- Carry out the plans and make changes and continue to evaluate their effectiveness and try out new teaching ideas.
- Regularly reflect on the course to decide whether it needs refreshing, or an overhaul such as new content or delivery option. Making these changes can be daunting and time consuming; however, it may improve your instruction and increase your enjoyment in teaching the course.

The process of collecting evidence about student learning, identifying gaps, providing feedback to students, and adapting instruction is continuous. When a gap is closed, the teacher creates new learning goals for the student to meet and continues ongoing informal assessing. Based on continuous formative assessment, the educator can be thinking of what kind of questions to ask next to promote higher understanding. If assessment is saved until instruction is completed, the teacher has lost the opportunity to reteach and differentiate instruction during the lesson. Formative assessment is about continuous practice and meeting the needs of all students.

Summative Assessment

Summative assessment takes place after the learning has been completed. It provides feedback about the teaching and learning process. There are two types of summative assessments that are important to consider. The first is the summative evaluation of what learners accomplished based on the objectives—what they learned during the course. A second summative evaluation is also necessary to gain constructive feedback to improve the course.

Summative assessments are graded, and they indicate whether the student has achieved an acceptable level of knowledge. It is product oriented and assesses the final product. Different types of summative assessment include graded texts, the final examination, term papers, projects, and portfolios. Rubrics are also often used for summative assessment. In addition, course assessments help the instructor recognize gaps or weaknesses in the course and build upon its strengths. An infographic in figure 5.2 shows a comparison between formative and summative assessment.

Formative and Summative Assessment Tools

There are numerous tools to use for online assessment. Here are just a few.

Graphic Organizers

These graphic representations, such as concept maps, flowcharts, timelines, pie or KWL charts, and infographics, help make complicated information simpler and easier to understand. They show key ideas and relationships among ideas. They might be hierarchical at different levels of specificity; they might clarify the meaning of a concept; and they might draw multiple connections. Electronic graphic organizers are becoming more useful in the visual world. They are used in activities and as part of content, but they can also be used in assessment, whether for learners to create them to demonstrate their understanding or as powerful tools to examine student thinking and learning during the course. See the graphic organizer example in figure 5.3.

Collaborative Activities

Although traditional instructor-created exams are a familiar type of assessment even in online courses, active participation and interaction during online courses is even more important to engage learners due to the lack of an instructor present. Collaboration among students has been shown to enhance the effectiveness of online learning, so it is important to consider both content learning and development of collaborative skills—the process and outcome goals that encompass individual and group learning in the assessment of the online course. Collaborations, including peer reviews and small-group activities, give stu-

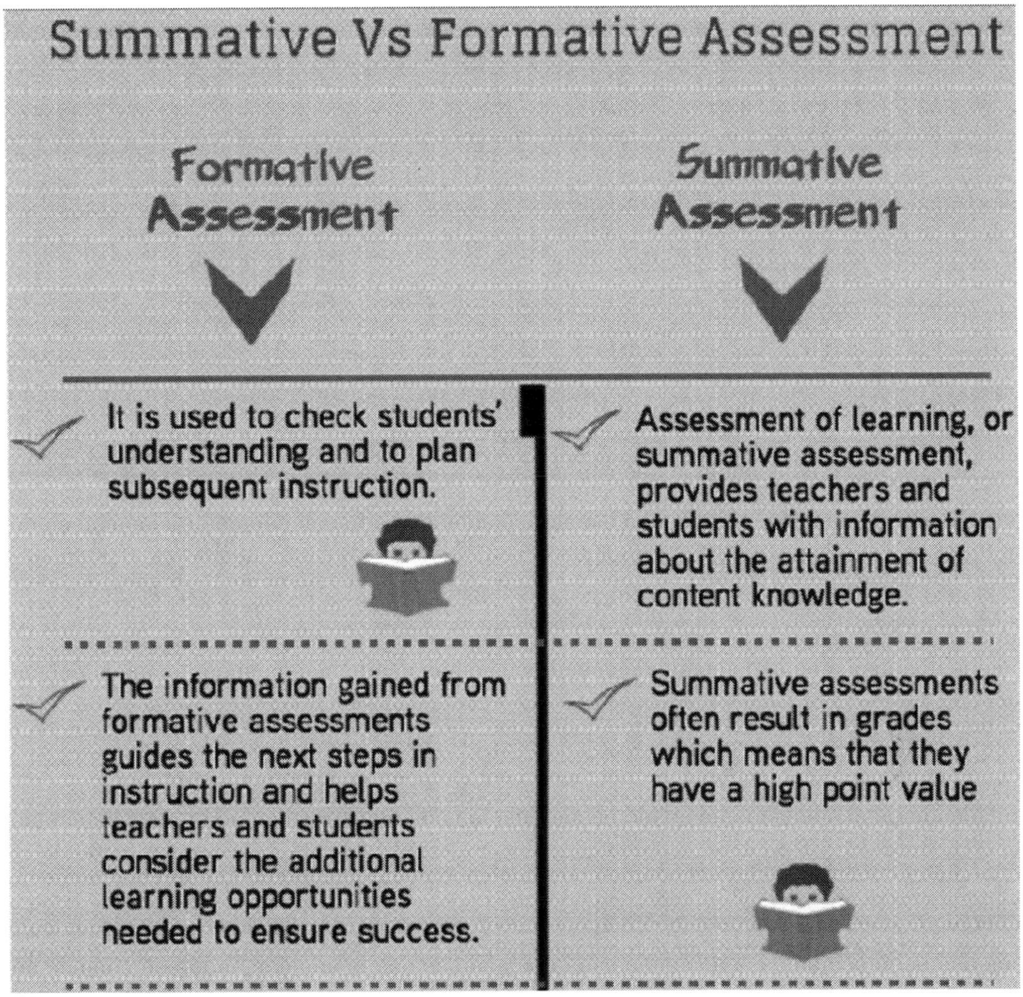

Summative Vs Formative Assessment
Formative Assessment
Summative Assessment
It is used to check students' understanding and to plan subsequent instruction.
Assessment of learning, or summative assessment, provides teachers and students with information about the attainment of content knowledge.
The information gained from formative assessments guides the next steps in instruction and helps teachers and students consider the additional learning opportunities needed to ensure success.
Summative assessments often result in grades which means that they have a high point value

Figure 5.2. Summative vs. Formative Assessment. *Used with permission, Med Kharbach, Editor, Educational Technology and Mobile Learning. http://www.educatorstechnology.com/2014/02/a-visual-chart-on-summative-vs.html. Based on Frey and Fisher's book "Literacy 2.0: Reading and Writing in the 21st Century Classroom" and Eberly Center*

Radio
TV
e-books
Electronic Media
Databases
Internet
Information Sources
Magazines
Maps
Books
Printed Sources
Newswires
Newspapers
Graphs
Charts
Relatives
Experts
Individuals
Friends
Teachers
Librarians

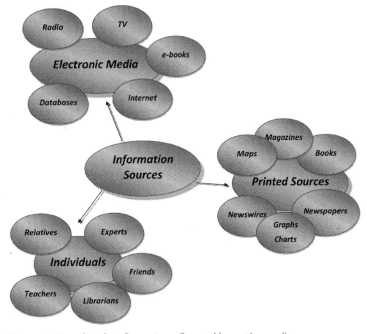

Figure 5.3. Graphic Organizer. *Created by author online*

dents the opportunity to communicate with others as they develop and demonstrate their understanding of concepts. Regular sessions with the instructor during the course via Google Hangouts or Skype can also create more personalized instruction. Online polls also provide a means to assess student knowledge and attitudes as the course progresses.

Discussions are a way of promoting interactivity in the course; therefore, assessing discussion participation has to count for a significant portion of the course grade. Not all comments and postings need to be individually assessed; in fact, they should not be. Often the instructor poses a question or comment and requires a specific number of postings per week or in each module on discussion boards. One problem with this approach is that students may not put thought into their responses, nor add anything meaningful to a threaded discussion. If the discussion breaks down with few responses, you can determine that the quality of commenting is not engaging nor does it offer insights into the content discussion. Often when students start new topics of discussion, they become more involved, and the quality of commenting may encourage others to add their postings.

To avoid responses that are not targeted, rubrics are often used to promote more effective comments. For example, an excellent response on a graded rubric might include the following: "Comment is accurate, original, relevant, teaches something new, and well written." A totally unacceptable rubric response might indicate that the comment adds no value to the discussion. You will review rubrics in more detail next.

This type of assessment might be a good individual assessment, but evaluation of group work is also necessary. One method for small-group work is to also give a group grade. This requires both individual accountability and group interdependence (Johnson and Johnson, 1992). For example, group members might be asked to collaborate on a discussion summary, a case analysis, or a solution to a problem. In such activities, both individual and group assessment could be given. This would also help to incorporate the social aspect, a group identity, or sense of community into the online learning environment. Students also experience teamwork, communication, time management, and technology use. One caution is to establish a group identity through activities such as icebreakers before beginning the collaborative group work. Note, too, it is not adequate to evaluate a collaborative, project-based assignment by rating just the quality of the final product of the group, but rather the process as well.

One way to collect both processes and products is through portfolio assessment. In portfolio assessment, students prepare collections of documents that demonstrate their understanding of content or key skills throughout the online course. Students must practice higher-order thinking skills by organizing, synthesizing, and communicating their achievements, as well as demonstrating their participation in collaborative processes. Both group and individual assessments are essential.

Rubrics

An often used assessment tool just mentioned, a rubric is a scoring key to clarify what level of work will earn a particular score. Objectives outlined at the beginning of a course let students know what they are aiming to learn during the course. Rubrics describe the performance expectations for an assignment, presentation, project, papers, and more. They can be used for pre-assessment, formative, and summative assessment in both face-to-face and online learning.

Rubrics contain three pieces: criteria, the parts of performance that will be assessed (e.g., evidence, clarity, skill); descriptions, characteristics associated with each criterion (e.g., authoritative evidence, non-biased); and a rating scale that identifies level of mastery within each criterion. They should avoid the use of comparative language like "better than" or "more than" in describing the differences in performance. The level of performance may range, for example, from a score of 1 to 5, based on the most essential criteria. The user receives a score out of the possible total points.

Rubrics can help students understand the instructor's expectations right from the start, use feedback to improve their performance, monitor and assess ongoing progress toward course goals, and identify their strengths and where they need to direct their efforts. They can also help the instructor to create consistency across grades, adjust instruction based on student strengths and weaknesses, and reduce uncertainty that often accompanies grading. Figure 5.4 provides an example of a rubric to assess instructional design and delivery, created at Chico State University.

A number of checklists have been created that ask questions about different aspects of an online course. The Instructional Design Review Checklist (http://elearningindustry.com/a-compact-instructional-design-review-checklist), created by eLearning Industry, lets you ponder important questions about objectives, structure, content, assessment, and technology design. These checklists could also be used to formulate both formative and summative evaluations.

Table 5.3 provides a list of additional assessment tool resources.

Category 3	Baseline	Effective	Exemplary
Instructional Design & Delivery	A. Course offers limited opportunity for interaction and communication student to student, student to instructor and student to content.	A. Course offers adequate opportunities for interaction and communication student to student, student to instructor and student to content	A. Course offers ample opportunities for interaction and communication student to student, student to instructor and student to content.
	B. Course goals are not clearly defined and do not align to learning objectives.	B. Course goals are adequately defined but may not align to learning objectives.	B. Course goals are clearly defined and aligned to learning objectives.
	C. Learning objectives are vague or incomplete and learning activities are absent or unclear.	C. Learning objectives are identified and learning activities are implied.	C. Learning objectives are identified and learning activities are clearly integrated.
	D. Course provides limited visual, textual, kinesthetic and/or auditory activities to enhance student learning and accessibility.	D. Course provides adequate visual, textual, kinesthetic and/or auditory activities to enhance student learning and accessibility.	D. Course provides multiple visual, textual, kinesthetic and/or auditory activities to enhance student learning and accessibility.
	E. Course provides limited activities to help students develop critical thinking and/or problem-solving skills.	E. Course provides adequate activities to help students develop critical thinking and/or problem-solving skills.	E. Course provides multiple activities that help students develop critical thinking and problem-solving skills.

Figure 5.4. Rubric. *Licensed under the Creative Commons Attribution 3.0 United States License*

Table 5.3. Assessment Tools

DESCRIPTION	URLS
Group work assessment example	http://www.cmu.edu/teaching/assessment/assesslearning/groupWorkGradingMethods.html
Classroom assessment techniques that can be used online	http://www.cmu.edu/teaching/assessment/assesslearning/CATs.html
Concept maps as assessment	http://www.cmu.edu/teaching/assessment/assesslearning/conceptmaps.html
Observations, surveys	http://www.eberly.cmu.edu/services/faculty/#observations
Clickers for assessment	http://www.cmu.edu/teaching/clickers/
Rubrics	http://www.cmu.edu/teaching/assessment/assesslearning/rubrics.html
Web tools for assessment	http://evscicats.com/blog/web-tools-for-teachers-assessment/
Formative assessments and online tools for formative assessment	https://nz.pinterest.com/pin/378795018639963779

Reflection

Reflection is an important way to improve online instruction. Through reflection you can identify reasons for changing the course. Possible problems you noticed when you last taught the course include whether, for example, student performance measured up to what you wanted it to be. Does student feedback on the course offer suggestions or concerns to address? If you changed the format from a traditional course to an online format, is there a student or administrative demand for this type of delivery?

As a result of your reflection and, especially if the online course will be taught again, you can begin to gather ideas and resources to make possible changes. Meet with colleagues, students, and administrators to ensure they are satisfied with the learning. Visit a colleague's online class; review online materials, such as a course syllabus, videos, case studies, or tutorials. Search digital resources online (e.g., Khan Academy, YouTube, the National Science Digital Library) to find new resources not currently part of your course. Look for images from Creative Commons or Flickr that are not copyright restricted. Monitor any technical issues that may need to be addressed. This may involve meeting with the technology group. Determine if anything needs to be changed: timing, instructions, objectives clarified, too much or too little content, student motivation during the course.

Next, plan the changes. Add new resources, incorporate technology, introduce new readings, change the format to more active learning with team projects and assignments. Depending on the complexity and depth of changes, start small and develop a step-by-step plan to implement them over a period of time.

Finally, continue to reflect on learning: the process, course quality, obstacles, benefits for student and teacher, practice, and assessment. Then make changes and test out the online course and/or materials again. Review links in table 5.4 for more resources.

Table 5.4. Additional Resources for Chapter 5

DESCRIPTION	URLS
Best practices for creating elearning	https://elearningindustry.com/tags/elearning-development-best-practices
An instructional design review checklist	http://elearningindustry.com/a-compact-instructional-design-review-checklist
Instructional design—spreadsheet sample	https://docs.google.com/spreadsheets/d/1mKWT6Td1fFoZJKvep0oodbFeREKGmIQtSeWPo72UUK8/edit?hl=en&pref=2&pli=1#gid=4
Using elearning templates: benefits and tips	http://elearningindustry.com/top-9-benefits-of-using-elearning-templates
Beginning checklist from University of Central Florida (use as model)	https://online.ucf.edu/teach-online/develop/create-course/semester-checklist/
Articles on formative and summative assessment	http://elearningindustry.com/summative-assessment-in-elearning-what-elearning-professionals-should-know
List of assessment strategies—53 ways to check for understanding	https://www.edutopia.org/pdfs/blogs/edutopia-finley-53ways-check-for-understanding.pdf

ⓖ Key Points

This chapter has focused on the third phase in creating an online course, that of implementation, assessment, and reflection.

- Part of implementing the designed course is identifying a delivery method, such as a learning management system (LMS).
- The LMS is used to incorporate all parts of the online course—content, assessment, communication, resources, and data collection and analysis.
- Learning assessments—formative, done before and during the course, and summative, occurring at the end of the course—are important ways to gauge a learner's comprehension.
- Assessment must align with course objectives.
- Assessment should offer a variety of ways, including multiple choice, true/false, polls, and cases studies, to evaluate knowledge, skills, performance, and/or behavior.
- Conducting summative assessment and peer review help to ensure the quality of an online course.
- After conducting the online course, quality checks and ideas from the learner's perspective enable the designer to reevaluate the course.

Chapter 5 has discussed the final components—implementing, assessing, and reflecting—necessary when you create an online course. Reflect on the visual representation of online course elements in figure 5.5 before you begin part 3: "Practical Examples for Public, Academic, Special, and K–12 Libraries."

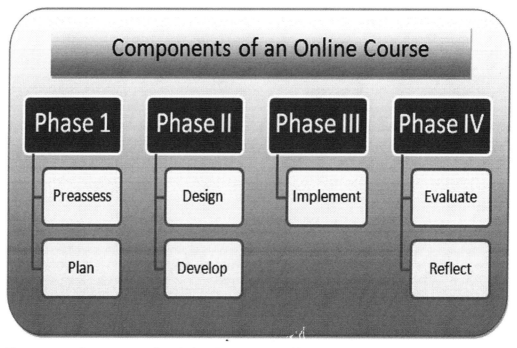

Figure 5.5. Components of an Online Course. *Created by author online*

ⓖ Exercises

To reinforce information in chapter 5, try the following:

1. Review at least two learning management systems listed in table 5.1. Create a table comparing features, benefits, and challenges of each.
2. Create an online mini-course.
   - Select a skill (e.g., create a search strategy, evaluate a website, write a résumé) you want your students/patrons to be able to perform.
   - Write an objective and outcome you want them to achieve.
   - Outline at least one or two formative assessments you might use to evaluate their ongoing progress and one summative assessment to determine if the outcome has been achieved.
   - Test your mini-course with a colleague. Reflect with your colleague on revisions necessary. Keep a continuous commentary on the process in your journal.

Apply what you learned in part 2 by creating your own short online course. First, create your own reflective journal to keep track of ideas, strategies, and activities that you want to include in your own elearning course. Divide the journal into three parts: pre-assessment (1–3), design (4–6), and implementation/assessment (7–12). Now complete the following steps:

1. Review instruction currently given in your library (e.g., school, academic, public, or special); identify one topic that could be offered via a one-session, synchronous, online course. Analyze why this topic is needed by your audience.
2. List characteristics of the audience you anticipate teaching.
3. Write at least one goal, two or three objectives, and two outcomes for the session. At the same time, identify a summative assessment to measure the outcomes.
4. Write and/or assemble the content and resources and determine the total amount of time for the course and time needed for each concept.
5. Include at least one interactive task among learners (e.g., discussion, perform skill) and one formative assessment (e.g., peer or self-assessment).
6. Create your design, including specific design elements (e.g., color, font, images).
7. Select a delivery method (e.g., LMS, organization online delivery).
8. Create learner assessment, self-assessment, and course assessment tools.
9. Review the checklist at http://elearningindustry.com/a-compact-instruction al-design-review-checklist.
10. Deliver the course to a small group of other librarians and have them complete assessments.
11. As follow-up, discuss the session with learners in the course to receive constructive feedback on all aspects of the course.
12. Write reflections in your journal. In a chart, summarize what went well, what problems arose while creating and/or delivering the course, and changes needed for delivering to an audience of students/patrons. Identify what you would do differently when creating your next course.

References

Atkin, J. Myron, Paul Black, and Janet Coffey, eds. 2001. *Classroom Assessment and the National Science Standards.* Washington, DC: National Academies Press.

Black, Paul, and Dylan William. 1998. "Inside the Black Box: Raising Standards through Classroom Assessment." *Phi Delta Kappan* 80, no. 2: 139–148.

Johnson, David W., and Roger T. Johnson. 1992. "Positive Interdependence: Key to Effective Cooperation." In *Interaction in Cooperative Groups: The Theoretical Anatomy of Group Learning*, edited by Rachel Hertz-Lazarowitz and Norman Miller, 174–99. Cambridge: Cambridge University Press.

Further Reading

Chappuis, Jan. 2005. "Helping Students Understand Assessment." Assessment to Promote Learning, *Educational Leadership* 63, no. 3 (November): 39–43. http://www.ascd.org/publications/educational-leadership/nov05/vol63/num03/Helping-Students-Understand-Assessment.aspx.

Chappuis, S. 2005. "Is Formative Assessment Losing Its Meaning?" *Education Week*, 24, no. 44: 38.

Hanna, G. S., and P. A. Dettmer. 2004. *Assessment for Effective Teaching: Using Context-Adaptive Planning.* Boston: Pearson.

Shank, P. 2006. *Developing Learning Assessments for Classroom, Online, and Blended Learning. Workshop Materials.* Centennial, CO: Learning Peaks.

Stiggins, R., J. Arter, J. Chappuis, and S. Chappuis. 2006. *Classroom Assessment for Student Learning: Doing It Right—Using It Well.* Portland, OR: Educational Testing Service.

PRACTICAL EXAMPLES FOR PUBLIC, ACADEMIC, SPECIAL, AND K–12 LIBRARIES

THE TWENTY-FIRST CENTURY HAS BROUGHT with it many changes in teaching and learning. Computing and telecommunications technologies have facilitated new ways to access and enhance learning, and learners now have access to the tools and the desire to look for new ways to learn. Libraries must continue to update their services made possible by advances in technology. For example, traditional students attended higher education in brick-and-mortar institutions and used on-campus libraries, and while some non-traditional students or "distance" learners took electronic courses, this was not the norm.

Now efficient, cost-effective learning can be delivered no matter the time or location. Online learning is increasing, and results of studies indicate the potential of elearning making it a viable learning option. As a result of changing technologies and in response to learner needs, libraries are changing as well. In addition to online catalogs or indexed databases, they now offer more resources online (e.g., journals, e-books, theses, dissertations, class materials, news). Users can access these sources on demand 24/7 from remote locations from traditional computers to mobile devices.

Online teaching is now taking many forms. Instruction and materials are available synchronously at specific times and places with an instructor, asynchronously in on-demand courses and self-paced materials, and in blended formats where part of a course may be online along with sessions in a traditional building.

Libraries that are leaders in information technology have joined the online revolution to distribute many resources that formerly could be obtained only by visiting the library. Now the library is open 24/7, and users can fulfill their needs at their convenience and pace. Distance, time, health problems, and age are no longer a deterrent to visiting the library. Finally, changing demographics shifting patterns of education and employment require that libraries focus on user demands for their services. Because libraries have the responsibility for identifying, developing, coordinating, and providing library resources and services, they must undertake new roles, revise their traditional services, and form partnerships with others, such as university faculty, parents, patrons, and organizations.

Part 3 provides practical applications for online teaching and learning for public, academic, special, and K–12 libraries. Each chapter describes a particular type of online learning and uses examples of how it is being used in different libraries. Finally, step-by-step models in the chapters illustrate how to set up a particular type of online instruction in a specific type of library.

- Chapter 6 covers asynchronous learning, both on-demand courses and self-paced materials. The step-by-step illustration shows creating an on-demand course for a public library, as well as examples of different types of self-paced materials.
- Chapter 7 focuses on embedded librarianship with examples in academic and special libraries and details the role of an academic librarian partnering with a faculty member.
- Chapter 8 describes an increasingly popular form of online teaching and learning: blended instruction. The focus of the detailed course is an academic library.
- Chapter 9 discusses online flipped instruction, a form of blended learning. The lesson plan is for use with K–12 students.
- Chapter 10 describes MOOC instruction, an alternative form of online teaching and learning. Focused instruction includes examples of parts of a MOOC for special libraries.

The applications in part 3 reinforce learning theory from part 1 and the detailed information on course design from part 2. When you finish part 3, you should have the foundation to be able to create your own online learning courses and materials.

The final chapter concludes the book with a look at trends and challenges for librarians in K–12, public, academic, and special libraries in the future. It also points out the many opportunities that will open up for librarians.

Asynchronous Teaching and Learning

IF YOU SEARCH THE INTERNET, you will find many examples of online learning created by and for public, academic, special, and K–12 libraries. You may be tasked with creating online learning for your library. So, what should you create? What are the benefits of each? Which one fits the learners at your library? These are all important questions to ask so that you won't waste your time going in the wrong direction.

This chapter attempts to answer these questions and more about the different types of online learning. Examples of courses and materials from different libraries will provide models of asynchronous instruction you might consider for your own audience. And, the step-by-step on-demand course will help you get started creating your own asynchronous learning.

Synchronous versus Asynchronous Learning

In part 2, you learned about synchronous teaching and learning, such as live webinars and the steps involved in creating an online instructor-led course. A quick review of the definition of synchronous learning will give you the basis for differentiating it from types of asynchronous instruction in this chapter (Hrastinski, 2008). Similar to classroom learning, synchronous teaching takes place at a specific time and place and is led by an instructor; however, the course occurs totally online. Common types are guest lectures, demonstrations, and discussions that occur at a set time when learners are expected to be present. These sessions are made possible by technology, such as screencasts, webinars, and videoconferencing interactive learning models. More details and examples of specific types of synchronous learning are described in later chapters.

Asynchronous learning is student centered and uses online learning materials located in an electronic network to facilitate interaction among learners without the limits of time and location. It requires learners to take responsibility for their learning and be actively involved. For example, users must be proficient with the technology required for the course as well as becoming comfortable with new methods of communication and collaboration with their peers. They must be able to interact online by posting and replying to messages and uploading and accessing multimedia. A facilitator may or may not be involved.

Asynchronous learning encompasses many different kinds of courses, such as an on-demand course or a self-paced course, as well as self-paced materials. Online learning resources that support asynchronous learning include e-mail, threaded discussions on online discussion boards, wikis, and blogs. Sometimes communication is supplemented with synchronous videoconferencing through Google Hangouts or Skype or telephone conversations.

Synchronous and asynchronous learning complement each other. It is possible to use asynchronous and synchronous learning activities so students and instructors can exchange information, collaborate on work, and remove the feeling of isolation that sometimes comes with online learning. So, what are some important differences in types of asynchronous learning?

- In an **asynchronous course**, learning takes place within the confines of a course, but learners can interact at different times. They may have an instructor who communicates through a learning management system (LMS), such as Moodle. For example, a learner might complete assignments and participate during the week with other students and the instructor through discussion forums.
- A **self-paced course** is more restrictive. It is created in advance, and learners participate in it at their own pace, usually without the benefit of a specifically named instructor. The only feedback may be through the technology in response to questions that are part of the course.
- **On-demand courses** may be live webinars that have been archived so they are able to be viewed at a later time. They may also be referred to as a self-paced course that is created in advance.
- **Elearning materials** combine various technologies, such as videos, LibGuides, screencasts, and many more. For example, online learning collections distributed in public libraries include elearning through subscription services such as video tutorials on technology and software from a private company such as Lynda.com or instruction on databases from vendors like Gale in its Online Learning Library or through online course collections like those from the Los Angeles Public Library.

Benefits of Asynchronous Teaching and Learning

Libraries began asynchronous learning years ago with the advent of online public access catalogs (OPACs) and paid databases. Long past this early beginning, new delivery systems allow students to access class materials online, hold group discussions, make presentations, interact with instructors, and pose questions to the librarian, all online. Online asynchronous learning has numerous benefits for twenty-first-century learners (Haslam, 2012):

- They can access information and all parts of a course when it is convenient for them.
- They can also proceed at their own pace so that when they move forward in the course they have acquired the knowledge necessary.
- They can review the material completely until they master it before moving on.
- They can take more time to formulate answers or consider different sides of an argument before offering an opinion.
- Its flexibility adjusts to work schedules and outside activities like sports or music or health issues.
- Asynchronous technology tools, such as discussion boards, social networking, e-portfolios, wikis, blogs, and virtual libraries (containing repositories of documents, graphics, audio, and video files) provide the connections and engagement missing in earlier versions of online learning and help to prevent user isolation.

Both learning types offer different benefits and limits for online learning. Some studies (Er, Özden, and Arifoglu, 2009) suggest that the two learning methods be integrated (i.e., blended learning) and used to support student needs. Chapter 8 discusses blended learning, providing examples, and the structure of a blended learning course for an academic learning environment.

Examples of Asynchronous Teaching and Learning

Different types of asynchronous teaching and learning are used for diverse purposes in all libraries—public, academic, special, and K–12. Examples are many. They include online on-demand courses as part of the academic or K–12 curriculum or to teach life skills in a public library. They may be asynchronous courses with facilitators. Self-paced materials of all kinds, such as infographics, videos, LibGuides, and many more provide teaching and learning tools, often as part of online courses. In the following examples, read how libraries are using asynchronous learning as part of their teaching and learning tool kits.

On-Demand Courses

Example 1—Self-Paced Course for Librarians in Public Libraries

One important task of a librarian in a public library is to advocate for the library. Advocacy requires special skills. Turning the Page website is designed to support libraries and strengthen communities. The Advocacy Training Curriculum, part of a program developed by the Bill & Melinda Gates Foundation, contains fifteen training sessions, each with a script, PowerPoint presentation, and handouts for the instructor. An Advocacy Training Implementation Guide and an Advocacy Action Plan Workbook are also provided.

This free, self-paced online training program can help librarians, other staff, board members, and patrons gain the skills and confidence they need to advocate for their libraries. Asynchronous materials show how to tell the library's story, deliver effective presentations, build partnerships, and develop a case for the library. See more about this project at http://publiclibraryadvocacy.org/. Start by reading the Implementation Guide and then review the other materials on the site. These materials provide a strong model for librarians as they create online materials for other tasks they must perform at their libraries.

Example 2—Public Library Association Online Courses and Materials

The Public Library Association (PLA) offers live webinars and on-demand seminars, archived versions of the live ones at http://www.ala.org/pla/onlinelearning/webinars/on demand. Available 24/7, many courses are free; others are available for digital download for a year at a small fee. Online sessions on topics such as literacy, technology, collection development, and more also offer librarians professional development. In addition, self-directed online workbooks on topics like literacy; how to find, use, and evaluate information; services for immigrants; and job and career development, are useful for public library patrons.

Example 3—Asynchronous Library of Congress Course on Primary Sources

Much asynchronous material can be used for different purposes. For example, Using Primary Sources, at http://www.loc.gov/teachers/usingprimarysources/, is an online course developed by the Library of Congress. It uses a variety of resources to show how primary sources facilitate inquiry. For instance, in the inquiry overview at the beginning of the course, a three-minute video (http://tinyurl.com/hckxjcd) illustrates how three educators used Library of Congress primary sources in a unit of study based on the New York draft riots of 1863. They used these sources to engage students and develop critical thinking. In the video, the director of school libraries for New York City schools acts as the guide when she deconstructs practical applications using primary sources in the classroom. Interactive activities have learners pre-assess their knowledge of inquiry, then watch videos, answer questions, and review at their own pace, if necessary. Showing videos of teachers actually working in classrooms with students at PS 153 in New York aligns the content more closely to the educator viewers of the video. Teacher reflection is also shown as the teachers work on classroom activities with their students. Reinforcement continues as the learner progresses through each of five chapters. The same list of concepts presented when introducing inquiry at the beginning of the course to check learners' prior knowledge is again shown to check for understanding at the end of the course. A list of additional resources to delve deeper into the topic of inquiry appears at the end. Other similar modules include ones on copyright and primary sources, and analyzing and finding these sources. Figure 6.1 shows the beginning of the Library of Congress video on primary sources.

Example 4—Online Public Library Course

Professional development for librarians is another way to make use of online courses and self-paced materials. An example of using asynchronous learning for staff development comes from the Baltimore County Public Library (BCPL). The library has a virtual orientation tool designed to orient staff and volunteers using technology, such as podcasts,

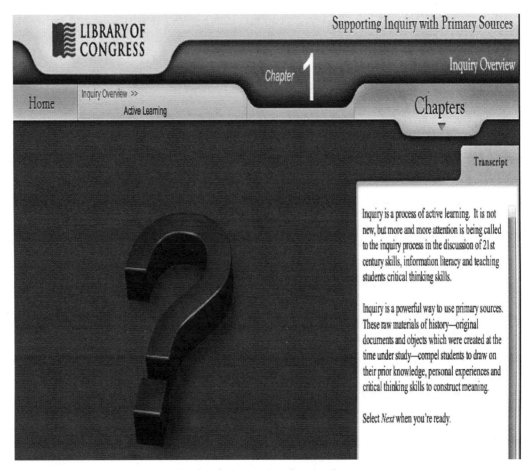

Figure 6.1. Primary Sources. *Used with permission, Creative Commons*

text, photos, and an interactive quiz, to present the information. The two-and-a-half-hour session can be completed all at once or over several sittings during the first month of employment. This method allows part-time staff to be trained, shortening the time between hiring and completion of the program (Van Noord, 2010).

Example 5—State Libraries Asynchronous Courses and Material

State libraries offer training support and materials to local public libraries. For example, the Texas State Library online training site at https://onlinetraining.tsl.texas.gov/ contains how-to videos and courses pertinent to public libraries. Accessible to local library staff, two-minute videos cover topics like searching the course catalog, accessing webinars archived on the website, and others. The videos also serve as models librarians can use to create their own videos for patrons. A guest log is available for such archived courses as one on makerspaces, or another on 3-D printing (shown in figure 6.2). This course contains videos, presentation slides, and a webinar recording, and you can receive a certificate of completion.

Self-Paced Materials

Libraries are increasingly creating new resources to help people of all ages become informed literate. Reviewing resources created by librarians for a variety of purposes to

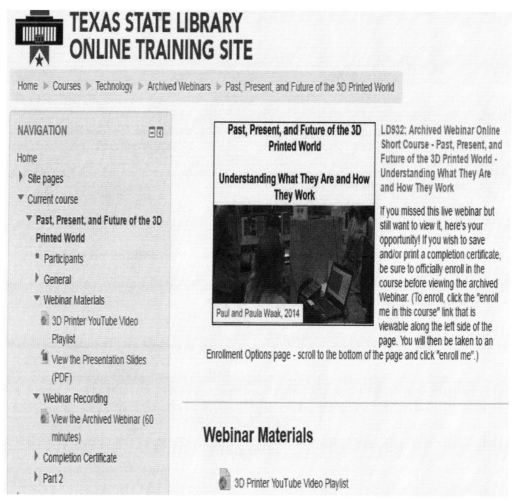

Figure 6.2. 3-D Printing Course. *Used with permission, Creative Commons*

serve as models is an effective way to help in creating your own. Start with the following examples that illustrate self-paced materials created by librarians, as well as some from vendors who service libraries.

Example 6—Texas A&M Libraries Self-Paced Materials on Fair Use

The Texas A&M Libraries have created self-paced materials on the important and often misunderstood topic of fair use. On their web page, titled Fair Use Week at http://fairuse week.org/texas-am-libraries-fair-use/, they have a two-minute video explaining what fair use is, when to use it, and how it is often misconstrued. The video also provides a message for Texas A&M faculty on how they should consider applying fair use. To reinforce the concept and make it available visually, they have also created an infographic outlining the fundamentals of fair use, including why it's important and examples of fair use. Figure 6.3 illustrates a portion of the infographic that can be shared via Creative Commons.

Example 7—Using Screencasts for Online Teaching and Learning

Hamersly Library at Western Oregon University has created numerous self-paced materials, among them research guides to teach literacy skills, as well as content subjects. Topics

Figure 6.3. Fundamentals of Fair Use Infographic. *Used through Creative Commons*

of the guides arranged in categories at http://research.wou.edu/cat.php?cid=48629 range from A to Z, from art to education, health, and many more. For example, a three-minute video demonstrates how to search Google Scholar for academic articles and for those articles within references. A demonstration illustrates creating a search strategy by selecting keywords and using advanced techniques to narrow a search. It also shows how to retrieve and cite articles and search within citing articles to get related articles. The video has audio, video, and a text script to accommodate special-needs users.

A four-minute YouTube video at https://www.youtube.com/watch?v=NQ0wvoquq3s discusses primary sources in the natural sciences. This video shows learners how to do the research important to classes they are taking. The video also differentiates between primary and secondary sources, as well as review articles. It then lists types of these sources, such as technical papers, dissertations, and theses, to name some, and explains the differences between the three types so students can pick the sources most pertinent to the purpose of their research. Another useful aspect of this video is that it takes a real-world scientific example and demonstrates primary, secondary, and review articles on the topic.

Access to these tutorials, research guides, and videos are all available from the library website. Students, faculty, and staff can also obtain access to authoritative databases, including MEDLINE, ScienceDirect, Biological Sciences Collection, and other resources online with their library identification and password. Western Oregon University is just one example of college and university self-paced resources available online.

Example 8—Vendor-Created Self-Paced Materials

Vendors of library products and services also offer diverse online self-paced courses to library staff and volunteers that are available 24/7. For example, OCLC WebJunction creates courses in categories such as social media, youth services, and library services with topics like designing web-based instruction, teaching technology to technophobic patrons, and Pinterest for libraries. An archive of past courses is also available at http:// learn.webjunction.org. Other vendors like ProQuest (www.proquest.com) offer instructional videos, illustrating how to search their databases.

Synchronous and asynchronous courses and self-paced materials in the twenty-first century will often be designed by teams rather than individual subject specialists. The academic library is at the center of a liberal education, so librarians must pursue opportunities to partner with teaching faculty and others to create and deliver these new online courses. Librarians are accustomed to functioning in a collaborative environment and can draw on their experiences to design and share in the online teaching and learning environment. Table 6.1 provides additional resources for asynchronous teaching and learning.

Table 6.1. Additional Resources for Chapter 6

DESCRIPTION	URLS
University of North Carolina (UNC) course with different styles, how, when, why to cite, exercises on types of cites, video on citing sources, quiz	http://tinyurl.com/j6mkj25
UNC Libraries research tutorials repository; contains short videos on content and how-to library topics	http://tinyurl.com/l6wf3h8
Ways to make content interesting	http://tinyurl.com/kwbkwcl
Free assets to use in elearning	http://tinyurl.com/h5r4epy
Free elearning templates	http://tinyurl.com/hnurteh
Elearning interactions—visuals	http://tinyurl.com/jhpmb8n

Tips for Creating Asynchronous Learning

When you start creating an asynchronous learning course, you want it to motivate your students by keeping them engaged. Keep the following in mind to create an effective elearning asynchronous course strategy:

- Make interaction a vital part of an online course. Having an online forum encourages collaboration among members of the class and the class and instructor (if there is one). This discussion vehicle also helps students to feel connected and less isolated without a "sage on the stage."

- Add social learning such as Facebook and Twitter so that learners gain knowledge and experience from their peers and communicate with an online facilitator, while still accessing the content at their own pace. Study questions or responses to comments can generate online discussion. Students should also be posting their opinions as part of the course, enabling the facilitator to evaluate learners' participation and progress.
- As discussed in chapter 2, set learning objectives and expectations before the course begins. Use the syllabus or online course outline to clarify what is expected of learners, skills they should develop, communication methods to use, and deadlines they must meet. Knowing expectations encourages learners to stay on track and motivates active learning.
- Consistently communicate with learners through e-mail or other updates. Set expectations on how quickly and often they will receive a reply. A facilitator might decide to have regular online "office hours" when learners can expect to reach him or her, but at the least provide a time period (e.g., forty-eight hours) for responses. Also, indicate the format, such as chat via e-mail or discussion forum. If an issue surfaces that affects the entire group, make sure users know how they will receive that message.
- Create an elearning community for student discussion and interaction. Blogs and wikis work well for asynchronous learning. A page on the LMS might also be the vehicle for regular updates. Whatever method of communication used, most important is that learners feel comfortable stating their ideas and opinions as a valued part of the course.
- Resources outside the course content are important to its success. Include links to relevant material that will help in understanding the content, spark new ideas, and facilitate discussion. Links to materials placed directly in the LMS might include webinars, articles on the subject or related topics, and infographics, to name some.
- Include interactive activities, such as podcasts, videos, games, and audio presentations to enhance activity while at the same time informing and engaging learners.
- Based on the structure of the asynchronous course, have the online facilitator (if there is one) monitor and guide the online experience. This person can moderate discussion, ask questions to move student discussion forward, and keep it on topic, thereby providing guidance for those who might need extra support.

You've looked at diverse examples of asynchronous teaching on-demand courses, as well as self-paced materials used in different types of libraries. It's time now to prepare your own on-demand course on a topic that a public library might be called upon to create.

Creating an On-Demand Course to Prepare for a Job Search

With the recent economic downturn, public libraries have become an important presence for job and career development. They are often called upon to help patrons with life skills, such as preparing for job searches or interviewing. To meet this need, librarians may be called upon to provide training for patrons who are first-time employees, for those looking to change jobs or who have been laid off, or for others who are reentering the workforce.

This part of chapter 6 demonstrates with a step-by-step example how to create an on-demand course on the topic of searching for a job. It begins by showing librarians aspects to consider as they preplan the course. Next, Module I: Writing a Résumé and Module II: Writing a Cover Letter present detailed instructions to the librarian to direct patrons through the course content and activities. To accompany the librarian's instructions, sample handouts are posted on the course site as part of each module. They provide patrons with information about each topic and activities and assignments as they progress through the course. The final steps include a wrap-up, evaluation of course outcomes, and reflection about the course.

Consider this example as a model to provide information on this topic and show you how you might construct your own online asynchronous course. Of course, you might decide to add other topics to this course, such as completing a job application form and preparing for an interview that are all part of job searching. Exercises at the end of the chapter offer suggestions to get you starting writing such additional modules for the course.

Step 1: Preplanning Your Course

As you get ready to begin creating instruction, what should you consider? Should it be synchronous led by an instructor; an interactive, on-demand training; asynchronous materials; or some combination? These questions need to be answered as you preplan your course.

Conduct a Needs Assessment

A needs assessment of your patrons will help you decide on the kind of instruction and what to include. Your analysis indicates that the audience is quite diverse. Some patrons are just getting started in the job market; others have been laid off, and a small group is looking to reconnect to the workforce with part-time employment. You have also identified three areas of need: documents to prepare, such as a résumé and cover letter, application forms to complete, and tips to prepare for an interview for those who are so fortunate.

Questions to address include when and where to hold instruction and what format it should take. Because of the varied background of the audience, you have decided that an on-demand, self-paced course is most suitable because of its flexibility to take at a time convenient to learners and a place of their choosing whether at home or using library computers.

Because of the range of experience of your patrons, you also plan to include main course content in the two areas of need, as well as asynchronous materials that can be used to reinforce points that the more inexperienced job seekers may use to supplement their knowledge. Your plan for the course is based on adult learning principles, discussed in part 1 of this book: active participation so patrons can learn from each other, team learning, and experience-based opportunities with materials chosen to reflect learning styles. Having a facilitator available to promote discussion, answer questions, and direct learning when needed will help guide learners during the course and offer help to new job seekers. However, learners will be responsible for completing activities and exercises in the modules on their own with the Internet and discussion boards for support.

Create a Scenario for the Course

Based on the needs assessment, the following online course is one that a public library might be called upon to create for its patrons to show them how to apply for a job. It takes the prospective employee from the beginnings of reviewing possible job types to creating a résumé and cover letter for a specific position. This model can be used as you prepare asynchronous training for your own library whether it is an online on-demand course and/or asynchronous materials to complement the course. You could also create separate learning sessions for each of the above-mentioned needs.

This three-week on-demand course described is divided into two modules:

- Module I: Writing a Résumé
- Module II: Writing a Cover Letter

The two modules provide the librarian with detailed instructions about course content and patron activities and assignments. The librarian will post information on topics and activities on the course site so that patrons can proceed through the course at their own pace. Figure 6.4 provides a blueprint of the course, showing goals and objectives and activities students will need to complete to demonstrate proficiency in learning the material. In exercises at the end of this chapter, you will be tasked to create Module III: Completing a Job Application and Module IV: Preparing for an Interview to reinforce what you learned as you reviewed Modules I and II.

Set Up Course Structure

An on-demand course needs to be accessed online. Your library may have a website or an LMS (see chapter 5 for more on LMSs) where the course content, materials, activities, and assignments are posted prior to the beginning of the course. As the course moderator, you will set up a date for the course to begin, and a sign-up page will display on the library website. As part of the sign-up, learners will be assigned a number that they will use in place of their name when posting activity assignments.

If you decide to combine synchronous and asynchronous teaching, you will also need access to an interactive interface, such as Google Hangouts or Skype. See chapter 8 for links to information about these technologies. As a last thought, you may also decide to offer this course so that it can be accessed without the peer review activities. If so, remember that without the collaboration, learners may lack a feeling of community that promotes learning.

Gather Materials

The following three types of materials will be used in each module to provide information about the topics, instructions you provide learners so they can complete activities, and tables of links to additional resources on topics in each module. Handouts are on reproducible pages within each module. Prior to the course, these materials should be posted on the course site under their respective modules:

1. **Content Handouts** contain information about the topic of the module (e.g., résumés, cover letters), such as what they should contain, how to format them, and what to consider when writing them.

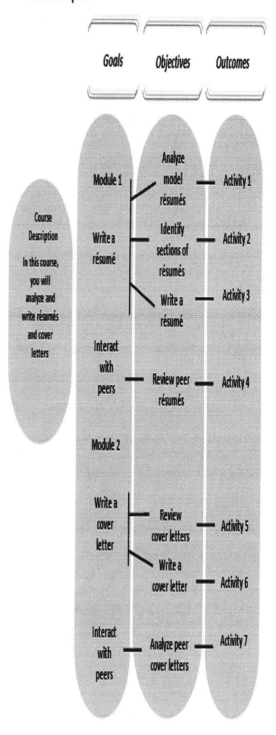

Course Blueprint

Figure 6.4. Course Blueprint. *Created by author online*

2. **Activity Handouts** give step-by-step instructions to complete sample activities. Working through the activities enables learners to practice the skills needed to achieve the learner outcome. Some tasks outlined in the handouts will require interaction with members of the course through the course online discussion forum. Other activities assess how well learners achieved the module objectives.

3. **Tables** provide links to additional resources on the module topic. Use these tables as examples to re-create your own materials on the course site.

Step 2: Write Course Goals, Learning Outcomes, and Specific Objectives

Based on your analysis of the audience's needs, you are ready for Step 2, to write goals, objectives, and learning outcomes for the course. You might want to review information about goals, outcomes, and objectives in chapter 3 before beginning to write your own. Here are some sample goals, objectives, and outcomes for this job search course as outlined above:

Goals

At the end of the course, learners will be able to:
- Write effective résumés in response to specific job descriptions
- Write cover letters that match résumés written for specific job descriptions
- Interact with peers in the online class
- Participate in an online learning environment

Learning Outcomes

At the end of the course, learners will be able to:
- Write appropriate résumés for specific job descriptions
- Write accompanying cover letters that align with the same specific job descriptions

Specific Objectives

After completing these modules, learners will be able to:
- Analyze model résumés for strengths and weaknesses
- State components that should appear in a well-written résumé
- Identify parts of an exemplary cover letter and write a cover letter
- Review résumés and cover letters of peers and provide constructive comments

Note that the objectives are more specific than goals and outcomes and provide more specific tasks that will help learners achieve the outcomes of the course. You are now ready to create each of the modules in this course. Goals, outcomes, and objectives should be posted on the course site prior to the beginning of the course so that learners understand what to expect to do, see, and hear during the course.

Step 3: Create Module I: Writing a Résumé (to Be Completed during Week 1 of the Course)

In Module I, learners must complete tasks to enable them to create one of the documents they need to begin their job search. One of the most important is to know how to create a résumé. As you create the on-demand course, remember that for each module you must provide learners with all elements necessary to achieve the outcomes for the course:

1. Objectives that will enable them to attain the outcomes by the end of the module
2. Content Handouts with information about résumés
3. Examples that model a well-written résumé to show what they are trying to achieve
4. Activity Handouts with instructions to tasks and assignments so they can practice creating a résumé for the job they are interested in

Directions on Activity Handouts will also instruct learners on how they will interact with other learners in the course to complete module assignments.

Finally, learners must be assessed so they will know they have achieved the outcomes you stated at the beginning of the module. Module I has two assessments: a rubric for peer evaluation of a résumé, and a quiz over material about résumés.

The storyboard in the textbox shows the sequence of instruction for Module I and how all elements relate and fit together. Instructions to librarians will guide them through the objectives, content, activities, and evaluation. Handouts provide learners with content about résumés and directions for activities to practice writing résumés.

MODULE I STORYBOARD

Course: Prepare for a Job Search					
Module I: Writing a Résumé					
	Course goals, objectives, outcomes	Instructor-generated content, communications	Readings	Class interactions and activities	Assessments—quizzes, posts, projects
Week 1: Creating a Résumé					
Introduction		Have learners give name and job interests	Icebreaker		Post "Who I am" to discussion forum
Module I: Writing a Résumé					
Activity 1	Analyze sample résumés	Have learners read different sample résumés	Content 1 Handout: Résumé Analysis	Select category & analyze 2 résumés	Answer questions on Activity 1 Handout
				Activity 1 Handout: Analyze Sample Résumés	Post to discussion forum
Activity 2		Have learners read about résumé sections	Content 2 Handout: Résumé Sections		
	Write résumés	Have learners write résumé content responding to job descriptions		Activity 2 Handout: Write Your Résumé Content	Post résumé content on discussion board

Activity 3	Interact with peers	Explain what a rubric is and why use it	Table 6.2: Sample rubrics	Review rubrics in table 6.2	Post questions/ comments about rubrics
				Activity 3 Handout: Review Peers' Résumés; review & proofread content of 1 peer résumé	Post reviewed peer résumés on discussion board
				Review & incorporate peer comments	Repost reviewed résumés
Activity 4	Format résumés	Have learners format their résumés	Content 4 Handout: Résumé Formatting; table 6.3: Formatting Résumé Content	Activity 4 Handout: Format a Résumé; have peers review formatted résumés	Post peer-reviewed formatted résumés for discussion
				Have writers revise formatted résumés	Post writer-revised résumés
Evaluation	Formative, summative	Have learners complete short quiz on Module I content			Assess on assignments, posts for Activities 1–4. Assess based on quiz at end of Module I.

Write Module I Goals, Outcomes, and Objectives

The goals and objectives for Module I should form the basis for the outcomes you want your learners to be able to do at the end of this module. Here are some samples you can adapt and place under Module I on the course site:

Goal

After completing Module I on writing a résumé, learners will be able to:
• Write an effective résumé in response to a specific job description

Objectives

After completing Module I, learners will be able to:
• Analyze model résumés and point out strengths and weaknesses
• State components that should appear in a well-written résumé

- Write a draft résumé
- Format a résumé
- Review résumés of peers and provide constructive comments

Introduce the Course

Start the module off with a warm-up exercise so that learners get to know each other, feel less isolated in the online environment, and begin to form a learning community. Design an icebreaker activity with specific objectives in mind that are appropriate to the audience so learners can get acquainted. Here's a sample activity:

- Have learners write a post in the discussion forum to introduce themselves. Have them share their name and two interesting facts about their current job or the one they hope to acquire. Through this activity they will get to know others with similar interests and facilitate conversation during the course.
- Have learners read the posts and find at least one person who seems to have an interest in common and respond to the post in the discussion forum. This activity will also familiarize participants with the course structure and how to use the discussion forum.

Begin Module I Learning Activities

Now you will create activities and strategies to achieve each module objective. You learned from the needs assessment that your learners will be a diverse group in their job experience and their knowledge about seeking a job. Therefore, you must make sure that those with little prior knowledge have enough information about a résumé that they will be able to write one for a specific job description.

Module I has four activities. Prior to the course, you will have posted content and instructions for each activity in Module I on the course site. Your instructions will direct learners to the Content and Activity Handouts they will use as part of their assignments. Each Content Handout covers information learners should know about résumés. Activity Handouts contain instructions for completing activities and assignments to enable learners to write résumés. Tables or links provide more resources on the topic for those who need extra help. All handouts are provided as reproducible pages and are located throughout the chapter, as noted by page number.

Activity 1: Analyze Sample Résumés For the first assignment, have learners review the Module I, Activity 1 Content Handout: Résumé Analysis, located on page 105. It provides background on the importance of résumés and tips on creating a résumé. The information contained in the Content Handout can also take other formats. Ideal for this type of information would be short videos, less than five minutes. Other options include PowerPoint slides, containing predominantly graphics, or visuals like infographics that also map out the information visually. To provide you with background about résumés to help you write the content and create the learner activities, review different YouTube videos about creating résumés at http://tinyurl.com/hahlooc. Note that in an on-demand course, users can skip information with which they are already familiar, and you can add or eliminate information from your course depending on audience characteristics.

Module I, Activity 1 Content Handout: Résumé Analysis

To be successful in applying for a job, you will need a résumé. It should be targeted to the organization to which you plan to apply. First, take time to research organizations you are interested in to learn what prospective employers want in new employees. You will then have the information you need to tailor your résumé to emphasize the qualifications you have that meet your prospective employer's needs. The document should convey who you are, what you know, and what you have to offer. Your goal is to create a résumé that best displays your skills, knowledge, and abilities in order to attract employers and lead to an interview.

Tips for Writing a Résumé
The following tips will help you to create a professional résumé that an employer can peruse in seven to ten seconds. This is the average time for scanning an initial résumé.

- Read through the entire job description before submitting your résumé. The résumé should address specifically the requirements listed in the job description. When writing your résumé, you can make sure you cover everything the employer desires.
- Especially if you don't have too much technical knowledge for the job, make sure to include employability skills. These cover skills, such as communication, teamwork, problem solving, planning and organization, initiative, self-management, learning, and technology. Job-specific skills are not the only ones employers look at on résumés. Place employability skills under qualifications or experience.
- Include the following components in your résumé: contact information, immediate career objective, skills, experience, such as volunteer work, detailed education, and interests.
- Print your résumé on good-quality, white, or light-colored paper.
- Carefully check for typos and misspellings.
- Format and organize the content clearly on one page, if possible.
- Create a PDF of the résumé because opening a PDF attachment is universal and does not need a specific program. For example, if you created the résumé in Microsoft Word and the employer tries to open it in a different program, the formatting may be misaligned.

Reproduced from *Online Teaching and Learning: A Practical Guide for Librarians*, © 2017 Rowman & Littlefield Publishers

After learners have completed the readings in Module I, the Activity 1 Content Handout: Résumé Analysis offers them some practice in looking at résumés. Have learners select a category close to the type of job they are interested in and have them review at least two different résumés at http://tinyurl.com/zo4k76e. These will serve as models. Note that this link has numerous sample résumés in different categories. You can limit the number based on your learners and provide links for specific ones on Module I, Activity 1 Handout: Analyze Sample Résumés. Have learners complete the questions on the Activity Handout. This activity helps to achieve Objective 1 and prepare them to begin writing their résumés.

Module I, Activity 1 Handout: Analyze Sample Résumés

Looking at model résumés will help you determine what to put in the résumé you will be writing next. From the résumés at http://tinyurl.com/hcobyuu, select the category that most closely aligns with a job you are interested in, and choose two résumés to review. Analyze them, identifying what stands out most that you think might attract an employer. Compare and contrast the résumés and answer the following questions. Post your answers and any comments or questions you have in the discussion forum. Remember to put your course number on all posts.

Answer the following questions about résumés.

1. Is the content on target (e.g., catch an employer's interest, key skills and strengths highlighted, represents your overall qualities)?

2. Is the résumé neat, attractive, and easy to read (e.g., headings consistent, key phrases easy to identify)?

3. Is the résumé complete and accurate (e.g., grammar and spelling checked, typos eliminated, dates and complete contact information provided)?

Reproduced from *Online Teaching and Learning: A Practical Guide for Librarians*, © 2017 Rowman & Littlefield Publishers

Activity 2: Résumé Sections   This activity requires learners to use information about résumés to compile and write the content for their personal résumés. Have learners read the Module I, Activity 2 Content Handout: Résumé Sections, located on page 107, to learn about the specific sections to include in a résumé. Next, tell them they are going to assemble personal content to use in their résumés.

Module I, Activity 2 Content Handout: Résumé Sections

The information that follows is content you may want to include in your résumé. First, decide whether to write a chronological or a functional résumé. A chronological résumé emphasizes your jobs in date order, the most recent job first. A person with extensive employment history in a specific field might want to use this type of résumé to emphasize past positions held, perhaps within the last 15 years. A functional résumé is focused on your skills and is appropriate for a person seeking an entry-level job, a person without much employment history, or one who is changing careers. In this résumé, you list skills, regardless of when or where those skills were acquired.

The following are sections that are common to include in most résumés:

- **Header.** Include your name, phone number, and e-mail address. Make sure the e-mail address is professional with no nicknames or unusual tag names.
- **Objective statement.** State the job that you are applying for and what you are after. Customize the objective based on the job you are applying for. To personalize, you can also add the company name.
- **Skills.** Use short bullet points, targeted to the job you are applying for, that can be skimmed quickly.
- **Experience.** Include companies you worked for in chronological order, most recent first; add job title and your accomplishments when you worked at the job with details that would relate to the job you are applying for. Keep it short.
- **Education.** Enter school name and location, degree received, and date of graduation. Also, include certificates for special training.

Other sections you may incorporate are interests, awards, military service, or volunteer experience as shown next.

- **Interests.** Include several sentences about your interests, such as you like working with computers.
- **Volunteer experience.** Add organizations you volunteered for, their locations, and dates.
- **Military duty.** Identify military background and duty, including locations and dates.

When you have compiled all information for the résumé, review, edit, and proofread your draft; then have several others read it and give you their advice. Post it on the discussion forum under Module I, Activity 2.

Reproduced from *Online Teaching and Learning: A Practical Guide for Librarians*, © 2017 Rowman & Littlefield Publishers

Using Module I, Activity 2 Handout: Write Your Résumé Content, located on page 108, have learners list their personal content under each section heading. They should be familiar with the categories from reading Module I, Activity 2 Content Handout: Résumé Sections. Indicate that they should select either a functional or chronological résumé type based on their job experience. Have them post their résumé content in the discussion forum. If you have set up a Facebook page, learners can respond to each other's résumé on Facebook in Activity 3.

Module I, Activity 2 Handout: Write Your Résumé Content

Complete an outline of the content you want to include in your résumé. Incorporate your own personal information under each of the following sections that you reviewed on the Content Handout. Omit areas that are not applicable (e.g., military, volunteer). Be concise!

Post the résumé content on the course site under section Module I, Activity 2. Make sure to put your individual course number on the résumé before posting.

Header.

Statement of career objective.

Skills.

Experience.

Education.

Interests.

Volunteer experience.

Military.

Reproduced from *Online Teaching and Learning: A Practical Guide for Librarians*, © 2017 Rowman & Littlefield Publishers

Activity 3: Review Peers' Résumés   Interaction is especially important in an on-demand course to generate community among learners and eliminate the feeling of isolation. This activity requires learners to do a peer review of another learner's résumé. Rubrics are useful to facilitate peer review by setting non-judgmental evaluation standards. Some participants may not be familiar with rubrics. Explain what a rubric is and how to use it. Create a table with URLs of sample rubrics from table 6.2 and post it on the course site. Request they post any questions or comments on rubrics in the discussion forum.

Table 6.2.   Sample Rubrics

DESCRIPTION	URLS
Detailed rubric for résumé	http://tinyurl.com/jc7trfx
Detailed rubric with bulleted points for each section of résumé	http://tinyurl.com/htrsgjl
Detailed rubrics for résumé and cover letter	http://tinyurl.com/zxkfnd4
Cover letter rubric divided by parts of the letter	http://tinyurl.com/j7sj7ve
Samples of résumés and other how-to advice on résumés	http://tinyurl.com/hz2fwmj
Comprehensive information about educational rubrics	http://tinyurl.com/pqgkqnm

Using Module I, Activity 3 Handout: Review Peers' Résumés, located below, have learners analyze and proofread the résumé content of one of their peers. Have them select a rubric from the table of rubrics you placed on the course site and use the rubric to comment on points that are done well and those that may need improvement or are missing. On the course site under Module I, Activity 3, set up a section for peer-reviewed résumés and one for revised résumés. Have learners post their completed reviews under peer-reviewed résumés. Instruct writers of the résumés to review peer comments and incorporate those that they think make their résumés better and note reasons for not using specific suggestions. Have writers post their résumés with corrections under revised résumés under Module I, Activity 3. When learners post their résumé content in Module I, Activity 3, it is identified with their individual course number as are any responses. The numbers take the place of their names on the posted assignments.

Module I, Activity 3 Handout: Review Peers' Résumés

In this activity you will conduct a peer review of another person's résumé. Rubrics are useful to facilitate peer review by setting non-judgmental evaluation standards. If you are not familiar with rubrics, review information at http://edglossary.org/rubric/.

Peer Review

- From the table on the course site under Module I, Activity 3, select one of the sample rubrics to use to evaluate the résumé content of your peer.
- Select a résumé of one of your peers from the course site under Module I, Activity 2. Identify the résumé with your course number.
- Analyze and proofread your peer's résumé content.
- Use the rubric to comment on points that are done well and those that may need improvement or are missing in the résumé you are reviewing.
- Post any questions or comments on rubrics in the discussion forum.
- Under the section for peer-reviewed résumés, post your completed review of your peer's résumé content.

Writer Response

- As the writer, you should now review peer comments made on your résumé and incorporate those comments that you think make your résumés better and note reasons for not using specific suggestions.
- Post résumés with corrections under revised résumés under Module I, Activity 3.

Reproduced from *Online Teaching and Learning: A Practical Guide for Librarians*, © 2017 Rowman & Littlefield Publishers

Activity 4: Format a Résumé There are various ways to format a résumé. Table 6.3 provides information on résumé formatting principles. Have learners read Module I, Activity 4 Content Handout: Résumé Formatting, located on page 110, and select a résumé sample based on their industry and job at https://resumegenius.com/resume-samples.

Table 6.3. Formatting Résumé Content

DESCRIPTION	URLS
Creating and formatting a résumé	http://tinyurl.com/zutpk2y
Steps to create a basic chronological résumé using a Microsoft Word template	http://tinyurl.com/jkss8yl
Creating a custom formatted résumé	http://tinyurl.com/mznl2rb
Format résumé in Microsoft Word 7	http://tinyurl.com/jcbbl7c
Format electronic résumé	http://tinyurl.com/zgpqnf2
Résumé chronological samples and writing guide	http://tinyurl.com/jpfjv97

Module I, Activity 4 Content Handout: Résumé Formatting

Employment managers often receive hundreds of résumés for each job they advertise. Therefore, they can spend little time perusing each résumé, perhaps seven to ten seconds each. It is important, therefore, that the look of your résumé catches readers' attention as they scan it. Formatting is very important to getting noticed by the employer. Formatting tips will help you in presenting yourself. Ready-made templates available in your word processing program and online can also save you time and produce a professional-looking document.

Consider these formatting tips:

- Résumé designs can vary by discipline. Research your area of interest for résumés in that career field preferred by the employer.
- Neatness counts. White space between sections of the résumé will enable the employer to locate the different sections quickly. A cluttered display with little white space will be difficult to scan so that your qualifications for the job will not stand out. One page and no more than two pages is a preferred résumé length.
- Either find a template on the web and follow the formatting standards or design it yourself in a program like Microsoft Word. Designing it yourself may be difficult and time consuming.
- If you design your own résumé, you can use typical standards:
  - Header. Center name in large, easy-to-read font type and large size (e.g., 14-point Arial). E-mail address and telephone number is in smaller font (e.g., 11-point Times New Roman). You may want a line separating the personal information from the rest of the content.
  - Headings like Career Objective. Left justify and bold with double-space headings under the personal information block and a line to separate.
  - Skills. Start each bullet with a strong verb and keep them short. Include universal skills and responsibilities.
  - Check for typos and misspellings.

Reproduced from *Online Teaching and Learning: A Practical Guide for Librarians*, © 2017 Rowman & Littlefield Publishers

Using Module I, Activity 4 Handout: Format a Résumé, located below, have them take the résumés reviewed in Activity 3 and format them based on similar job résumé samples and post them in the forum under Module I, Activity 4. Also, have learners read and comment on one formatted résumé under Activity 4. Remind learners to use their course number on all posts to the course site.

Module I, Activity 4 Handout: Format a Résumé

Finally, it is important to make your résumé look as professional as possible. In this activity, you will be formatting your peer-reviewed and revised résumé.

- Under Module I, Activity 4 on the course site, read Module I, Activity 4 Content Handout: Résumé Formatting.
- The table listed under Activity 4 on the course site contains URLs with examples of formatted résumés for different occupations. Review several formatted résumés and make a list of common formatting features.
- Review at least two or three résumé samples based on your industry or job at http://tinyurl.com/hz2fwmj. Use your peer-reviewed résumé that you then revised in Activity 3 and format it based on similar job résumé samples and the information on Content 4 Handout.
- Post your formatted résumé in the forum under Module I, Activity 4. Remember to use your course number on all posts.
- Review and comment on at least one formatted résumé under Module I, Activity 4, and repost it on the course site.

Note that your instructor will also be reviewing each formatted résumé.

Reproduced from *Online Teaching and Learning: A Practical Guide for Librarians*, © 2017 Rowman & Littlefield Publishers

Possible task: Depending on the features available in the course LMS, have learners interested in similar jobs form a group online and discuss and review the formatting of the group's résumés. They should identify formatting issues and create a list of common concerns to post in the discussion forum.

Evaluate Module I

Learners have now completed activities for Module I on creating a résumé. You already have some assignments on which to base evaluation of learner outcomes. Learners have written and formatted their own résumés, and they have done a critique of a peer's résumé. Have learners complete a short five-question quiz to assess whether they can identify sections of a résumé and important considerations when formatting one.

Step 4: Create Module II: Writing a Cover Letter (to Be Completed during Week 2 of the Course)

A cover letter should always focus on the job the learner is applying for and be included with the résumé. The following activities provide tasks to help learners practice writing a cover letter to match the résumé they just completed. As in Module I, the storyboard for Module II shows the sequence of instruction and how all elements relate and fit together within Module II. Applications are more common for some jobs and a cover letter may not be necessary; however, it is important to know how to complete one. See the exercises for chapter 6 on page 120 for more on completing an application form.

MODULE II STORYBOARD

Course: Prepare for a Job Search

Module II: Writing a Cover Letter
Assessment and Evaluation

	Course goals, objectives, outcomes	Instructor-generated content, communications	Readings	Class interactions and activities	Assessments — quizzes, posts, projects
Week 2: Writing a Cover Letter					
Module II					
Activity 5	Learn about, write, and review cover letters	Have learners read information about cover letters		Activity 5 Content Handout: Cover Letter Sections	
		Have learners write a cover letter		Complete Activity 5 Handout: Learn about, Write, and Review Cover Letters	Post cover letters
		Have learners review cover letters of peers and writers make revisions		Continue Activity 5 Handout	Post peer-reviewed letters and then revised cover letters

Evaluation		Have learners complete short quiz on Module II content			Assess on assignments, posts for Activity 5. Assess based on quiz at end of Module II.
Week 3: Evaluation, Reflection					
Course Evaluation	Formative, summative	Write objective assessment on entire course content			Assess assignments, posts for Activities 1–5. Assess based on quizzes at end of Modules I, II. Objective assessment covering entire course
				Course Evaluation Rubric	Complete Course Evaluation Rubric
Reflection		Complete self-evaluation of course			Self-evaluation of course

Write Module II Goals and Objectives

The goals and objectives for Module II should be written the same way as those for Module I. Here are some samples you can adapt:

Goal

After completing Module II on writing a cover letter, learners will be able to:
• Write effective cover letters in response to specific job descriptions that align with the résumé

Objectives

After completing Module II, learners will be able to:
• Review sample cover letters and point out strengths and weaknesses
• State sections that should appear in a well-written cover letter

- Write a draft formatted cover letter
- Review cover letters of peers posted in the discussion forum and post constructive comments for at least three letters

Begin Module II Learning Activities

You have finished writing information for Module I so patrons can create a résumé for a specific job. You are now ready to show patrons how to write a cover letter to align with the résumé they just wrote. Just as with a résumé, the cover letter should be specifically written for a particular job. Generic cover letters take away from the detailed résumé already written. The letter must complement the résumé. Because the employer will view the cover letter prior to reading the résumé, it must pique interest and encourage further reading. The activity you provide patrons in Module II should give them details about analyzing, writing, reviewing, and formatting a cover letter. You will have learners use Module II, Activity 5 Content Handout: Cover Letter Sections and Module II, Activity 5 Handout: Learn about, Write, and Review Cover Letters for this module.

Activity 5: Learn about, Write, and Review Cover Letters Explain the importance of the cover letter, and then have learners read Module II, Activity 5 Content Handout: Cover Letter Sections on page 115 that provides a synopsis of what a cover letter should contain and how it should be formatted.

Based on Module II, Activity 5 Content Handout: Cover Letter Sections, have learners review both poorly and well-written sample cover letters for jobs in different industries. Post questions in the discussion forum that you want learners to consider about the examples (e.g., "If you were an employer, what in each letter would catch your attention? Was anything missing?" "Based on what you read about cover letters, is there anything you would change in these examples?"). Ask them to post answers to your questions and also put in their own comments about cover letters they reviewed to further the discussion.

Based on the cover letter discussion online, have learners write their own cover letters. The letter should be targeted to the same job for which they wrote the résumé. It should be no more than one page. Have them post the letters on the discussion forum under Module II, Activity 5.

Using the rubric at http://tinyurl.com/zxkfnd4, have learners review at least three peer cover letters and evaluate them (e.g., How could the letter be better, or what was particularly successful?). They should post their rubric cover letter reviews in the discussion forum under Cover Letter Reviews under Module II, Activity 5. As facilitator, review learner posts, and write your own general responses identifying the comments that appeared most often as problems, and what learners seemed to do most successfully.

Module II, Activity 5 Content Handout: Cover Letter Sections

A cover letter should always be included with your résumé when applying for a job. In the twenty-first century, cover letters and résumés are often sent via e-mail with the résumé as an attachment. No matter what the mode of delivery, if a résumé is requested, a cover letter should accompany it. The cover letter, no more than one page, should be targeted to the job that you are applying for and emphasize the benefits you bring to that particular position in that organization. A generic letter will not get you an interview!

The cover letter contains three parts: a brief opening, a longer middle, and a brief closing. All paragraphs should be left justified with no paragraph indents. Paragraph 1 is the header and contains:

- Personal information, including your name, address, telephone number, and a professional e-mail address. It is formatted with a one-inch margin, using a readable font type and size (e.g., 12-point font, for example, in Times New Roman).
- Date
- Information on the person to whom you are writing—the name and/or title, if known—(e.g., Dear Ms. X: or Dear Hiring Manager:), followed by a colon and one blank line
- Position you are applying for and how you learned about it
- Skills or strengthens, using strong verbs like "know," not "think," to identify the skills

Paragraph 2 expands on your skills and shows your experience through specific examples. Pull out things from the job description to focus on as qualifications. It shows what work you did for your previous company; add education, if possible. The goal here is to show that you know the company you are applying to. Each point focuses on a different set of skills with details of past jobs that are linked to this new one you hope to be hired for. These examples and your skill set show you are ready to assume the new job immediately. You are focusing on what you have to offer the company, not what you hope to gain from being employed by it. At the end of paragraph 2, you should ask the employer to review your attached résumé.

Paragraph 3 emphasizes your enthusiasm to learn more about the position through an interview and asks that they please contact you. Mention that you will follow up in a week. Show you are confident. The final sentence thanks them for their time and for considering you for the position.

The end brings the letter to a close with a "Sincerely," and your first and last name. Add "Enclosure" so they are aware that a résumé is attached.

Module II, Activity 5 Handout: Learn about, Write, and Review Cover Letters

- Review some actual cover letters at either of the following links (some are well written; others are not as good) and answer questions under Module II, Activity 5 in the forum. Remember to use your course number when posting all assignments for Module II.
    ◦ http://tinyurl.com/z45sznt
    ◦ http://tinyurl.com/hg4b3nj
- Write your own one-page cover letter, targeted for the same job for which you wrote the résumé in Module I.
- Post the cover letter in the forum under Cover Letters under Module II, Activity 5.
- Based on the rubric at http://tinyurl.com/zxkfnd4, review at least three peer cover letters and evaluate them (e.g., How could the letter be better, or what was particularly successful?). Post your rubric cover letter reviews in the discussion forum under Cover Letter Reviews under Module II, Activity 5.

Reproduced from *Online Teaching and Learning: A Practical Guide for Librarians*, © 2017 Rowman & Littlefield Publishers

Evaluate Module II

Learners have now completed activities for Module II on creating a cover letter. You already have some assignments on which to base evaluation of learner outcomes. Learners have reviewed cover letters; written and formatted their own letters; and they have done critiques of cover letters of several colleagues. For a final assessment in Module II, have learners review a cover letter. You can use a short five-question multiple-choice format to evaluate their knowledge of points to include in a cover letter, what the letter does well, and what could be improved.

Step 5: Provide Follow-Up: The Next Step (to Be Completed during Week 3 of the Course)

Touched on briefly in this chapter was the ability to identify jobs, find documents online, and transmit cover letters and résumés electronically. Remind your learners about some tips to think about when using electronic documents:

- Electronic résumés, simplified versions of a printed résumé, are designed to stand out in an e-mail message or on a web page. Instructions for converting a print résumé into an electronic one are available on various sites, such as at http://www.ceswoodstock.org/job_search/jobleadseresume.shtml
- An applicant may submit an electronic résumé and be asked to bring a print résumé to an interview, so be prepared for both.
- When applying online or via e-mail, the cover letter should still be properly formatted, readable, and mistake-free.
- Even if there are specific requirements for submission, the cover letter still needs to cover each of the job description's requirements and show time was taken in its composition.

- An online cover letter format may be less structured, but the opportunity to make it unique and provide impact is still important.
- Online application forms are common, but make sure to take time to complete them and proofread carefully before sending.

Step 6: Evaluate the Course

Formative assessment of learners' assignments has occurred throughout the course through peer reviews and quizzes following each module. Depending on the technology used in the course, the summative evaluation will also determine whether attendees have met the learning outcomes you set out at the beginning of the course. This assessment covers material from the entire course. It should be accessible for learners to complete at the end of the course.

Participants also should complete a course evaluation form to give you feedback on the course overall—its objectives, content, structure, activities, and assignments. It should also address the interactivity required in the course. A reproducible example Course Evaluation Rubric is provided here for your use as the instructor (i.e., not for students). In this evaluation form, learners would need to select one response from each line.

Step 7: Summarize, Wrap Up, and Reflect

Make sure you bring the course to a conclusion. Have a brief summary of what you covered, for example, listing the top mistakes made when writing a résumé and cover letter. See common mistakes at https://www.youtube.com/watch?v=bFoDMTYIcyU.

Follow-up is an important part of any training. In a concluding portion on the course site, point out any other documents, such as a certificate of completion or other information that shows learners they successfully met the requirements of the course. Indicate that materials from the course will be available for further review on the library website. Tell learners that the course will be repeated during the upcoming year and to watch for announcements.

Reflect on how the course proceeded in a self-evaluation. Review and revise your course materials while everything is still fresh in your mind. What questions did learners ask that were not answered by the course? Were they able to use the technology or should you have a video or more instructions to get them started? This will help you decide what you like or dislike and what you might do differently if you repeat the course.

Course Evaluation Rubric

Circle one entry from each row (adequate, effective, or exemplary) of the Course Evaluation Rubric to provide your feedback on the course. Your comments are valuable in making this a better course. Post any additional comments about the course on the course website.

	Adequate	Effective	Exemplary
1	Students are not certain about what is expected of them in an online environment.	Students can understand the components and structure of the course; it is organized and easy to follow.	Students clearly understand all components and structure of the course; it is well organized and easy to follow.
2	Course structure (e.g., website or LMS) and format are inconsistent.	There is consistency in some aspects of the course (e.g., website or LMS).	There is consistency in all aspects of the course (e.g., website or LMS).
3	Learning objectives are vague and may be incomplete. Performance expectations are unclear or absent.	Learning objectives are identified and performance expectations are implied.	Learning objectives and performance expectations are clearly defined.
4	Opportunities for interaction and communication are limited.	There are some opportunities for interaction and communication among students, between students and instructor, and between students and content.	There are multiple opportunities for interaction and communication among students, between students and instructor, and between students and content.
5	Some course objectives, instructional strategies, and assessment techniques may be aligned.	Course objectives, instructional strategies, and assessment techniques are somewhat aligned.	Course objectives, instructional strategies, and assessment techniques are closely aligned.
6	Opportunities for students to receive feedback about their performance are infrequent.	Opportunities for students to receive feedback about their performance are provided.	Students' peer feedback opportunities exist. Regular feedback about student performance is provided in a timely manner.
7	Course uses a few technology tools for communication and learning.	Course uses technology tools to facilitate communication and learning.	Course uses a variety of technology tools that are appropriate and effective for facilitating communication and learning.
8	Some technology is used for its own sake.	Technology is mostly used to support student learning.	Technology is used to enhance student learning.
9	Additional resources outside the course content are largely absent.	Additional multimedia resources are available to engage learners in the learning process.	Multimedia elements are relevant/optimized for student Internet users and effectively engage learners in the learning process.

◎ Key Points

This chapter has focused on asynchronous teaching and learning, one form of elearning.

- Asynchronous learning is student centered and uses online learning materials located in an electronic network, such as a website or LMS, to facilitate interaction among learners without the limits of time and location.
- An instructor may or may not be part of asynchronous teaching and learning.
- Self-paced materials, such as videos, LibGuides, PowerPoints, and infographics provide on-demand instruction when used as part of a course or as stand-alone materials in on-demand courses without a facilitator.
- Public libraries are being called upon to create life skills courses and materials for face-to-face and online training to help first-time job seekers, those changing jobs, and the unemployed as they seek jobs.
- The model asynchronous course illustrated in this chapter can help those looking for jobs to create résumés and cover letters tailored to specific job descriptions.
- Exercises illustrate how a job applicant can complete a job application and prepare for an interview, vital parts of a job search.

With the increase in elearning, different methods of online teaching and learning are gaining traction in all libraries. Asynchronous learning that you learned about in this chapter provided an on-demand environment where learners in a public library could prepare for a job search. Embedded teaching and learning, another popular form of online learning, allows the librarian to work together with faculty members in an academic library, customers in special libraries, and teachers in the K–12 environment. Chapter 7 provides an in-depth look at this promising online partnership.

☉ Exercises

It is always important to practice and thus reinforce what you learned. In chapter 6, you learned about asynchronous teaching and learning and worked on creating an on-demand course to teach patrons who might come to the public library to create documents necessary to prepare for a job search. Patrons may also need to complete an application form and learn interviewing skills. Completing the following exercises will give you more information to add Module III: Completing a Job Application and Module IV: Preparing for an Interview. You could also use answers to questions in the exercises to create a totally new on-demand course.

Job Application Form

Applications differ greatly depending on the career area, and some jobs may not require an application. Put yourself in the place of the job applicant and complete the following tasks and answer the questions about job application forms. The information you gather will enable you to write Module III.

1. Decide on the outcome you want learners to be able to do at the end of the module. Write objectives that will achieve that outcome.
2. Review different types of applications in different industries. Look at some appropriate to first-time job applicants.
3. Look at sites where application forms can be submitted online. Jot down the process for filling one out and sending it online. Make a short video showing how to obtain and fill out a form and post it on your library website for learners to review.
4. Review application "Hints for Success" page by ColoradoCollege.org at http://tinyurl.com/zkwm65m/. You might incorporate these into a Content Handout.
5. View several videos on completing applications. Complete several sample application forms for different types of jobs. The application "Hints for Success" page (http://tinyurl.com/zkwm65m/) also has some samples to use as models.
6. Write at least one interactive activity you might include in this module. Write two or three questions related to applications to put in a discussion forum for learners to respond to.
7. Think about the assessment. Write some sample questions with answers to include in a quiz.

Completing these tasks gives you information for each step to create Module III on job application forms.

The Interview

The interview provides the opportunity to present oneself, so the potential employee must prepare carefully for the interview. Role-play an interviewee by completing the following tasks and answering the questions in this exercise. The content you gather will start you on the way to creating Module IV on preparing for an interview.

1. Gather several job descriptions to serve as models for job interviews. You want learners to be completely knowledgeable about the position, skills needed, and

responsibilities. Create a three-column form where the interviewees can list the requirements of the position in Column 1 and their skills, education, and prior experience that meet those of the job requirements in Column 2. Column 3 should list any weaknesses for each requirement and an alternative to minimize the problem.

2. Create a form in which the interviewee can put the details of the search about a job (e.g., look at the website, company products and services).

3. Employers also look for life skills (e.g., enthusiasm, confidence, dedication). Create a table to list characteristics in one column and descriptions of each trait with specific examples to use in the interview in a second column.

4. Find videos that show persons in interviews who are providing concrete examples of times that demonstrated being a team player or collaborating with colleagues, or showed how their actions benefited the organization.

5. Make a list of typical questions that usually come up in an interview, such as the following:
   - Tell me about yourself.
   - Why do you want to work for us?
   - Why should we hire you?
   - Why do you want this job?
   - What are three of your weaknesses and strengths?
   - Why did you leave your last job?
   - Where do you want to be in five years?
   - Job related: How do you sell to someone? How do you handle customer complaints?

6. Write up a mock interview that could be completed among learners.

Once you have completed these exercises, you have content that will start you off in writing Module IV.

References

Er, E., M. Özden, and A. Arifoglu. 2009. "A Blended E-learning Environment: A Model Proposition for Integration of Asynchronous and Synchronous E-learning." International Journal of Learning 16, no. 2: 449–60.

Haslam, Josepf. 2012. "Synchronous vs. Asynchronous Classes." *e-Learners.com* (blog). April 2. http://www.elearners.com/online-education-resources/degrees-and-programs/synchronous-vs-asynchronous-classes/.

Hrastinski, Stefan. 2008. "Asynchronous & Synchronous E-Learning." *Educause Quarterly* 31, no. 4: 51–55.

Van Noord, Rachel. 2010. "Virtual Staff Orientation Reduces Time to Bring New Staff Up-to-Speed." WebJunction. https://www.webjunction.org/content/dam/WebJunction/Documents/webJunction/CaseStudy_BCPL.pdf.

Embedded Librarianship: Partnering outside the Library

A ROLE TYPICAL FOR THE LIBRARIAN, no matter what type of library, is the "one-shot" presentation about the library. Whether in the library or in the classroom, the session has usually consisted of a face-to-face rundown of materials available in the library and services offered by librarians. For example, if the audience is students, the librarian may point out the types of special databases available, technology tools and a brief overview of what each does, and resources to help students when they use the library. Unfortunately, this short overview has left library users with inadequate knowledge about topics, such as how to do searches or select, evaluate, and cite sources. Librarians also feel frustrated because they have so little time to cover so much that their audience needs. In addition, because the Internet is the source of choice for student research, they do not seek out further information; thus their research skills and resulting projects, papers, and presentations often lack authoritative, diverse sources. These are information literacy skills that twenty-first-century learners need in their work and daily lives.

More and more academic libraries are adopting embedded librarianship as an approach to creating an integrated and sustained library instruction presence in classes across the curriculum. This approach is also being used in businesses, medical institutions, professions such as the law, and other for-profit and non-profit organizations. Embedded librarians work closely over time with non-librarian groups, whether by joining a semester-long course, maintaining an ongoing presence in online courses, participating in broad curriculum planning efforts, or joining the staff of academic departments, clinical settings, or corporate teams.

⊚ What Is Embedded Librarianship?

Embedded librarianship involves focused, customized instruction, materials, and/or presentations to a specific group. An embedded librarian is a librarian who is integrated into an online class for a period of time to support the students in their research process. For example, the librarian might be working with undergraduate students in English, an upper-division psychology class, or a group of aspiring patent attorneys. Of course, much of the subject content will come from the faculty member in an academic setting, but examples of library sources, searches, databases, and other materials will need to align with the content. The level of support the librarian performs will determine how much work is involved. However, as an equal partner, the librarian has more opportunity to provide the information literacy skills students need to utilize in a twenty-first-century workplace.

A definition of embedded librarianship was first presented in 2004 by Barbara Dewey. Her definition states: "Embedding requires more direct and purposeful interaction than acting in parallel with another person, group, or activity" (2004: 6). David Shumaker and Mary Talley (2009), in a report funded by the Special Libraries Association (SLA), define embedded librarian as one "focused on the needs of one or more specific groups, building relationships with these groups, developing a deep understanding of their work, and providing information services that are highly customized and targeted to their greatest needs."

The SLA research report characterizes embedded librarians in corporate environments as being located with a customer group, partially or fully funded by that group, and supervised by a non-library manager. The embedded librarian is encouraged to build relationships by meeting with the customer to gather and share information, support the group's work through collaborative activities, and meet with group leaders to review performance. The goal is to deliver value-added services, targeted to the group's work needs.

The SLA report also points out that the audience for special embedded librarians is quite diverse and widespread within the SLA membership, especially in larger organizations where they provide specialized services, such as training on information resources in the customer's office, conference room, or classroom. Often the embedded librarian has expertise in librarianship, the subject matter of the organization, and/or work experience in a field related to the customer's work.

Embedded librarians continuously learn themselves. They perform value-added services, as well as basic library services for different organization types and industry sectors. Academic, government, corporate, and non-profit organizations report widespread adoption of the embedded model across educational, legal, biomedical and pharmaceutical, media, and technology sectors.

Embedded librarianship is not a traditional question-and-answer model of reference service. The goal is collaboration and shared responsibilities to achieve outcomes. Embedded librarianship differs from that of the traditional librarian in several ways. A primary

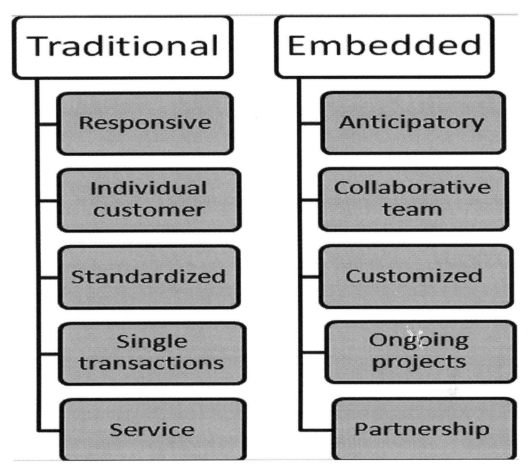

Figure 7.1. Traditional vs. Embedded Librarianship. *Adapted from Shumaker and Talley, 2009*

difference is the emphasis on relationships, discussed in more detail later in this chapter. Shumaker and Talley's report identifies five categories of differences as shown in figure 7.1.

Both in academics and the corporate world, working in teams, such as a student project or a research group, is now more often the norm. Because teams have different needs, flexibility on the part of the embedded librarian is essential. By establishing a working relationship with team members, the embedded librarian can better understand team needs and customize the solution to meet those needs. No longer is the number of questions a librarian answers in a day the measure of success. In the embedded model, the customized contributions to meet group or project needs are measures of success. Librarians still receive requests, but responses are often disseminated in a virtual discussion board or workspace among team members as part of a student or work project. The shared resources prompt new questions and further research. The embedded librarian provides value that can be assessed through learner outcomes or team success. Embedded librarians are now providing service as a partner in a team relationship, making them key players in the organization. Although librarians are often embedded in traditional classes, the focus in this chapter is on librarians embedded in elearning environments. An example later in this chapter entails an embedded librarian who is integrated into an online class for a period of time to support students in their research projects.

In summary, embedded librarianship is becoming widespread in all libraries and growing especially in large organizations and academic institutions. Much of its success depends on the librarian's ability to build relationships and collaborate with customers and faculty. Knowledge of their organization, whether an engineering department, a corporation, or a medical institution, is vital, as is understanding the subject. Embedded librarians must perform a variety of both value-added and basic activities and contribute to the groups with which they are working. Embedded librarianship succeeds because of the outstanding skills and exemplary dedication, motivation, and hard work of each embedded librarian. Librarians are now moving from a supporting role into partnerships with their clientele, enabling librarians to develop stronger connections and relationships with those they serve.

⊚ Why Use Embedded Librarians?

With the information explosion, students with computer skills are assumed to have research expertise. This is not necessarily the case. As often as not, they don't have knowledge of available resources or the ability to locate sources in their subject area. Students considered to be web savvy have difficulty evaluating the credibility of information online. They need instruction to find information in scholarly resources, create search strategies, evaluate information, understand plagiarism, and cite the information they use. The information now available is overwhelming, so students most often use Google to pick up the first few sources in their search that retrieved many thousands of records. Students need the help of librarians, and what better way to gain that expertise than for the librarian to work together with a faculty member. Often if their instructors do not require students to use library services, they do not.

As the number of online classes increases yearly, many students may never go to campus, never visit the library, nor have any idea what online library resources are available for their use. These online students need library research instruction classes as much as or more than a freshman in early undergraduate classes. As a result, academic institutions are increasingly incorporating embedded librarians into online classes.

Embedded librarians can facilitate student research and use of library resources during an entire course or just when needed. Depending on the degree of the collaboration, they can:

- Offer individual attention to students during any stage of their research process
- Serve as an online contact regarding library or research questions
- Work with students to quickly resolve access issues
- Provide customized designed content for the course, including suggested resources, tutorials, search strategies, and research guides
- Teach portions of the class in partnership with a faculty member

The benefit of embedded librarians is their engagement, so they are considered an integral part of the class, team, or learning community.

⑥ Characteristics of the Embedded Librarian

Embedded librarians must strengthen their traditional skill set and develop some new skills and attitudes at the same time—qualities that are extensions of their traditional roles. Strengths that librarians use every day—their knowledge of library research and reference skills, information technology, and information organization skills—form the foundation for work they will do as embedded librarians. In addition, knowledge of the customer's subject area is necessary. But, there is more.

One of the most important goals of an embedded librarian is to build relationships with his or her clientele—students, community groups, corporate teams, physicians, and more. In so doing, the librarian will better understand the group's values, culture, and goals and be able to share these qualities to collaborate to solve problems and achieve the group's goals.

Besides relationship building, embedded librarians must exemplify certain critical skills to foster these contacts:

- **Interpersonal communication skills.** Being able to communicate with all the players is essential to building relationships. For example, in an academic setting, the embedded librarian must communicate with staff, undergraduate and graduate students, faculty, researchers, and administrators from the department where the librarian is embedded. Both online (e.g., e-mail, discussion boards, wikis, blogs, social media) and offline (e.g., committees, off-hour activities), communication is necessary to ensure successful long-term relationships and success as an embedded librarian.
- **Socialization** is a key aspect of embedded librarianship. Success is linked not just to working in the same location as users in an academic area or organization. Embedded librarians who successfully integrate become an integral part of the communities they serve. They hold online office hours and communicate via e-mail, distribution lists, and web pages. Even outside of regular hours, they attend social as well as official functions to build relationships. Embedded librarians find ways to be present and socially involved with users to learn about their needs.
- **Services and activities** are already to some degree embedded electronically into online reference chat, use of and instruction on Web 2.0 social networking applications, such as Twitter and blogs, as well as collaboration in online classrooms (Ramsay and Kinnie, 2006). Embedded librarians also provide personalized online asynchronous services, including effective tutorials, interactive guides and links, and chat functions.
- **Collaboration** is vital for the embedded librarian. Today, libraries of all types do more than just store books. They are becoming more like social spaces for multitasking, group work, and expert assistance. Faculty members can work more effectively with librarians to design research projects and to develop collections that support the undergraduate curriculum where they must learn how to write a research paper and critically evaluate sources (Benton, 2009).

To sum up, the ideal embedded librarian possesses certain specific attributes, including the ability to be creative and flexible, being committed to service, possessing excellent interpersonal skills, advocating for the interests of the groups the librarian serves, and having the ability to achieve in both traditional library and non-library settings.

Roles of Online Embedded Librarian

Embedded online librarians are becoming more entrenched in academic and special libraries. The embedded role is a dynamic set of interactions between embedded librarians and patrons, faculty, or employees, to name some. What are some characteristics of an embedded program? Embedded librarianship can take several forms, from being an equal partner with a faculty member, to supplying additional help in teaching information literacy, to providing occasional assistance to students who are struggling with their research. Depending on the type of library, the role of the embedded librarian may not be the same, requiring different skills and work on very diverse tasks.

Academic Libraries

Faculty members are using online embedded librarians in the following ways:

- **Guest class librarian.** A typical approach has been for the librarian to work online with students on one or two research projects for a particular week or time period within the semester. The librarian assists students with the specific project during the week(s) of this assignment. Instruction is more effective if students have their assignment and submit it before the online librarian's session. Then the assigned librarian has time to review and discuss it with students during the class.
- **Semester-long class librarian.** A librarian maintains a discussion board forum throughout the semester to post helpful instructions, answer questions, and work with students on various assignments and projects.
- **Partner with faculty member.** The librarian works as an equal partner to create the online course, including setting objectives, creating activities, teaching and reviewing some of the assignments, collaborating on a discussion board, and providing and perhaps grading formative and summative assessment.
- **Course developer.** The librarian is also playing an integral role in the curriculum and instructional design process of online courses. In this role, the librarian works with faculty to design successful online courses that emphasize the value of the library. The embedded librarian not only teaches information literacy skills but also provides library instruction or tutorials on searching and finding resources through the library in support of course assignments.

Specifically, embedded librarians help students by assisting them in finding credible sources and writing citations. Or, when students need to narrow topics or identify keywords and search terms for a topic, the embedded librarian is the ideal authority for assistance. Other tasks include providing information about the library's authoritative databases like ProQuest and EBSCO*host*, and subject-specific ones, such as MEDLINE and legal files. They also assist students with the online catalog and answer questions about other library services and research.

Some activities that can solidify a partnership and increase the librarian's role include:

- Having librarians' contact information on the syllabus within a course
- Creating a discussion forum topic for the librarian to answer specific questions related to particular assignments in a course

- Establishing a blog in a course to answer questions for the class as a whole, not just for individual students
- Conducting a library instruction session for a course through an online classroom
- Embedding library resources into a course, such as tutorials or videos on information literacy and other topics, or including tip sheets and handouts as part of online class resources

Special Libraries

Embedded librarianship has been adapted by a diverse number of industries, ranging from biomedical to legal to educational. In order to become a part of their users' culture, embedded librarians are encouraged to build relationships by working with the client to gather and share information, supporting the group's work through collaborative activities, and meeting with group leaders to review performance. The goal is to deliver value-added services, targeted to the group's work needs.

Embedded librarianship in corporate and specialized organizations depends on the ability of library managers and embedded librarians to do several things (Shumaker, 2012):

- Establish relationships with key decision makers at all levels
- Continue to increase contributions and value within the organization
- Cost-effectively perform necessary tasks
- Provide evaluation consistent with the organization the librarian is embedded in

Librarians who are embedded with units and work groups also maintain connections with their peers across the enterprise.

Five services are common for these online embedded librarians. Most services relate to reference and in-depth subject research, such as evaluating and synthesizing the literature and current awareness. Technology is also high on the favorites list. However, teaching about conducting research is often necessary, and a part of training is to create learning materials that can be placed online, such as how-to manuals and pathfinders.

Embedded librarians may be called upon for the following activities:

- Meet with senior members of the customer group to discuss information needs and services
- Attend meetings, classes, and conferences devoted to customers' area of expertise
- Attend customer group meetings to learn about customer work and information needs and provide work products, such as online training or resources
- Collaborate on the group's electronic communication, including e-mail, wikis, blogs, and other web-based platforms

They also may have to undertake specific tasks:

- Assist with research, such as analysis and summary of research findings, develop and contribute to current awareness
- Create ways to offer research education like identifying keywords and search terms to help narrow topics or brainstorm ideas for further research
- Provide information about the library's databases, e-books, and services

- Help researchers, clients, and staff find credible web sources
- Assist with citations
- Assist users in using the online catalog

Key concepts for successful embedded programs include location, communication, services, flexibility of librarians, and collaborations. In an academic library, they may be among librarians and faculty, staff, researchers, and students. In special libraries, partnering may occur with researchers, clients, administrators, and distant employees. These concepts, combined with non-traditional socialization opportunities, encourage embedded librarians to provide specialized programs for their subject-focused users.

Best Practices from Libraries Involved in Online Embedded Librarianship

Collaboration between faculty and librarians is growing in academia, as well as in corporate and medical organizations, for-profits and non-profits. In academic environments, for example, neither librarians nor faculty can adequately teach the research process in isolation. The partnership between librarians and faculty can motivate students and provide them with current library research information. The examples that follow illustrate academic, K–12, and special libraries that are implementing the varied roles of the embedded librarian. Public libraries are also involved in embedded librarianship, but many of the examples involve the librarian actually going out into the community to provide the library's services.

Embedded Online Academic Librarianship

Most electronically embedded librarians in academic settings are associated with online courses. The following exemplify academic programs with an embedded format.

Example 1—The University of Central Florida Libraries

The University of Central Florida (UCF) library instruction program for distance education classes employs an embedded component. Faculty requests and students' needs initiated the development of the online library instruction program. The program has two aspects: research modules created by librarians and the librarian working with the class during the semester.

Research Modules   Created by the librarian (Bozeman, 2008), library modules provide online students with information to improve their research skills, resources available at UCF libraries, and the opportunity to make a connection with one librarian. There are also stand-alone modules that can provide information for class-specific instruction. Topics include creating search strategies, finding articles from peer-reviewed journals, searching databases and the Internet, and understanding plagiarism and APA citation style. One module also contains general information about the library.

The modules are interconnected so they can be used by both the librarian and faculty member. Courses can be modified to accommodate the unique differences required by each class. Practice exercises are also included and can be created and graded by both the librarian and instructor. Located on the library servers, modules and assignments can be accessed by students throughout the course. A final graded library assignment is part of the course. Students' reaction to the modules has been quite positive.

Embedded Librarian The embedded librarian must be closely involved with the class to understand the needs of the online students and faculty. The librarian has access to course materials and e-mail, can set up and monitor a class discussion forum, and answer questions. By monitoring discussions, the librarian is integral to the course and can determine where students are having research problems and provide help.

Results The library online embedded instruction program was deemed successful mostly because of the collaboration between librarians and faculty. Needs of the students were better understood so that instruction could be structured to meet them. See more details about this program at http://tinyurl.com/jzjsebg. Figure 7.2 shows a slide from a PowerPoint program presentation about the UCF program.

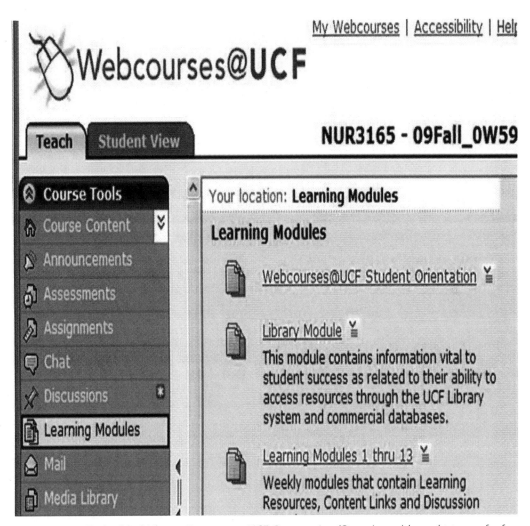

Figure 7.2. Embedded Library Program at UCF. *Presentation (Open Access) brought to you for free and open access by Digital Commons@Georgia Southern*

Example 2—Community College of Vermont

The Community College of Vermont (CCV) serves its online students by having librarians join a classroom virtually. Given the rapid growth in the number of online courses at the college—from eight courses in the fall of 1997 to 181 courses in the spring of 2006—the lack of library instruction for online students became a problem. The embedded librarian idea was first implemented by incorporating library instruction into one online psychology class (Matthew and Schroeder, 2006).

How It Works   The librarian entered the online discussion forum and opened the discussion by introducing herself and explaining her expected availability and involvement in the class. Students could then ask questions. The librarian responded to the student requests and advised, for example, about databases and other resources and also gave instructions on how to use them. Questions ranged from basic requests to those requiring more specialized research.

Answering students' questions within the forums is just one service of the embedded librarian. The librarian also posted tips about finding and narrowing topics, choosing and using library databases and resources, and incorporating research using American Psychological Association (APA) and Modern Language Association (MLA) citation styles. Students appreciated and used the support so much that the program was expanded to all online instructors for subsequent semesters. Faculty was also impressed with the results students achieved on their research projects.

The program has grown from a beginning with two classes to forty-three in spring 2006. The librarian also advertised the program at the beginning of the semester through e-mail to all online faculty, describing the embedded program and giving examples of how it worked. Variations of the initial model have appeared. For example, CCV's Seminar in Educational Inquiry capstone class has incorporated an Ask the Librarian thread in its weekly discussion forum so the librarian is available to help throughout the project. Other models include working with classes in different subject areas for one week to several weeks per semester when they are learning how to do research on the Internet. For example, in a law class, the embedded librarian was involved for three weeks to assist students in locating Vermont statutes.

Results   The embedded model has proved most effective for classes that are actually working on specific research-focused projects, not those that had to make up a question that was unrelated to their coursework. Students were also more likely to use the librarian during a week when they were working specifically on a project. In order to foster engagement, faculty members also had to play a part by stressing the benefits of the embedded librarian. Finally, the Ask the Librarian worked best when it was included in the discussion forum so students had one point of entry to post questions, receive answers, and find all aspects of the course. Posting to a discussion forum also established a community, enabling all class members to gain insight from questions and responses.

Future Ideas   Because of the popularity of the program and the limited number of librarians, other approaches are being piloted. Library courses have been created for specific curricular areas. In this way, discussion forum interactions are accessed by all online students in a specific curricular area (e.g., education). CCV's embedded librarian program demonstrates how, through a partnership approach with faculty, comprehensive library instruction can be provided for online students in a meaningful, integrated way. Learn the details of this embedded program at http://er.educause.edu/articles/2006/1/ the-embedded-librarian-program (see figure 7.3).

Example 3—K–12 Embedded Online Librarianship

Embedded librarianship in the K–12 arena refers to the practice of school librarians integrating their expertise into content area classrooms. This can include co-teaching,

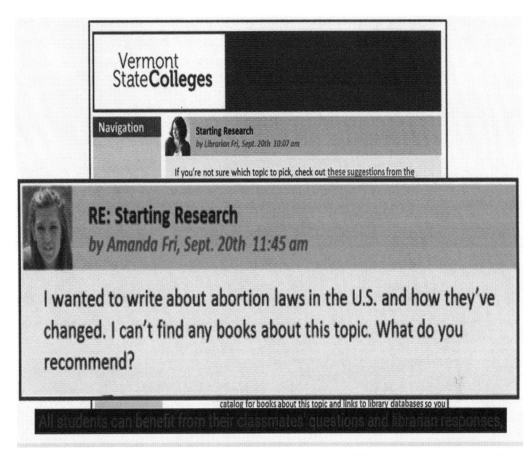

Figure 7.3. Embedded Library Program, Hartness Library at CCV. *Licensed under Creative Commons. http://tinyurl.com/hwyrwxg*

providing research instruction for course projects, co-evaluation of projects, describing library resources, conferencing with students, and more. As K–12 online environments increase, the teacher librarian has one more role to play. This example describes how one high school librarian partnering with an English teacher worked with tenth-grade students in an honors literature/ composition course (Hamilton, 2012).

How It Works The goal was to incorporate information literacy as an essential standard in subject area classes. Achieving this goal necessitated that the librarian collaborate with subject area teachers. Beginning in 2009 and continuing to the present, the librarian, working in partnership with the English teacher, has been involved in the instructional design, teaching, and assessment of student learning for tenth graders for approximately 75 percent of each academic year. Through the use of social media and cloud computing, the partners assisted students in creating their own personal learning environments (PLEs) and information dashboards to help them manage their own learning. Together, the two educators wrote content-based and information literacy outcomes they wanted students to master, collaborated on a draft of learning activities and tools to use, and put together a master list of materials. They created instructional handouts, LibGuides for content, assessment rubrics, and the daily calendar of learning activities and resources. The librarian incorporated technology tools ranging from Google Sites to hosting course content to Wordpress.com as the course blog for instructions, communication among educators and students, as well as for reflection. Technology tools, such as wikis, NoodleBib for creating bibliographies, and Scoop.it for curating and collecting resources, were introduced.

Results   An important factor in the positive outcome of this embedded relationship was the teacher's willingness to share ownership of content, pedagogy, and assessment practices to help establish the librarian as a co-teacher of the course. Review the entire project at https://journals.ala.org/ltr/article/view/4367/5049.

Special Libraries Embedded Online Librarianship

Although the embedded approach in academic libraries is growing rapidly, various forms of embedded librarianship for for-profit and non-profit organizations, government organizations, and other special libraries or information services are also taking shape. Because special libraries are so diverse, however, the ways their librarians support their organizations is tailored to each environment. Two types of approaches are often used: project based and programmatic. Projects have a start and end date, and the librarian is involved until the project concludes. In programmatic-based embedded librarianship, a librarian is hired by an organization on a full-time, ongoing basis and supports multiple projects within the organization.

Example 4—The Mitre Corporation

The Mitre Corporation, a government organization that works with a number of U.S. government agencies, has used an embedded librarian as part of a team approach.

How It Works   One of the librarians from the main library at Mitre was embedded into the Systems Engineering Process Office (SEPO) (Moore, 2006). As part of the SEPO team, his office was relocated in the building with the rest of the team. The librarian's responsibilities also evolved from managing a collection of documents and links to providing multiple services: tagging and linking content, providing news alerts, and researching subjects specific to SEPO, to name some. Much of the information the librarian provided was then funneled virtually throughout the company. This approach was a win-win situation whereby the librarian developed comprehensive knowledge to be able to respond to questions on systems engineering subjects requested by the engineers and create connections with the information analysts as well.

Results   Mitre Corporation's embedded librarians provide the vehicle to mentor and share expertise, enhance collaboration, identify and connect in cross-organizational projects, and link research and knowledge management needs across the corporation (Shumaker, 2012).

⊚ Tips for the Online Embedded Librarian

Leaving the comfort and familiarity of the traditional library and moving into an unfamiliar environment with new responsibilities, although rewarding, can be a daunting task initially. Here are some tips for the embedded online librarian taking on this new role (Carlson and Kneale, 2011):

- As a team player, know your roles and responsibilities, but also understand the roles of the other team members and how you will interact with, support, and receive support from them.

- Solicit the understanding and approval of both the library administration, who may need to adjust your responsibilities, and your colleagues, who may also be affected by your new role.
- Be proactive in identifying and pursuing opportunities (e.g., by attending university seminars and talking with speakers), thus indicating what you can contribute as a librarian toward new knowledge-based practices.
- Accept risk as part of the new, unfamiliar role and its responsibilities. Tasks you perform may have both direct and indirect benefits.
- Translate library work into other disciplines explaining your knowledge, skills, and expertise to others in ways that are relevant and meaningful to them and their situation—not necessarily an easy task.
- Build relationships to talk and listen with the researchers that you serve, with an emphasis on teaching and learning from each other. Researchers need to be able to get to know you and you them and what you can do so that they will seek you out as a valued colleague and resource and build the relationship.
- Move outside your comfort area. The library environment is well known to you; however, ask for help when you need it. It also helps to develop a network of colleagues to confer with when things are uncertain. In addition, remember that this may not only be outside your comfort zone, but out of your faculty member's as well. The rapidly changing nature of research in the twenty-first century means that faculty is also confronting new and unfamiliar situations themselves. Keep in mind that you have skills and a perspective that your collaborators likely do not possess and that you are adding value.

The embedded librarian model offers the potential for librarians to apply their knowledge and expertise in new ways that can influence the value of librarians. Embedded librarianship is a powerful way to show the impact that librarians can and do have beyond the traditional functions of the library, and why librarians are needed now more than ever.

Setting Up an Online Embedded Library Program

As you consider whether or not to become an online embedded librarian in an academic course, there are several steps to follow. Starting with a pilot project can work out all the problems prior to testing the regular online course. The steps that follow outline an online course with an embedded librarian involved. The format is that of two equal partners.

When working with partners, it is critical to set clear expectations from the beginning. What does the instructor think your role as online librarian will be in the course? How much involvement will you have with the assignments, with grading? Careful analysis of the syllabus, along with detailed conversations with the instructor, forms an excellent pre-embedding strategy.

The steps that follow outline an online course with an embedded librarian involved. Activities are developed in detail in the implementation step. The format of the course uses the ADDIE model, discussed in chapter 2 (see figure 7.4).

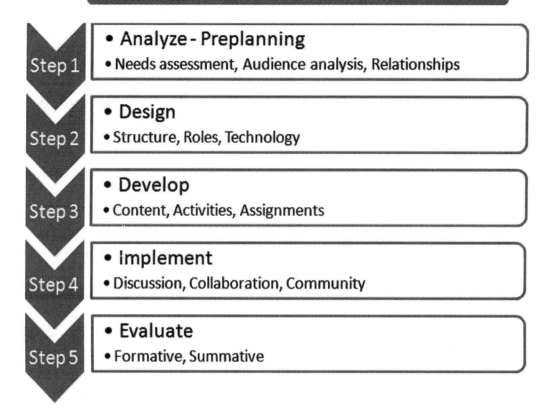

Figure 7.4. ADDIE Model. *Created by author online*

Step 1: Analyze: Preplanning

Identify Campus Needs and Goals

Analyzing the need of staff, time, budget, and students is the initial step done through a needs assessment. The academic mission and priorities of your institution should guide your planning efforts. You may also implement formal needs assessments, surveys, and focus groups to learn more about what kind of embedded project will be most effective and best address the needs of students and faculty. Meeting with subject departments can expand existing partnerships into more formal embedded projects. Prioritize when to use an embedded librarian according to the academic mission, goals of the library, and perceived need of librarian presence. For example, an online embedded librarian might be better used in a class with a heavy research component and a general education information literacy requirement than in a survey course with minimal research work.

It's also important to let online instructors know about the library embedded service. You can market that service through e-mail to faculty personally or to liaisons the library has with specific academic departments. For faculty to determine how the embedded service fits with a class, you might even include a checklist (e.g., http://tinyurl.com/z8oulqu). Any new programs in development at your institution are an opportunity to build the presence of a librarian throughout a degree program. This is especially true when academic programs develop a new online presence. Departments in the midst of major curriculum changes are also excellent partners for expanding an embedded project with goals that:

- Build strong relationships with members of a specific information user group
- Focus on understanding their work and information needs
- Share their goals and actively contribute to the achievement of those goals
- Become an integral and indispensable member of the group (Riccio, 2012)

Ask Questions to Help Analyze Need

The reasons for choosing an online class are varied. Often it is because students are not able to visit the physical campus. Thus, they do not have the same exposure to the library as a resident student. Determine that an embedded component is needed in the online class and then how to implement it given the constraints of staff, time, and budget. Questions to consider even before class preparation begins include:

- Who is the audience? Get as much information about the class ahead of time as possible. What is their knowledge of research? Have they had classes before requiring research papers or projects or presentations requiring them to conduct research? The needs assessment might provide answers.
- Is a librarian available who is knowledgeable about the course content? What will be the online embedded librarian's role? Librarians' roles in courses can be divided by length of involvement (e.g., one-shot versus semester-long) or by purpose (e.g., library instruction, answering reference queries, discussion board maintenance). To be a partner in the class, librarians require knowledge of the course content and time to work together with the faculty member. Relationship building is an important part of obtaining the knowledge necessary to decide on the level of the embedded librarian's participation.
- How does research fit into the course requirements?
- How much time will collaborating with the faculty member take? How will the time be budgeted? What other librarian duties, if any, are required?

These and other questions must be worked out between the library and department into which the librarian will be embedded. Again, relationship building is important to resolve these issues.

Result: For this course, a request has come from a science department indicating that the librarian will be embedded into a science course for the semester.

Step 2: Design the Course

When it is determined that a librarian will be embedded in a specific online course, the course design begins. First, the librarian and instructor must clearly negotiate and define the librarian's role. In this example, together as equal partners, they will design, develop, teach, and evaluate the course.

In order for the course to run smoothly, many decisions must be made in the design phase related to goals, objectives and outcomes, course content, communication, interaction, technology to use, activities and assignments, and assessment. Working together, the instructor, librarian, and any other team members might want to create a storyboard that incorporates all aspects of the course and how they fit together. See storyboard examples in chapter 6.

Goals, Objectives, and Outcomes

The instructor and embedded librarian should collaborate on writing goals, objectives, and outcomes. For example, the instructor might focus on ones for the content he or she is writing and the librarian for the research aspect of the course. Create one or two goals to achieve the outcomes you determine for the course. Objectives should be more specific with tasks broken down into discrete units to achieve the outcomes. Complete a joint review to make sure the course forms a cohesive unit. If the course is divided into modules, you'll want to create goals, objectives, and outcomes for each module. See chapter 3 for more information on writing goals, objectives, and outcomes.

Course Content

For the embedded librarian, it is not enough to have an online presence, for example, having the librarian contact information available in the LMS/CMS. The librarian must have total access to the LMS (e.g., Moodle, Blackboard) or website that hosts the course to be able to communicate with students and post and review items online. If the librarian is writing a research component for the course, then all information needed to teach the content, including any handouts, instructions for activities, interactive tasks, and additional resources, must be a part of the LMS or of each module or an individual module depending on the way the course is structured.

For this example course, the librarian's content focuses on teaching and expanding students' information literacy skills. The total course will cover the following topics: developing a search question or research statement, identifying keywords and selecting them from the search statement/question, developing several search strategies, searching general or specific databases using Boolean operators, searching the Internet for scholarly information, distinguishing between peer-reviewed journals and magazines, evaluating resources, and providing an overview of citation guidelines. Depending on the extent of the research component in the course, these items can be covered in more or less detail or taught in separate courses. Online self-paced resources can be used to provide some of this information.

Communication

Expectations about time and availability are key to put in place before the embedded project begins. Virtual office hours for both faculty and librarian should be designated in the syllabus, on the LMS, and in the discussion forum. Librarian contact information should be alongside that of the instructor. Keep these next tips in mind as you set up what the discussion board will contain, how often students will post, and when or whether the librarian and/or the instructor will respond.

- Communicate class assignments and other deadlines for the course. This helps you and students plan ahead if several due dates occur at the same.
- Check to see if the LMS you are using gives e-mail notification when posts to the discussion board are delivered. This gives you a heads-up to log in when responses are needed. Chapter 5 provides detail on the LMS.

- Set expectations by setting up specific days and times each week to log in to the LMS to respond to e-mails and posts.
- Save e-mail messages and posts for future use. It will save time and show areas where additional communication is needed in subsequent courses. They can also be used for assessment.

Resources

Place additional resources (e.g., links, videos, white papers, websites) in the LMS to offer more in-depth information about topics discussed in the course. If students are struggling or if they are interested in delving deeper into the subject, they can explore further at their own pace. Links to additional resources that are part of the course are also ideal to stimulate online discussion and motivate learners to actively participate.

Step 3: Develop the Course

During the development phase you will develop the rest of the storyboard you designed earlier. As a team you've identified all components you plan to implement in your online course, and they are ready to be transferred online into the LMS. Your storyboard should also contain the order, how the content fits together, transitions from one part to another, timing for each part, reinforcement through practice, and, of course, assessment. You have to identify the pieces—how they are located on the course site, whether the activities and assignments will enable learners to achieve the objectives, what formative evaluation you will use within the course, and what the summative assessment will be. Since this is a synchronous course with two equal partners, one may act as instructor providing subject content, for instance, on the solar system for science, while the other performs the role of facilitator and focuses on the information literacy aspects. Note that the roles may reverse depending on the emphasis of the course, for example, if the course focus for the learners is on conducting research.

Interaction

Having interaction in a course creates community where online users might otherwise feel isolated. It gives learners an online platform to share ideas, questions, and concerns, as well as receive feedback necessary to achieve learning outcomes. Some questions to consider are: What are the objectives and outcomes of the activities? Who takes charge of different activities? How much time will each interaction take? How will you know if outcomes have been achieved?

Both types of these next interactions involve online student communication; however, students' ability to write creative posts, ones that further the discussion, will improve the course. One focus in this chapter is how to make sure learners know how to use postings to make the most of the online discussion.

- **Online forums or a discussion board** in the LMS/CMS or an organization's course site can provide the vehicle for this interactivity. Setting up and/or monitoring the discussion forum is often an ideal role for the embedded librarian. Prior to the course, the instructor and librarian should work together to develop guidelines, such as instructions on student posting like netiquette rules, post frequency, guidelines for commenting, and consequences for disrespectful posting, to name some.

Setting up the LMS sections for the course may also take help from the IT department. Chapter 6 provides a detailed example of module setup on a course site.
- **Social media** can be an alternative form of discussion during the course. If students are reluctant participants on the discussion forum, they may more readily contribute to Google+, Facebook, LinkedIn, or Twitter because many are used to responding in this media.

To have a truly interactive component to your online learning, the quantity and quality of questions, responses, and comments make all the difference. As the facilitator, you must provide guidelines for posting in an online discussion forum. Once students understand what is expected, they often can lead the way.

Consider the following as you set up your online discussion forum:

- Decide on the forum venue. Think about the goals, objectives, and outcomes you want learners to achieve. They may determine the type of forum you create. For example, posting articles and having students comment on them or create their own posts might be better with a blog format. Short responses such as on Twitter with the 140-character limit or using a threaded message board might be other choices.
- Set guidelines in advance. Learners must know what you expect from them in the online forum and how they should behave when interacting with their peers. For example, how often are they expected to post and to whom? Can they initiate a new thread? How will you deal with students who are not participating?
- Set a specific schedule that requires posting on a regular basis at least once a week by a specific day of the week. If possible, provide a list of topics for discussion so students have flexibility in creating their posts. This will foster more in-depth comments. Make sure all class members are participating. If some are not, contact them privately and address their concerns. Involvement emphasizes the interactivity in the course.
- Guide the discussion by posting questions or ideas so that students will take that idea further and add their own thoughts. Create questions to encourage thinking. Socratic questions require students to think deeply about the topic and necessitate thoughtful responses to the questions. Consider these types:
  ○ Clarifying that requires an explanation in response—Why do you believe . . . ?
  ○ Probing assumptions of an argument—Tell me why . . .
  ○ Probing reasons and evidence, often used as follow up—Give an example . . .
  ○ Analyzing different sides to a question—Why is your solution better?
  ○ Probing consequences of a theory—What do you think might happen?
  By posing such questions, you can then let learners take control to spark the online discussion. For more on Socratic questioning, go to http://tinyurl.com/bqoum.
- Write clear, concise, open-ended questions with a focus on higher-order thinking on Bloom's Taxonomy (see chapter 2).
- Monitor the dialogue and add a new post when you think the current idea has been examined. Sometimes one discussion thread leads to another that a small group may want to explore in a new thread. You will also need to keep an eye on the posts so that they do not get off topic.
- Try to link to multimedia resources (e.g., videos, online scenarios, infographics) outside the course and also to the learning materials you have created. Such visuals also spark interest.

Once you have outlined the purpose of your forum and what you want it to contain, you must consider your audience—how much do they know about posting to an online academic forum and what are your guidelines for posting? The reproducible Content 1 Handout: Netiquette Advice for Posting can be placed on the LMS for students to download as a guide.

Content 1 Handout: Netiquette Advice for Posting

For more effective, constructive, and interactive discussions, consider these tips when writing posts to discussion boards:

1. Be constructive in your feedback and comments to others.
2. Don't type in ALL CAPS. It's rude!
3. Post on one topic at a time and don't wander from the topic in links, comments, and graphics.
4. Don't write anything that sounds angry or sarcastic: the tone of your voice is not conveyed online—only your words.
5. Be polite, using "Please" and "Thank you" when requesting help from others.
6. Review postings to make sure your question has not already been asked.
7. When answering a question from a classmate, make sure your answer is accurate; guessing does not help.
8. Respect the views of others. Disagree respectfully and acknowledge valid points in an argument. Everyone is entitled to their own perspective.
9. Be brief. Questions and responses are more likely to be read if they are simply written.
10. Summarize multiple responses to your question and post as a summary.
11. Check recent comments before replying to older ones because the issue may have been resolved.
12. When referring to an earlier post, quote a few lines for reference.
13. Check spelling and grammar before posting to the discussion board. This is an academic forum.

Reproduced from *Online Teaching and Learning: A Practical Guide for Librarians*, © 2017 Rowman & Littlefield Publishers

Activities

As students begin their course research, the librarian creates activities that provide content on best practices in conducting research, as well as practice actually doing the research that focuses on the subject content of the course. The research goals reinforce information from the instructor. Each session is tailored to a specific class assignment, and librarians are present to answer questions as students conduct their research. For example, depending on the online course design mutually agreed upon, the librarian might provide a guest lecture on one day and assign searches to be posted in the discussion forum for another activity to be reviewed by peers and the librarian, who both provide feedback for an interactive assignment. Such sample activities will be discussed in Step 4.

Step 4: Implement the Course

During implementation, all components of the course are available to the developers and audience. It is now accessible to view on the course site or LMS. Often, a short test run is conducted and monitored to ensure no problems arise when the course goes live. Adjustments can then be made before the entire audience obtains access. The following is a detailed sample of activities where the faculty member and the embedded librarian would work together to introduce information literacy to an online class.

Online Example

In this academic course, there is a research component. An overview of information literacy is necessary to introduce students to conducting online research at the college level. An embedded librarian is working with a faculty member to explain what information literacy is to this class of university students. The embedded librarian will take the lead to select the content, compile materials, decide upon assessment, and structure activities. The activities could be part of a webinar that the librarian presents, feature self-paced materials, be conducted in a self-paced format, or use a combination of these strategies. Table 7.1 includes some materials that will be used for this sample introduction to information literacy.

Table 7.1. Materials for Information Literacy Activities

	DESCRIPTION	URLS
1	Video 1 on integrating information literacy into courses	http://tinyurl.com/hcedmfx
2	ACRL Information Literacy Standards, Performance Indicators, and Outcomes	http://tinyurl.com/hhdsr2l
3	Video 2 explaining 5 components of information literacy	http://tinyurl.com/hkwfh2m
4	Video 3—Module 2 of a 3-module series on information literacy (find information, search strategies, keywords)	http://tinyurl.com/gnptwck
5	Information literacy lesson on credible sources, Boolean operators, and tips for searching the Internet	http://tinyurl.com/zbl43jh
6	Examples of micro-lesson models	http://tinyurl.com/jlws8ju
7	Google Scholar search tips	http://tinyurl.com/j5bhfn3

Sample Activities

The embedded librarian and faculty member can use these next sample activities to introduce information literacy to the online class.

- Both faculty member and librarian begin by viewing Video 1 in table 7.1, row 1. It provides an introduction that both instructor and librarian should consider together at the beginning of the activity. In an entertaining way, this video outlines information the instructor may think students know (but don't!) about information literacy. Note that some of the examples in the video may be helpful to the librarian who is creating the content and will provide practice examples for students.

- Table 7.1, row 2 presents the Association of College & Research Libraries (ACRL) Information Literacy Standards, which faculty members may not be familiar with; this also provides a quick review for the librarian. Some of the standards will be addressed in the activity.
- The librarian now takes the lead to determine what the overview to information literacy should contain so students can get started on their research. The overview should include content, practice, and interaction.
- The librarian gathers content to help students learn about keyword search for credible sources.
- Video 2 in table 7.1, row 3 conveys the content clearly—the five components of information literacy—and includes examples so students can see how they might apply their knowledge in real life.
- Numerous videos are available on information literacy—what it is, why it's important, and how to teach it. These may be useful as models to see different ways librarians are teaching their students about information literacy. Review some in table 7.1, rows 5 and 6.
- Micro-lessons are mini-lessons that can be taught in a few minutes. For example, you might do a micro-lesson on what Boolean operators are and how to use them when searching authoritative databases. Review some samples of micro-lessons in table 7.1, row 5 as models for creating your own.
- Students need practice to reinforce what they learned about searching. In Practice 1 students will determine a topic and create a concept map to narrow the search.
  - Have them read about concept maps and review examples on using concept maps to narrow a search on the topic of sustainable development at http://tinyurl.com/ha6j75t.
  - Place Content 2 Handout: Search Strategy Preparation on the course website. Have students read it as a model showing them how to create concept maps and identify search terms. A completed concept map is shown on the handout.
- For interaction in this module, students will do Practice 2 and review concept maps and search strategies of peers.
  - With the concept map in Activity 1 Handout: Prepare a Search Strategy as a guide, have students identify their own topic, and following the Content 1 Handout example write a sentence explaining what they want to discover about the topic.
  - Have them create their own concept map by narrowing the topic to at least three levels.
  - Have them select two or three search terms from the sentence or the concept map to use in a search. Note if you want them to search specialized library databases, you will need to explain Boolean operators and how to use them to connect terms to retrieve results.
  - Have students post their Activity 1 Handouts to the discussion forum under a section labeled Activity 1.
- At the end of Practice 2, have students do another activity. Have them conduct a review of three of their peers' concept maps. Have them provide comments on keywords used and how well creating the concept map prepared them to select an appropriate topic. As students write their comments, have them refer to Content 1 Handout: Netiquette Advice for Posting. Have them post their peer responses in the online forum under Activity 2.

Content 2 Handout: Search Strategy Preparation

This handout shows a step-by-step example of brainstorming to create a concept map about your research topic, narrowing the topic, and using the map to identify search terms for the online search.

1. Write the topic you plan to search for in one question: What are some alternative energy sources currently in use?
2. When deciding on the topic, answer these questions:
   • Is the topic too broad? Do you want to narrow it to one energy source?
   • Is it too narrow? Do you just want to know the name of the type of energy?
   • What do you want to know about that energy source? How is it being used? What are the benefits? What are the disadvantages of its use?
3. Read about concept maps and review examples on using concept maps to narrow a search on the topic of sustainable development at http://tinyurl.com/ha6j75t.
4. Brainstorm a list of possibilities for the topic alternative energy sources.

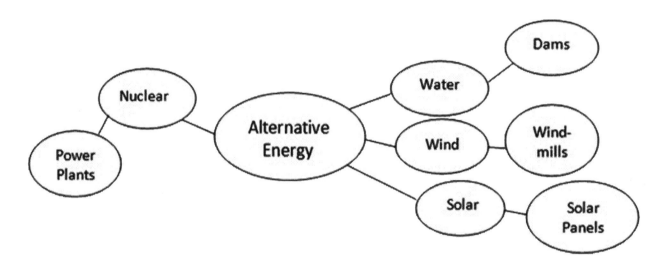

5. Select keywords (important concepts from the search question or your brainstorming) to use in your search. Put different concepts under separate columns. Put synonyms in the same column.

Concept 1	Concept 2	Concept 3
alternative source, alternative sources	wind	windmills, windmill
	nuclear	power plants, power plant
	water	hydroelectric power
	solar	solar panel, solar panels

6. Enter these keywords in the search box in your search engine.

Reproduced from *Online Teaching and Learning: A Practical Guide for Librarians*, © 2017 Rowman & Littlefield Publishers

- Note that you should also add suggestions on search structure, and post common suggestions in the online forum, as well as replying individually to students. The faculty member might also wish to comment.

The micro-lesson just outlined forms a foundation for an in-depth course on teaching the components of information literacy in separate online modules.

•Activity 1 Handout: Preparing a Search Strategy

Complete Activity 1 Handout: write a topic question, answer questions to refine the topic, brainstorm keywords and synonyms to use as search terms. Put different terms in separate columns.

1. Write the topic you plan to search for in one question _____

2. Answer these questions about the topic:

    - Is the topic too broad? How can you narrow it?
    - Is it too narrow? What more do you want to know about it? How is it being used? What are the benefits? What are the disadvantages of its use?

3. Brainstorm a list of all possibilities for this topic.

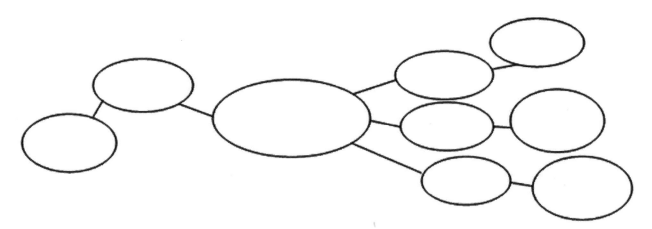

4. Select keywords (important concepts from the search question or your brainstorming). Put different concepts under separate columns. Put synonyms in the same column.

    Concept 1   **Concept 2**   **Concept 3**

5. Place your Activity 1 Handout on the course website under Activity 1.

6. Review three peers' search sheets, add comments to each sheet, and repost using your course number. Chapter 6 gives information about the course number.

Reproduced from *Online Teaching and Learning: A Practical Guide for Librarians,* © 2017 Rowman & Littlefield Publishers

Step 5: Evaluate the Course

Both formative and summative assessment should be built into the embedded online project from the planning stages forward. Evaluation must be planned when the course is designed and reflect the learning outcomes for the information literacy instruction, as well as support the main subject-matter goals and objectives of the course. Both the librarian and instructor should design and review the evaluation tools.

The assessment will confirm that students have achieved the learning outcomes. Both types of evaluation might include pre- and post-tests, student responses to forum questions, and number and quality of posts made, as well as activities and assignments completed. Since discussion forum posts will be part of the formative assessment, students should be aware at the beginning of the course of your grading plan. For example, if you plan to use a point system, the number of points associated with posts on the discussion forums communicates to learners the relative importance of that participation and your expectations on posting. Determine what percentage of the final grade will be assigned to discussion postings. You can set up a simple rubric that you can use for formative evaluation and that your students can also use for self- and peer evaluation of postings.

Feedback should be delivered throughout the course. Not only do responses assess your learners' progress, they also reinforce the concepts taught, which enhances retention. Constructive, non-judgmental comments have the greatest positive effect on students' learning behavior. Also, the more related the feedback is to the real world, the more helpful it is.

In your formative assessment, you want to test to see if learners have retained key ideas and skills over a short amount of time. Common types of formative assessment are knowledge checks or quizzes that are not graded. These typically provide immediate feedback and solidify the learner's knowledge on the subject. For formative assessment in the search strategy example, you can track improvements in student research questions, selecting search terms, and creating search strategies over the course of the embedded project.

Summative evaluation can include reflection essays on the search process; the quality of the research project, based on the information they retrieved with their searches; and a more comprehensive graded evaluation at the end of the course to assess learner outcomes.

Step 6: Reflect on the Course

When planning and prioritizing growth in an embedded project, librarians can reduce the time spent preparing for embedding by reusing content and recycling learning objects. One method for doing so is by tracking common questions and answers and storing them in a knowledge base during the course.

As an embedded online project grows in scope, it is critical to keep detailed statistics of classes served, time spent, and resources utilized. Areas of high demand and positive experiences should be noted, as should any problems encountered. This data can help refine a program and justify continued efforts in building embedded services. A major benefit of embedded projects is that you can measure student learning over time, which is much more informative than the snapshot of learning during a traditional library instruction one-shot session. Review more resources about embedded librarianship in table 7.2.

Table 7.2. Additional Resources for Chapter 7

DESCRIPTION	URLS
Blog written for embedded librarians	https://embeddedlibrarian.com/
Embedded librarianship in special libraries	http://tinyurl.com/jzdzwst
Conference presentation on embedded librarians at UCF	http://tinyurl.com/jzjsebg
Downloads on effective elearning—both research and application	http://tinyurl.com/j3oc9su
Models of Embedded Librarianship: Final Report from SLA	http://tinyurl.com/zsmm8ha
Grading posts	http://tinyurl.com/zbrxk89

⊚ Key Points

Chapter 7 has focused on the important embedded online role librarians are playing in the academic world, as well as in academic, K-12, and special libraries.

- An embedded librarian is a librarian who is integrated into an online class for a period of time to support the students in their research process.
- Embedded librarians assume various roles, from an equal partner with an instructor to the person who is in charge of teaching research skills, creating materials, and facilitating discussion forums, to name some.
- Embedded librarians are more engaged in the online teaching and learning process, so they are considered an integral part of the class, team, or learning community.
- A primary role of the embedded librarian is to build relationships. To do so, they must have the ability to be creative and flexible, committed to service, possess excellent interpersonal skills, advocate for the interests of the groups they serve, and have the ability to achieve in both traditional library and non-library settings.
- The ADDIE model—analysis, design, development, implementation, and evaluation—provides the framework for setting up a course with an online embedded librarian as an integral part of the process.
- Interactivity, an important part of any online course, can be facilitated by using online discussion forums of social media.
- Thoughtful posts to a discussion forum in an online course site are more beneficial if they forward the conversation, add new material, encourage interaction, and alleviate isolation that can be a problem in an online environment.

While the position of embedded librarian can take many forms, more academic institutions are opting for enhanced roles with the librarian as an integral part of online teaching and learning. Chapter 8 discusses blended learning, another type of teaching and learning instruction that combines both face-to-face and online instruction, and the important role the librarian can play in this popular form of instruction.

⊚ Exercises

As discussed in this chapter, it is important to reinforce what is learned through practice and interaction, as well as relate it to real-life experiences. Try the following activities based on what you learned in chapter 7 about embedded online librarians.

1. Based on the type of library you work in, review some online examples of embedded librarianship. Identify and list characteristics of the programs you think would be helpful if you were to start or participate in an embedded online program in your own library.
2. What characteristics required of an embedded librarian do you think you possess? Which ones would you have to work at? Write a reflection about these qualities.
3. Select a topic for your library environment that you think would work well for an embedded online program. Make a detailed list of specific steps you would take to get the program started (e.g., contacts, audience, content, role). Discuss embedded librarianship with others at your library and try to set a time frame for taking the first step.
4. Select an online embedded role (e.g., partner, facilitator, materials creator) and outline a storyboard of the objectives, content, activities, interaction, and assessment for a particular subject. Make it detailed enough so that you could present it to others at your library.

⊚ References

Benton, Thomas H. 2009. "A Laboratory of Collaborative Learning." *Chronicle of Higher Education.* August 7. http://www.chronicle.com/article/a-laboratory-of-collaborative/47518.

Boyer, Brenda. 2015. "Designer Librarian: Embedded in K12 Online Learning." *TechTrends* 59, no. 3 (May/June). http://link.springer.com/article/10.1007/s11528-015-0855-9#/page-1.

Bozeman, Dee. 2008. "Embedded Librarian: Research Assistance Just in Time." Annual Conference on Distance Teaching & Learning. Daytona Beach Campus. University of Central Florida. http://www.uwex.edu/disted/conference/Resource_library/proceedings/08_12912.pdf.

Carlson, Jake, and Ruth Kneale. 2011. "Embedded Librarianship in the Research Context." *College & Research Libraries News* 72, no. 3 (March 11): 167–70. http://crln.acrl.org/content/72/3/167.full.

Dewey, Barbara I. 2004. "The Embedded Librarian: Strategic Campus Collaborations." *Resource Sharing & Information Networks* 17, no. 1/2: 6.

Hamilton, Buffy J. 2012. "Embedded Librarianship in a High School Library." *Library Technology Reports* no. 2 (February/March). https://journals.ala.org/ltr/article/view/4367/5049.

Matthew, Victoria, and Ann Schroeder. 2006. "The Embedded Librarian Program." *Educause Quarterly* 29, no. 4 (January): 61–65. http://er.educause.edu/articles/2006/11/~/media/977531e54d784e87a2c9d8b8a6c1ee48.ashx.

Moore, Michael F. 2006. "Embedded in Systems Engineering: How One Organization Makes It Work." *Information Outlook* 10, no. 5 (May): 25. https://www.mitre.org/sites/default/files/pdf/05_1004.pdf.

Ramsay, Karen M., and Jim Kinnie. 2006. "The Embedded Librarian." *Library Journal* 131, no. 6: 34–35.

Riccio, Holly M. 2012. "Embedded Librarianship: The Library as a Service, Not a Space." *The New Librarian.* October 12. http://www.aallnet.org/mm/publications/products/aall-ilta-white-paper/embedded.pdf.

Shumaker, David. 2012. "Embedded Librarians in Special Libraries." *Information Today* 29, no. 7 (July/August). http://www.infotoday.com/it/jul12/Shumaker--Embedded-Librarians-in-Special-Libraries.shtml.

Shumaker, David, and Mary Talley. 2009. *Models of Embedded Librarianship: Final Report.* Chicago: Special Libraries Association, June 30.

◉ Further Reading

Clark, R. C., and R. E. Mayer. 2002. *E-Learning and the Science of Instruction: Proven Guidelines for Consumers and Designers of Multimedia Learning.* San Francisco: Jossey-Bass Pfeiffer.

Shumaker, David. 2012. *The Embedded Librarian: Innovative Strategies for Taking Knowledge Where It's Needed.* Medford, NJ: Information Today.

Blended Learning: Combining Two Worlds

IN PART 3 SO FAR, you have reviewed online teaching and learning from different perspectives—synchronous learning where an online instructor directs student learning, asynchronous teaching and learning including on-demand instruction with or without an instructor, self-paced materials that can enhance learning in any of these formats, and embedded online librarianship where the librarian works together with other educators to provide instruction.

Chapter 8 focuses on another type of online teaching and learning that has been successful in academic, K–12, public, and special libraries. In some instances, it can be an extension of embedded librarianship, yet there is more. What is blended librarianship? Why is it important that you understand how it works? How are librarians using blended learning to teach their users? You will obtain answers to these questions and more in this chapter.

⊚ What Is Blended Librarianship?

Blended learning and blended librarianship are not one and the same. Blended learning is a common term in education today. What is blended librarianship and how is it different from blended teaching and learning? A common definition of blended learning contains three parts. Learning takes place (1) in part through web-based content, instruction, and delivery where learners have some control over the time, place, path, and pace of the instruction; (2) at least part of the time is spent at a supervised brick-and-mortar location away from home; and (3) the two parts are connected to provide an integrated learning experience. If done right, blended learning engages learners, encourages deep thinking, and can enhance the quality of interaction between students and educators. The goal is to improve the learning experience by increasing personalization and control by the learner. Blended learning should focus on strategies that encourage active learning, communication, and collaboration. Technology is part of the learning environment, but just because technology is involved does not mean you are engaging in blended learning.

Blended librarianship, on the other hand, is less well known. Blended librarianship arose from the uncertain role that academic librarians would play and the future relevance of the academic library. Coined by Steven Bell and John Shank, the term "blended librarianship" also has three parts: librarianship, instructional design, and technology. These librarians proposed that blended librarians combine "the traditional skill set of librarianship with the information technologist's hardware/software skills, and the instructional or educational designer's ability to apply technology appropriately in the teaching-learning process" (2004: 373).

The principle that librarians can and should be integral, educational partners as well as a catalyst for students' knowledge enrichment and intellectual inquiry guides blended librarianship. Results of the 2015 national faculty survey by Ithaka S+R (Wolff, Rod, and Schonfeld, 2016), a non-profit consulting and research company, agree. Respondents ranked the importance of undergraduate support at 75 percent, the second most important service libraries provide. One reason is that faculty are concerned that undergraduates don't know how to locate and evaluate scholarly information. A summary of the survey's results further states that students have poor research skills, and faculty who participated in the survey saw the library's role as helping those students develop research, critical analysis, and information literacy skills. In fact, they said students should know more than just content; they should be knowledgeable in finding, sorting, analyzing, criticizing, and finally creating new information and knowledge. The librarian can lead the way to help students attain these goals.

Although the educational role is a primary goal of blended librarianship, it is not the only role. No longer is information scarce with the librarian as the gatekeeper. Today's society is overloaded with information both in quantity and formats. Add to the amount of information all the technology tools available to access and create information, and the librarian is positioned to become a facilitator, navigator, and teacher. The blended librarian can now assume the important role of guide on the side to assist users—faculty, other academic staff, and students—by instructing them in computer, media, and information literacies.

◉ Why Pursue Blended Librarianship?

Why is blended librarianship important? Online learning has been steadily increasing in higher education, as well as K–12. For-profit and non-profit organizations are teaching online to train users wherever they might be and with participants often learning at their own pace on a device accessible to them. Corporations and government agencies use elearning to bridge locations to communicate and teach employees, colleagues, and customers about their products and services throughout the world. Blended librarianship matters because it strives to position the library, through its greatest resource—its people and their related skills, knowledge, and relationships—as a central and essential part of the evolving teaching and learning environment in higher education.

As courses progressively become more blended (i.e., integrating more online components—learning activities, resources, communication technologies, and assessments), instructors will need to partner with librarians and other support staff to develop more effective courses that enhance student learning, retention, and success. Librarians can gain valuable insight into how learning takes place, how structures for effective learning are designed, and how learning outcomes are assessed by integrating a fundamental understanding of instructional design. This knowledge will be important to successful partnering with instructional designers and educational technologists, as well as faculty, in the goal to develop instruction and teach it effectively. Blended librarianship is essential to creating the partnerships and collaboration necessary to successfully develop an institution's information and learning. These partnerships are increasingly of critical importance in higher education today.

Blended librarians complement both the embedded librarian and librarian 2.0. The goal of blended librarianship is not to replace instructional designers and technologists. Rather, it seeks to strengthen the ties and relationship between these professional groups so that together effective cross-functional teams can be created to work with faculty to enhance student learning.

◉ Roles of the Blended Librarian

As mentioned in the definition of a blended librarian, the role can encompass three different parts: (1) traditional librarian skills, such as teaching information literacy; (2) the instructional design role; and (3) expertise with technology as a learning tool. Consider the blended librarian's three roles (see figure 8.1):

The traditional librarian's role forms the foundation of the blended librarian's services. Librarians are knowledgeable about skills, such as answering research questions, working with others, and components that make up information literacy. However, many librarians are thrust into teaching library workshops without experience; therefore, models of instructional design can be a great place to start. Instructional design is important for librarians because it provides an opportunity to perform an analysis of learning needs and the systematic development of learning materials. The blended librarian should be knowledgeable enough to talk the language of the instructional designer, if one is available on staff, as well as being able to adapt and design learning materials if needed—thus, assuming the second role of instructional designer. Librarians have also taken the lead in educating others about technology in most library settings. In blended librarians' third role, they must be able to have productive conversations and build a relationship with the

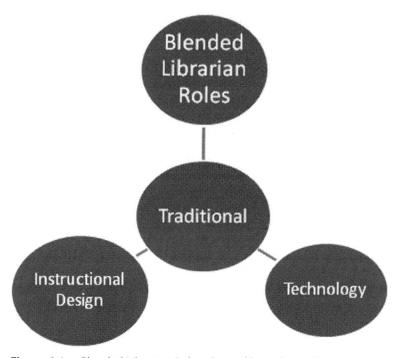

Figure 8.1. Blended Librarian Roles. *Created by author online*

technology staff person. Because librarians understand both design and technology, they blend in with these personnel.

Traditional Blended Librarian's Role

Academic librarians' primary role, as well as demonstrating the relevance of the library, lies in their ability to impact and facilitate knowledge acquisition, student learning, and the attainment of lifelong learning skills, all of which guides blended librarianship. They have also been trained in organizing, accessing, retrieving, and evaluating information to teach students to become information literate, which are examples of service and commitment to the information learner.

Higher education courses are increasingly combining a mix of face-to-face and online elements to become blended courses. One example of blended librarians' role can be to educate faculty and students about existing and new information. They can also demonstrate their expertise when it comes to blended learning resources. These might include research (e.g., white papers, case studies), workshops, blogs, tutorials and videos, and step-by-step design help.

Instructional Design Blended Librarian's Role

Instructional design has become an integral part of online teaching and learning. As Joan Giesecke summarizes, "By integrating fundamental instructional design skills and knowledge, blended librarians become partners with faculty and other academic professionals in designing courses and incorporating information literacy and research skills into academic programs to achieve student learning outcomes" (2011: 58). As a result, they become part of the instructional development team.

An important task of blended librarians is to help students and faculty achieve academic success. Librarians must work to blend library and information services into the teaching and learning process by understanding and applying design principles, which involves thinking as a user in order to understand how the learner can receive the best learning experience. For example, having a knowledge foundation in instructional design methods (e.g., ADDIE), instructional theories (e.g., Gagné's nine events), and educational psychology is vitally important. Knowing how to apply those skills in online learning settings is even more important. Chapter 1 reviews some of the learning theories (e.g., pedagogy and andragogy). Chapter 2 delves into instructional design theories and strategies.

Educational Technology Blended Librarian's Role

Being blended is more than having a set of technology skills. From the lowest grade level to the college graduate student, librarians have undertaken the role of technology leader. Faculty members are already seeking advice from librarians on technology and related resources. Library schools, however, have not always provided direction on this evolving librarian role, one that is part traditional librarian and part educational technologist. Blended librarians can help instructors incorporate and use new forms of multimedia, such as video, podcasts, digitized images, screencasts, and sharing tools, to engage students and enhance the learning experience. They can also provide education on learning materials, including games, simulations, and tutorials to assist users in locating, collecting, and organizing information. With their knowledge of Web 2.0 and social networking tools (e.g., Facebook, Twitter, Flickr), they possess skills to become instrumental in facilitating conversations between administrators, faculty, information technology staff, instructional designers, and other educational support staff about skills needed in the digital information age.

Some types of technology tools that blended librarians should have in their toolbox encompass Web 2.0, social networking, learning or course management systems, and data management tools. Some have been discussed in earlier chapters (e.g., LMSs in chapter 5). Some of the tools overlap in that they can be used for the same purpose. For example, Google Hangouts can be used for communication and collaboration. A description of each category follows, and table 8.1 contains links to other technology tools.

- Online communication and community-building tools (e.g., discussion forums, Google Hangouts, blogs, wikis) enable users to connect with peers, students, colleagues, and administrators. They can also be used to create communities of users to discuss topics they have in common.
- Social networking sites (e.g., Facebook, Twitter) connect to personal learning networks where followers can learn more from colleagues, share ideas, and discuss assignments.
- Web 2.0 tools (e.g., Flickr, YouTube Education, Vimeo Education) encompass a category of tools to provide ways to create, collaborate, edit, and share user-generated content online. They host videos as well as providing individually created materials to engage students and enhance learning.
- Presentation tools (e.g., PowerPoint, Prezi), especially PowerPoint, can be used to create interactive tutorials.

Table 8.1. Technology Tools

DESCRIPTION	URLS
List of 10 tech tools for librarian tech leaders	http://tinyurl.com/guk8gcn
TIM—guide for tech integration and evaluation process	http://fcit.usf.edu/matrix/
Edudemic—newsletter articles about connecting education and technology	http://www.edudemic.com/
Technologies for student engagement	http://tinyurl.com/jjp7mkd
Examples of blended learning schools	http://tinyurl.com/jmxglgv
Jing, Screencast-O-Matic—screencast and video tools	http://screencast-o-matic.com/home https://www.techsmith.com/jing.html
TED Talks—"Ideas Worth Spreading"	http://www.ted.com/talks

- Video creation and screencasting tools (e.g., Jing, Screencast-O-Matic, Captivate) are used to create videos, such as in a flipped environment or screencasts for presentations.
- Collaboration tools (e.g., Skype, Google Hangouts, Google Docs, Dropbox) provide online locations where learners sharing folders can work together brainstorming, editing writing, and creating projects.

Other tools, such as the following databases of content, are gaining importance. The blended librarian will be most knowledgeable about the information and how to search and retrieve it. These valuable tools are also part of the blended librarian's realm.

- Multimedia Educational Resource for Learning and Online Teaching (MERLOT) at http://www.merlot.org is a repository of multimedia educational resources. With information from this database, blended librarians can create multimedia tutorials, webcasts, screencasts, podcasts, online videos, and more that can be used in the blended library instruction process. They are ideally placed to inform students and faculty about these materials.
- The Open Educational Resources (OER) Commons at https://www.oercommons.org/ is an extensive curated, digital library of educational resources. It includes content from diverse subject areas. The resources are especially important for student and faculty research and may help in class preparation because they include articles, case studies, lecture notes, reports, and much more, with many of the materials available free under Creative Commons copyright. This information is another product that can be incorporated into a library commons as part of a blended program of study.
- Technology Integration Matrix (TIM) at http://fcit.usf.edu/matrix/matrix.php shows educators how to use technology to enhance learning for K–12 students. It contains information on using technology for active, collaborative, constructive, authentic, and goal-oriented learning. The matrix guides the educator through levels of integrating technology into the curriculum—again part of the role of the blended librarian.

These databases use different search techniques, and users would benefit from the blended librarian's expertise. Moreover, as libraries increasingly integrate learning and knowledge commons, they will offer digital and media commons services, too. While library personnel may not be directly in charge of this service, they will have to be able to provide adequate support for it.

As a result of diverse challenges and the need to deliver information literacy skills, blended librarianship offers focused, empowering roles for librarians. Bryan Sinclair explains that "the blended librarian is versed in both print and online tools and can help faculty meet course goals, regardless of the medium or technology" (2009: 505). By incorporating an understanding of and ability to use the ever-increasing number of digital technology tools (e.g., software apps and mobile devices), librarians can assist and enable use of these tools in information research, access, and creation.

In summary, they can build an online presence, promote expertise in instructional design, and assess and become problem solvers for faculty working with technology like the LMS. Blended librarians can lead rather than follow faculty as they embrace technology for developing new services and relationships.

Partnering is a triple win: for the faculty to obtain assistance with technology and information literacy from the librarian, for the librarian who assumes an important role in the university community and continues to learn from technology and instructional design staff, and most important, for students because courses that are developed will be more effective to enhance student learning, retention, and success.

ⓖ Blended Librarianship Examples

As shown in the roles of the blended librarian, blended librarianship can assume different formats.

Example 1—K–12 Blended Library Classes

White Bear Lake Area High School has offered blended classes from economics to health/physical education for three years. This Saint Paul, Minnesota, school of eleventh and twelfth graders provides blended in-class and independent study. More than 265 students in nine blended classes come to the school library and learning commons to work together to enhance learning. Teacher librarians take on many roles to build blended classes: blended librarian, instructional designer, creator of online resources, and teacher/subject-matter expert. Review more about the project at http://tinyurl.com/j7plaxj.

The first part of the project was to transform the library into a learning commons with comfortable chairs and tables that students could arrange to work in groups. Several other quiet areas were added so that students could work independently. There were also areas for faculty to work and collaborate in creating blended classes. The first class to use the new learning area was a blended American Government class focused on politics where students completed online surveys and participated in the resulting online discussions. See more about this project at http://tinyurl.com/gwb4lw9.

Example 2—University of Michigan Blended Library Course

In 2005 at the University of Michigan, the library staff determined it was necessary to expand their current research instruction so that students could expand their information literacy skills. Librarians and faculty in the College of Literature, Science, and the Arts (LS&A) partnered to develop and deliver a course geared to first- and second-year students. Previously, such instruction was integrated into a four-credit course and offered in single-session workshops by the librarian. As a result of the success of the course and growing enrollment, and to meet learning goals, a way to provide instruction for more students both on and off campus was needed. Librarians and LS&A faculty created a blended learning pilot whereby a team, including librarians, LS&A faculty, and a university educational technologist, would explore an online component designed to improve students' experience and accommodate more students. A group of librarians convened regularly to work out strategies for how to collaborate with others to create a hybrid course.

First, a large portion of the course materials was transferred to the university website so students could access it anytime from any location. Next, the team adopted a blended approach where three of the seven weekly sessions were offered online. An example on integrating sources that focused on academic integrity was one such session. As part of the online session to help students understand how to paraphrase, they were asked to read a portion of a scholarly article and paraphrase sentences from it (see figure 8.2). For the activity, the educational technologies librarian helped to determine the web tools to use to meet curricular goals. A local university LMS was used, and the team embedded tutorials, such as screencasts, online quizzes, and active learning activities into the course section of the LMS. A university instructional technologist participated as a consultant in the creation of screencasts and as a resource for technical difficulties.

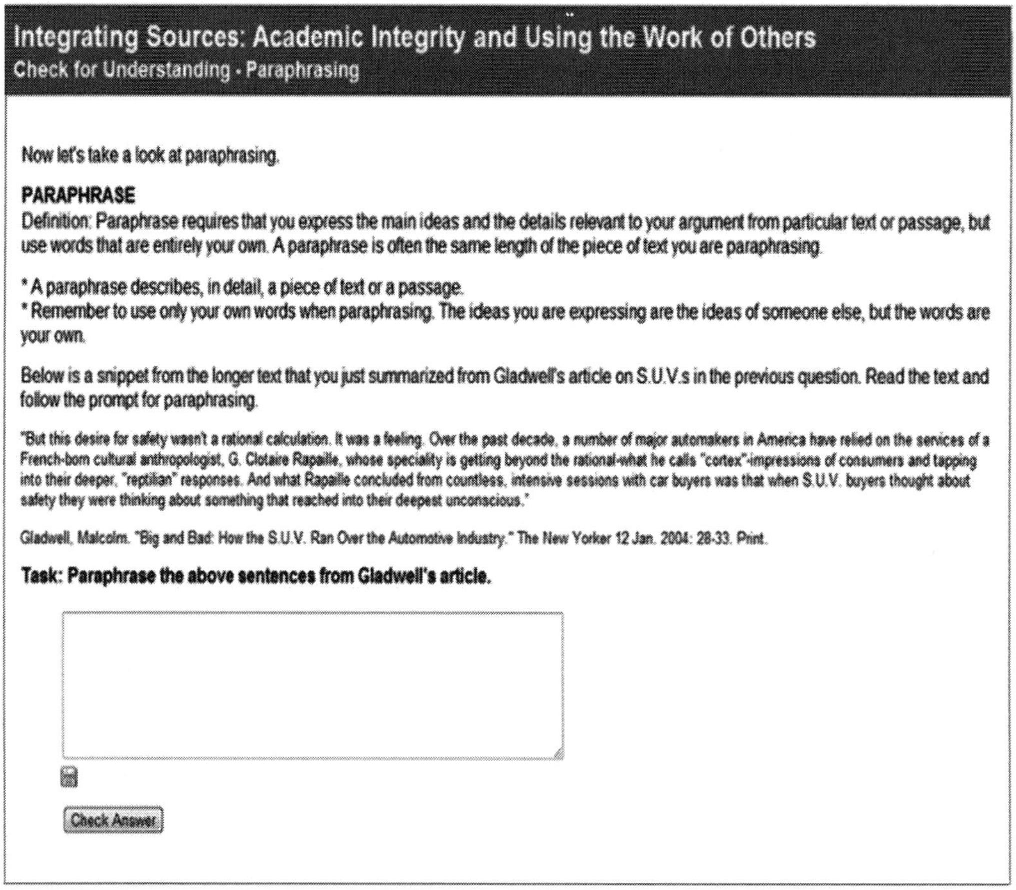

Figure 8.2. Online Paraphrase Example. *Used through Creative Commons license*

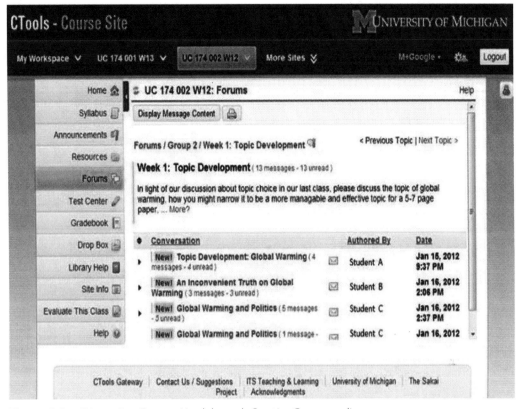

Figure 8.3. Discussion Forum. *Used through Creative Commons license*

Because interactive activities were deemed important, the instructional technologist suggested tools to use to design discussion forums to elicit participation online between students and students and instructor (see figure 8.3). Pre- and post-tests were used in assessment. As a result of the course's success, it is now being offered on a regular basis. Review more details about this project at http://tinyurl.com/js5jd63.

Example 3—University Blended Librarian Roles

A number of institutions of higher education have moved into a blended librarian role. Although each librarian encompasses the three roles of a blended librarian, each school may focus on one area more than another. For example, the role of the blended librarian at the University of South Florida emphasizes instructional design by creating tutorials, on-demand courses on research basics and information literacy. The librarian also works together with faculty, especially in the freshman English classes and has designed asynchronous courses for medical students. In addition, technology played a major part in creating some of these learning materials. The focus of a blended librarian at Georgia Tech was to work with the economics department. This librarian created interactive Lib-Guides to integrate chat boxes and enable students to conduct searches directly from the research guides. He also participated in creating a credit course for first-year students. Finally, a blended librarian at The Ohio State University (http://liblearn.osu.edu/tutor/) participated as part of a teaching/learning team to create tutorials, online credit classes, and instructional games, a goal for all materials being to create interactive learning.

As discussed earlier, many users, especially students, look for the easiest, fastest way to obtain information: the answer is usually Google. Therefore, to teach information literacy, it is important to create interactive activities that address specific aspects of the information literacy process. Dividing each part of the process into a separate module that includes objectives, content, activities and assignments, and assessment allows you to teach an entire course by covering each module or make each module an individual course. In either case, each module can use a blended structure.

One complete blended course, titled Evaluation Skills Needed during the Search Process, is shown in detail next and can serve as a model for other information literacy skills you may want to teach. Since students' search results on Google are usually in the thousands if not more, evaluating the information becomes an onerous process, most likely one where they will select the first few records as the information they will use for their topic. Another reason for selecting information evaluation is that it is a skill at the upper, more difficult level of Bloom's critical thinking ladder (see chapter 2 for more on Bloom). Moreover, university professors and employers will expect young people to know how to search the academic side of the Internet, a skill that for many students needs to be taught.

This course is divided into four modules necessary to cover the content for the entire course—to formulate a research question; to select search terms necessary to obtain relevant results; to evaluate websites based on specific criteria and assess the sources and results themselves; and to use Google Scholar, a more scholarly database. An outline of individual steps follows.

Step 1: Preplan the Course

Prior to starting the course, several considerations are important: the audience who will take the course, the task you ask students to undertake (e.g., the topic you select as the example), and sources students will search. For this example, they will be searching the Internet, not online authoritative databases.

- **Audience.** Consider the academic level of the students. Are they K–12 (elementary, middle, or high school); an undergraduate survey course, an upper-division or graduate class, or strictly a blended information literacy course? Age, prior knowledge of the content, interest, and engagement enter into your choice. For example, if this is a warm-up exercise, start with something students are interested in. Figure out their likes and dislikes. Is it trends in music, sports, video games, fashion, or celebrities? Gather feedback using a short poll to survey your class with Survey Monkey (https://www.surveymonkey.com/) or Poll Everywhere (https://www.polleverywhere.com/).

  Once you gain their interest and they enjoy the task, it is easier to weave in the content. The activity will be even more enjoyable if the topic is relevant to their world. For instance, at this writing, the music legend Prince had just died. Learning about his life, songs, and death might be of interest to many students at most levels. When you have students interested, then think about building the lesson and assessment around the content.

- **Task.** Ask students to solve problems related to their real world. For example, 2016 is a presidential election year. If this is a high school class on problems of democracy or an English writing class or a political science course at various college levels, this topic would provide real-world examples and should prove engaging to students.

- **Sources.** The topic offers many types of sources ranging from authoritative academic and primary and secondary sources from reputable news articles to debates, multimedia such as videos, infographics, websites, television, and more. It would be ideal for different grade levels and comparison of new to prior knowledge. The topic would also require recognizing bias, prejudice, and manipulation, the need to investigate differing viewpoints, summarizing and analyzing main ideas, and synthesizing ideas into new concepts. As part of the topic, students will have to apply new information and effectively communicate their research. Reflecting on the research process is also part of the project.

Step 2: Write Goals, Objectives, and Learning Outcomes for the Course

Prior to creating the course, you want to determine what you want learners to attain—what are the outcomes that your learning activities and assignments will achieve? Identify one or two general goals, and break each outcome you want students to master into individual objectives with outcomes. Note, too, that at the same time, you should decide upon formative and summative assessment tools. See chapter 3 on objectives and chapters 4 and 5 on how to implement them.

Goals

By the end of this course, students will be able to:
- Focus a general topic
- Compare and contrast sources
- Select appropriate search terms on Google

Objectives

After completing activities and assignments for this course, students will be able to:
- Narrow a broad topic using a concept map
- Write the topic clearly into a research question
- Select criteria for evaluating websites
- Identify search terms to find a variety of sources on their topic
- Using criteria, identify and explain the difference between authoritative and non-scholarly information

Outcomes

After completing the course, students will be able to:
- Write a research question
- Retrieve credible results to use in a project for an academic course

Step 3: Design the Course

A Pew Internet study (Purcell et al, 2012) on how teens research found that the amount of information they retrieve online overwhelms students. Results of the study indicate that (1) reliance is mainly on searches conducted on search engines like Google; (2)

ability to evaluate sources is limited; (3) better skills are needed to judge the quality of online information; and (4) assessing the reliability of the information they find online is questionable. Considering these results, the module should contain research assignments to develop research questions that require students to use a wider variety of sources, both online and offline.

As this is a blended course with part in a brick-and-mortar class and the other part online, the instructor will spend class time helping students improve their search skills and evaluate websites, as well as the results they retrieve. Online time can be used to review evaluation techniques and tips, conduct searches, and perform peer reviews of strategies and results that can then be discussed in class by colleagues and the blended librarian. Activities and assignments will produce outcomes that enable students to assess the quality of their search terms and the websites they use so that the resulting information will also be of high quality. Students will also work together on some of the tasks.

This four-week course is divided into four modules:

- Week 1—introduce the course, followed by a sample warm-up search example
- Week 2—select the search topic for a research project, including writing the research question and choosing search terms
- Week 3—evaluate websites and sources to use
- Week 4—use Google Scholar to retrieve more academic sources

Sample activities from each module show you how to get started designing your own modules for a course. Formative and summative assessments are determined by working through activities to complete assignments (e.g., search question, search terms, website choice, search results) and peer reviews built into the course. A course evaluation will conclude the summative evaluation.

Step 4: Implement the Course

During this stage of development, you will implement the design of the course you created in Step 3. The modular structure is separated into four weeks needed to complete the course. Each week's module outlines objectives for that week, activities and assignments to be completed both in class and online, interactivity among students and with the instructor, any materials needed to introduce content (e.g., readings, videos, websites), and formative evaluation. Samples of specific activities, along with student handouts, and tables with additional resources complete the information for each week.

Step 5: Evaluate the Course

Formative and summative assessment is part of the overall course. Formative evaluation for each module will take place in class and online to include weekly exercises, such as selecting a topic, formulating a research question, selecting search terms for the course project, evaluating websites, and analyzing search results. Peer reviews of a search strategy and short quizzes for each module must be completed each week. Summative assessment of the project, a course evaluation, and reflection on the search process also need to be done.

⊚ Create an Example of a Blended Online Teaching and Learning Course

This chapter has explained aspects of blended librarianship and the important part the blended librarian plays in teaching, designing instruction, and incorporating technology into blended learning. Having a model helps when you are trying to create instruction for your own library. This section describes instruction in a modular format. Each module covers one week in the four-week course, explained in detail for both online and in-class instruction. For each module, the topic, objectives, individual and interactive activities and assignments, technology, assessment, and additional resources are described. Reproducible student handouts are also included.

An outline of the content for this course designed to prepare students to effectively search the Internet is given in Step 3. Information for the instructor to discuss with students is outlined, as well as instructions so students can complete the tasks and assignments to achieve the objectives for each module in the course. Depending on your audience and time frame, each module could be separated into a short course or combined for a longer course of instruction on information literacy.

Module I: Introducing the Course (Week 1)

During the first week, the instructor outlines the design of the course so students know what to expect during each week. Since it is a blended course, in-class and online activities and assignments must be created. One objective for Week 1 is for students and the instructor to get acquainted, so the class will begin with a warm-up activity based on the topic of the course, evaluating aspects of the search process. This will give them a taste of searching and allow the instructor to evaluate students' search expertise as a formative assessment.

Using the sample topic on popular music that may interest students, conduct a warm-up exercise to model what students will do as they start to select their own topic, conduct searches, and choose appropriate sources during the coming weeks. The textbox contains objectives for Module I.

STUDENT OBJECTIVES FOR MODULE I

Students will be able to:

- Conduct a basic search in Google
- Explain the purpose of a concept map and why it can help in their research process
- Analyze a search strategy and provide constructive comments on its effectiveness

---

In-Class Activities (Twenty-Five Minutes)

The first part of class will enable the instructor and students to get to know one another. It also points out that there is more thought to a Google search than typing in a sentence or a few random words. It provides interactivity and illustrates preplanning that will help when they conduct searches on a scholarly topic later in the course.

- Introduce the course by reviewing your syllabus, stressing that (1) they will be working and completing assignments both in class and online each week, and (2) they will be working together, both in class and online, as they proceed through the course.
- Tell students that they are going to conduct quick searches on the Internet to learn about the sudden death of the popular musical rock artist Prince, who died in April 2016.
- Ask them what sources they would consider credible to find this information on Prince and what sources would not be authoritative.
- Draw a concept map on the whiteboard and explain what a concept map is and how it will help them narrow a topic to find better information online. Chapter 7 illustrates this process of creating a concept map.
- Based on the map, ask students to write down two or three search terms they might use in their own search in Google. Have them share their terms with a partner. Determine what the three most common terms are in the class. Ask students why they chose those terms. Review other suggested terms and have students indicate why they would or would not use those terms in the search strategy.

Online Activities (Thirty Minutes)

The online activity builds on what was discussed in class. It also reinforces the information students learned about search with immediate online practice and continues interactive learning as students work together.

- Depending on the technology available in the class, have students work in pairs and enter their search terms into the Google search box online.
- After they complete their searches, divide students into three groups and have each group review twenty results to identify the sources. Have each group select three different sources they think are credible for this topic and explain their reasons to other groups.

Wrap-Up (Five Minutes)

Enumerate the steps completed to conduct the above search. Emphasize that librarians create online materials that explain how to select keywords and also formulate research questions, which will be discussed next week in Module II. Tell students how they can find out what their university has to offer.

Assessment

Formative assessment for this week includes the search terms they selected and their participation with each other as a group. It also provides the instructor with an idea of the prior knowledge on searching they bring to the course.

Assignment

Assignments will require mostly online work this week. Emphasize that they will be discussing information from the videos and using the searches they will do online in class in Module II during Week 2. Put the information for the assignment in either a handout or online for students to access.

- Have students view these short videos on differences between a topic and research question and how to write a research question created by different libraries at (1) http://tiny.cc/mbqqfy, and (2) http://tinyurl.com/p9r4rzo.
- Also have them review a video about selecting keywords to show the difference between searching Google and library databases at http://tinyurl.com/z5jkq9s.
- Have students conduct a search on a topic that interests them following the Prince model. Have them post the topic and search terms they used and a few records under Module I (Week 1). Based on their results, have them write their research question. Have them post only their search terms and five results in the class discussion forum but not the research question.
- For a peer review, tell students to review the topic and search results for the student listed below them in the student list in the class discussion forum (last student reviews first on the list) and comment on the following: (1) Did your search terms retrieve results that you expected from the search terms used? If not, what search terms would you suggest? (2) From 1 to 5, with 1 being the lowest score, how would you rate the quality of your results for academic research? Give your reasons.
- Have them repost their answers to the questions below the student's work they reviewed, again under Module I (Week 1).
- After the review and considering peer comments, have students write their research questions to bring to class for discussion in Week 2.
- As instructor, review the searches and peer reviews and compile a list of common problems or successes you see in the searches to mention in Week 2.

Module II: Selecting Search Terms and Writing a Research Question (Week 2)

This module builds on the introductory searching students did in Module I. Some may have difficulty formulating the research question they will be working on this week.

STUDENT OBJECTIVES FOR MODULE II

Students will be able to:

- Narrow or broaden a research topic
- From their research topic, focus and write a research question
- Select search terms from a research question

In-Class Activities (Thirty Minutes)

The next activities are based on the assignment from Module I. Make sure you have a plan for anyone who does not complete the assignment. You will also want to deal with any technical problems that may have arisen when accessing the LMS. Point out where class members can get more information online about the LMS used in the course.

- Ask students if they have any comments or questions as a result of the homework searches and critiques. Have students discuss main points from the videos on search terms and topic selection. You may have questions you want students to discuss.
- In groups of three, have students review together research questions they wrote for homework. Have them make any changes to the questions based on the group's review. Discuss common problems as a class.
- From their research question, have each student create a concept map of search terms to use online and post it under Module II (Week 2).

Online Activities (Twenty Minutes)

Prior to discussing evaluation criteria in Module III, you want students to get some practice with their research question and see if they can identify appropriate websites in their results.

- Based on reviewed research questions and the concept map, have students conduct a search for one of the group members' research questions and review the records to see what kinds of results were obtained—too narrow a topic, too broad, off topic?
- Now is the time to refocus the research question, if necessary. Based on the results, ask each group member to rewrite the question, if necessary, and conduct the search again.

In-Class Follow-Up Activities (Five Minutes)

- Using the concept maps online in small groups, have them review search results together. Have them discuss any differences in the search results based on using a different search strategy.
- Post a new concept map, if needed, and the results of any new search under Module II (Week 2) in the discussion forum.

Assessment

Formative evaluation should be based on the quality of the research question and also a short objective quiz on writing a research question and selecting search terms.

Wrap-Up (Five Minutes)

Mention that one of the most difficult parts of research is writing the research question and that they now know the difference between just the research topic, the research question, and how writing the question will help them prepare a better search strategy.

Assignment

Explain that students will be evaluating websites and sources on Google in Module III during Week 3 and the assignments will prepare them for that task. Have students view the following videos to prepare for Module III assignments:

- Evaluating websites (videos)
  - Evaluating websites at http://tinyurl.com/grjpvqt
  - Critically evaluating websites at http://tinyurl.com/z7nn5hx
- Criteria to use to evaluate sources (videos)
  - CRAP (currency, reliability, authority, purpose) test in action at http://tinyurl.com/oovrfb5
  - CRAAP (currency, relevance, authority, accuracy, purpose) test and criteria at http://tinyurl.com/o3fhylk

Module III: Evaluating Websites and Sources (Week 3)

Evaluating websites identified by your search strategies and the sources on those websites requires a higher-level thinking skill on Bloom's Taxonomy.

STUDENT OBJECTIVES FOR MODULE III

Students will be able to:

- List reasons it is important to evaluate websites
- Identify types of websites
- Analyze websites based on criteria
- Analyze records based on criteria

In-Class Activities (Twenty-Five Minutes)

Evaluation criteria will be discussed this week in Module III. Criteria to evaluate websites in Module III Content Handout: Website and Source Evaluation Criteria can be used to evaluate websites, sources like articles and books, and other information. Make sure to post the handout on the course site under Module III.

- Explain the differences between information found in the library and information online.
- Give students Module III Content Handout: Website and Source Evaluation Criteria and discuss the general categories of criteria (e.g., authority, relevance). Have examples available you can show online for each point. Discuss the types of websites from the video they reviewed as homework (e.g., .edu, .gov, .com, .org) and the differences (especially credibility) for academic research.

Module III Content Handout: Website and Source Evaluation Criteria

Answering the following questions will give you the criteria you need to evaluate websites and sources.

Currency: Timeliness of information
___ When was the information published or posted?
___ Has the information been revised or updated?
___ Does your topic require current information or will older sources do?
___ Are the links working?

Relevance: Importance of the information to your needs
___ Does the information relate to your topic or answer your question?
___ Who is the intended audience?
___ Is the information at an appropriate level (e.g., not too advanced or basic)?
___ Have you looked at a variety of websites before deciding on this one?

Authority/Credibility: Source of the website
___ Who is the source or sponsor of the website?
___ What is the domain of the website?
___ Is the author an expert or qualified to write on the subject? How can you tell?
___ What are the author's name, title, credentials, and/or affiliation?
___ Is there contact information (e.g., About Us, Contact Us?)
___ Does the URL reveal anything about the author or source?
___ Are there citations to support the information on the site?

Reliability: Truthfulness and correctness of content
___ Where does the information come from?
___ Is the information supported by evidence?
___ Has the information been reviewed or refereed?
___Can you verify any of the information in another source?
___Does the language or tone seem unbiased and free of emotion?
___ Is the page free of advertisements or sponsored links?
___Are there spelling, grammatical, or typographical errors?

Purpose: Reason information exists
___What is the purpose of the information? Inform? Teach? Sell? Entertain? Persuade?
___ Do the authors make their intentions or purpose clear?
___ Is the information fact, opinion, or propaganda?
___ Does the point of view appear objective and impartial?
___ Are there political, ideological, cultural, religious, institutional, or personal biases?

Reproduced from *Online Teaching and Learning: A Practical Guide for Librarians*, © 2017 Rowman & Littlefield Publishers

Online Activities (Thirty Minutes)

Students will be practicing what they just learned about website and source criteria. Module III Activity Handout: Evaluate Websites and Sources should be posted online under Module III in Week 3, or you can also distribute it in class.

Module III Activity Handout: Evaluate Websites and Sources

Writer's name_____ Reviewer's name (Your partner)_____

Task 1 (25 minutes)

- As your partner describes his or her research topic, jot down some of the words and ideas you hear.
  Research topic:

  Search terms:

- You are searching Google (www.google.com). Below write the search terms you selected after hearing your partner's description of the topic and enter them in the Google search box.

- Review the results and answer the following questions.
  - How many records did you retrieve?
  - What is the type of site?

List your search terms. (Note: You may have had to do more than one search to get relevant results. If so, list terms for each search you conducted.)

Using Module III Content Handout, list at least five different websites from the records you retrieved and why you selected each site. Prioritize websites from 1 to 5 with 1 being the best site.

Task 2 (30 minutes)

- Use Content Handout: Website and Source Evaluation Criteria to analyze the sources on the website you selected as best and answer the following questions. Add comments you think will help your partner.
  - What type of source is it (book, journal, article)?
  - Based on the criteria on Module III Content Handout, list the criteria and how well your chosen source meets each criterion.
  - Evaluate at least five sources.

- Write a post in the discussion forum commenting on what went well in the website search, changes you had to make to your search strategies, and why. Also, comment on the credibility of the sources retrieved.

Reproduced from *Online Teaching and Learning: A Practical Guide for Librarians,* © 2017 Rowman & Littlefield Publishers

- In small groups, using instructions on Module III Activity Handout, have students practice evaluating at least two websites using criteria on Module III Content Handout: Website and Sources Evaluation Criteria. Have them post Content Handouts under Module III (Week 3) containing evaluations of their two websites on the discussion forum in the course site. Have groups review each other's posted website review handouts and provide comments, if needed.
- Next, have students review the sources about their topics they selected from the websites. Again, use Module III Content Handout: Website and Source Evaluation Criteria as an evaluation guide. Also complete the next task on Module III Activity Handout. Have students evaluate the sources on the websites they selected as the five best, pick at least five different sources that might be usable in their research project, and write down the URLs with the best listed first. Have them write reasons for selecting them and have them post their Activity Handouts on the discussion board under Module III (Week 3).
- Have the other members of the group review the same sources, rank them (e.g., 1 to 5, with 1 being the best), and provide reasons for their ranking. Post all completed handouts on the discussion board under Module III (Week 3).

Assessment

Review postings of website evaluations completed in groups and make suggestions as appropriate. Also, review sources they selected for their own research project and the peer reviews and comments.

Wrap-Up (Five Minutes)

Summarize points covered including criteria for evaluation and the need to evaluate websites and sources on the sites, mention the next assignment, and explain that students will be searching a database called Google Scholar in Week 4.

Assignment

- Have students review the videos on (1) types of scholarly articles at http://tinyurl.com/z8d2odf and (2) differences between scholarly and popular journals at http://tinyurl.com/hbqysaw.
- Have students review the videos on Google Scholar: (1) how to search Google Scholar and read scholarly articles at http://tinyurl.com/jng6zfs, (2) Google Scholar tutorial at http://tinyurl.com/jrgr9ed, and (3) how to use Google Scholar's advanced features at http://tinyurl.com/hv64yoq.

Module IV: Searching Google Scholar (Week 4)

In the previous three modules, the focus was on searching content with the Google search engine. Searching Google Scholar in this module will demonstrate differences between Google, a search engine, and Google Scholar, a database with more scholarly content.

In-Class Activity (Twenty Minutes)

Having viewed information on Google Scholar, which some students may not be familiar with, students will need to know why Google Scholar is important. This is also a time you might provide a brief overview of library databases.

- Have students discuss differences between Google Scholar and searching on Google. Reiterate why Google Scholar and library databases are important for academic research.
- Ask students what sources they normally use for their research.
- Make a comparative list on the whiteboard so students can see the differences.
- Give some examples of scholarly and non-academic journals either online or by physically showing copies of the materials.
- Point out some of the advanced features of Google Scholar and how using them will narrow a search and cut the number of results significantly to more academic sources.
- Review the parts of a scholarly article.

Online Activity (Twenty-Five Minutes)

Provide some practice for students using Google Scholar.

- Have students conduct a search on their research question in Google Scholar. Ask them to enumerate the differences—number of articles, type of journal, currency.
- If necessary, have students select different search terms or even a slightly different focus to their research question.
- Have them post results of their searches or any changes to their original research questions under Module IV (Week 4) on the course website.

Wrap-Up (Five Minutes)

Summarize what has been covered in the course based on original goals, objectives, and outcomes. Indicate they will be taking a test on the course content and completing a course evaluation form. And, of course, thank them for participating in the course.

Course Assessment (Ten Minutes)

The course assessment consists of an objective test on the entire content of the course. Questions in an online objective assessment should cover deciding on a research topic, selecting search terms, writing a research question, evaluating websites and records using criteria, and identifying differences between Google and Google Scholar. A course evaluation is also appropriate to judge the course. See a sample course evaluation in chapter 6. You may also want to complete a self-evaluation to use when reviewing the course before you teach it again.

After students complete this blended course, they should be more cautious when they count on a Google search to meet their academic research needs. If students selected a research topic for a course they were currently taking, they should have the techniques and some academic content to begin the class research project, as well as knowing how and where to find more information. See table 8.2 for links to more resources for the blended learning course.

Table 8.2. Additional Resources for Chapter 8

DESCRIPTION	URLS
How to search Google	http://tinyurl.com/p2bse
Entering a query on Google using special features	http://tinyurl.com/2kwcbh
Select search terms	http://tinyurl.com/p2bse
Using Google advanced search	http://tinyurl.com/pgv9v
How to use keywords in library databases	http://tinyurl.com/zgx2mt6
Fun "CRAPpy" test song to evaluate sources	http://tinyurl.com/j8jy8zk
Handout for evaluating websites	http://tinyurl.com/z955m3v
Tutorial on evaluating websites	http://tinyurl.com/gqwrtrw
Singapore Management University—good example of blended librarian role	http://tinyurl.com/h8edvxa

As blended librarians increase their conversations and strengthen their relationships with faculty, staff, and students who are increasingly being educated in a blended learning environment, they will continue to improve their place within the curricular structure of the university. As Bell and Shank (2004) point out in their article on the blended librarian, this will happen only when librarians understand the pedagogy of instruction and adopt principles of instructional design, theory, and practice. Versed in both print and online tools, blended librarians can help faculty meet course goals, regardless of the medium or technology. The goal of blended librarianship is "to partner with faculty, not simply support them" (Held, 2010: 156).

Key Points

Librarians in the role of blended librarian are taking on more responsibilities as they shift to this new role.

- Blended librarianship encompasses traditional brick-and-mortar library teaching and learning, as well as online learning and how they differ.
- Library services in the digital age must develop and use skills to meet the instructional needs of the learner population in physical, blended, and totally online environments.
- Three parts comprise the role of the blended librarian: traditional librarianship, instructional design, and technology.
- Although librarians have often taken the lead with technology, they must develop the knowledge to keep up with emerging technology tools so they can teach their users how, when, and why to use them.
- A new focus is in creating digital library spaces in which the blended librarian can develop skills and take the lead.
- Forming partnerships with faculty, instructional designers, and technology gurus in academic environments is the wave of the future.

Exercises

The following exercises will reinforce the diverse items covered by blended librarianship in this chapter—technology, instructional design, open educational resources.

1. Educational technologies are an integral part of a librarian's role. Set aside a place for notes about technology in your notebook. Explore at least three technologies each week (e.g., video tutorials, screencasting, podcasts, websites). Create a table and list the name and description of the technology, as well as the URL, and comment on how the technology is being used. Use library examples, if possible, or ones that you think might be important for your user group.

2. A number of educational groups offer free webinars, newsletters, and online conferences about using technology as a solution to a learning goal. Sign up for an educational newsletter, from websites such as Library 2.0 for K–12 (http://www.library20.com/), Learning Revolution for technologies for all academic areas (http://www.learningrevolution.com/), edweb.net (http://home.edweb.net/) or one from your own library association.

3. Create one module of an online blended course on a topic needed in your library. Use the model in this chapter as a guide.

References

Bell, Steven J., and John D. Shank. 2004. "The Blended Librarian: A Blueprint for Redesigning the Teaching and Learning Role of Academic Librarians." *College & Research Libraries News* 65, no. 7 (July/August): 372–75.

Giesecke, Joan. 2011. "Finding the Right Metaphor: Restructuring, Realigning, and Repackaging Today's Research Libraries." *Journal of Library Administration* 51, no. 1: 54–65.

Held, Tim. 2010. "Blending In: Collaborating with an Instructor in an Online Course." *Journal of Library & Information Services in Distance Learning* 4, no. 4: 153–65.

Purcell, Kristen, Lee Rainie, Alan Heaps, Judy Buchanan, Linda Friedrich, Amanda Jacklin, Clara Chen, and Kathryn Zickuhr. 2012. "How Teens Do Research in the Digital World." Pew Research Center. November 1. http://www.pewinternet.org/2012/11/01/how-teens-do-research-in-the-digital-world/.

Sinclair, Bryan. 2009. "The Blended Librarian in the Learning Commons: New Skills for the Blended Library." *College & Research Libraries News* 70, no. 9: 504–16.

Wolff, Christine, Alisa B. Rod, Roger C. Schonfeld. 2016. *Ithaka S+R US Faculty Survey 2015*. Ithaka S+R. April 4. http://www.sr.ithaka.org/publications/ithaka-sr-us-faculty-survey-2015/.

Further Reading

Bell, Steven J., and John Shank. 2007. *Academic Librarianship by Design: A Blended Librarian's Guide to the Tools and Techniques*. Chicago: American Library Association.

Shank, John D., and Steven Bell. 2011. "Blended Librarianship: [Re]Envisioning the Role of Librarian as Educator in the Digital Information Age." *Annual Reviews. Reference and User Services Association, American Library Association* 51, no. 2: 105–10. https://journals.ala.org/rusq/article/view/4025/4568.

Strickland, Beth, Laurie Alexander, Amanda Peters, and Catherine Morse. 2013. "Leveraging Emerging Learning Technologies to Promote Library Instruction." *Educause Review* (June 3). http://er.educause.edu/articles/2013/6/leveraging-emerging-learning-technologies-to-promote-library-instruction.

Flipped Online Teaching and Learning

A N IDEA HAS CAUGHT FIRE in the academic community—flipped teaching and learning. If you had to define it in one word, you would most probably say "video." However, if the method is just videos watched at home and homework completed in class, then it might not be a method you would want to incorporate into your teaching anytime soon. Flipped instruction is much more than watching videos!

Flipped learning has gained momentum as an educational strategy and is being implemented in an increasing number of K–12 schools and higher education institutions around the country. In 2007, concerned to find a way to keep absent students up to date on content they missed, Jon Bergmann and Aaron Sams, two high school chemistry teachers and pioneers in flipped instruction pedagogy, developed a strategy different from the traditional lecture-based delivery of content (Bergmann, 2016). About the same time, Salman Khan started the non-profit Khan Academy (https://www.khanacademy.org) to provide videos to teach math techniques. These two events have evolved into what is now being labeled as "flipped instruction," a model for improving students' learning experiences in universities and schools around the world.

In a discussion of flipped instruction, however, too often the conversation focuses only on videos as the magic bullet for student understanding of content. The real question, however, should be how educators are using time that used to be taken up with the traditional lecture to improve learning for students. What is the teaching role of the instructor in the flipped online classroom? What is the best way to maximize the potential of group learning when students are together? What are productive ways to engage learners in collaborative, student-centered activities and assignments? Even what is and isn't flipped instruction, why use it, how is it done, and why does it work? Chapter 9 discusses these and other questions related to flipped teaching and learning in an online setting.

◎ What Is Flipped Online Learning?

You can find different definitions of flipped learning, but they all encompass the following: a flipped classroom inverts the traditional educational model so that the content is delivered outside of class, while class time is spent on activities normally considered homework (Benjes-Small and Tucker, 2013). The most common scenario is for students to access course content through videos, podcasts, online tutorials, and other materials before the class meeting. During class time, students work on interactive group activities where they can apply what they learned. It is the interaction and the learning activities that occur in the face-to-face instruction that is most important. However, in an online environment, where there may be no face-to-face time, how does the flipped concept work? To flip does not necessarily mean to have in-class and out-of-class work but rather shifting the focus from the instructor as the center to students. What are students doing to communicate and collaborate with others, create knowledge, and build higher-level thinking skills? In this definition flipping changes the focus from the instructor to the students.

Flipped learning can occur in a course, an activity, one period of a class, or every class. It is not the length of the "flip" that is important; rather, the main goals are to (1) create a more interactive learning environment, (2) enable students to learn at their own pace, and (3) help the instructor tailor the course to individual student needs with the learner at the center.

Founders and other educators of the flipped learning concept provide a definition and describe their guiding principles or what they call The Four Pillars of F-L-I-P (Hamdan et al., 2013):

- F = flexible environment (e.g., variety of learning modes, flexible spaces, flexible expectations of student timelines for learning and assessments)
- L = learning culture (e.g., learner-centered approach, active engagement in knowledge construction)
- I = intentional content (e.g., content to teach and materials to use to achieve student-centered, active learning strategies for specific grades and subjects)
- P = professional educator (e.g., observe, provide relevant feedback, collaborate, and reflect on practice)

Learn more about these concepts and indicators to incorporate into practice at http://tinyurl.com/m44rbld (see figure 9.1).

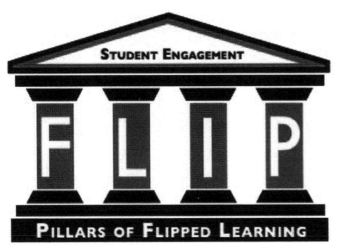

STUDENT ENGAGEMENT

F L I P

PILLARS OF FLIPPED LEARNING

FLEXIBLE ENVIRONMENT
LEARNING CULTURE
INTENTIONAL CONTENT
PROFESSIONAL EDUCATOR

Figure 9.1.   Pillars of Flipped Learning. *Flip Learning, 2014. http://flippedlearning.org/domain/46. Used with permission, Creative Commons*

Why Use Flipped Instruction?

How does flipped learning benefit teaching and learning? Students? Instructors? There are advantages such as personalized instruction for students, more extensive use of library materials, delivery of critical instruction despite lack of face-to-face time, and much more. Flipped instruction provides students with individualized instruction and more engaging active learning; instructors have more time to help their students one-to-one; and librarians have the opportunity to deliver immediate instruction in response to specific challenges of research assignments.

Benefits

As interest in flipped learning grows, more research studies are continuing to point out its educational success. Here are some of the benefits:

- Allows students to learn at their own pace. They can review any part of any lecture as many times as necessary. If they need further clarification, they come to class knowing that interactive questions and answers are part of the in-class experience and that the instructor will be available on a one-to-one basis to help them.
- Offers customized and engaging instruction. With material covering content reviewed before class, instructors have the opportunity to create learning activities that allow students to apply what they've learned. Group problem solving, student presentations, and whole-class discussions shift the focus of learning to students themselves so that they can learn through experience and critical discourse. These types of exercises help students ingrain what they've heard, test their comprehension, and master the content. Of course, this means that the activities must be a vital part of the model.
- Content easily accessed and controlled by learner.
- Helps student review for exams via recorded lectures. Hours of video content can be used as study material for tests.

- Provides content for students who have missed class due to illness, sports, other approved absences, and for special-needs students.
- Once recorded, videos can be reused in classes and repurposed for different library settings (e.g., self-paced, subject-specific, college-wide courses).
- Makes students responsible for learning, not the instructor.
- Ensures uniformity of content across all course sections.
- Collaborative activities can be better designed to further peer teaching.
- Engages students in the research process.
- Provides time for questions during application activities rather than after class.
- Provides data on the student pre-class experience. Many of the LMSs provide data on what students watched many times, indicating where they might have had problems. Formative assessment quizzes also provide data the instructor can use to determine in-class activities to use to personalize instruction for individual students.

To summarize, students benefit from the flipped classroom by being able to review lecture materials on demand and at their own pace, and by having their instructor and peers nearby to learn from during active learning. These benefits occur whether in a totally online or blended environment. Instructors benefit from the flipped classroom by being free to customize lessons and more directly engage individual students instead of "teaching to the middle." It also forces teachers to change the way they've always done things, and can motivate them to bring technology into their courses through the use of video and virtual classrooms. Through the use of on-demand video, peer-to-peer collaboration, and individualized instruction, flipping provides a more student-centered approach to learning and enables educators to engage with their students on an individual basis.

In an educational environment, flipped teaching and learning also strengthens opportunities for faculty members/teachers and librarians to collaborate on pedagogy, module content, accountability measures, assessment, and ideas to improve instruction. Librarians can also work together on implementing instruction, teaching, evaluation, and improvement of instruction.

Challenges

As with any new teaching strategies, there are always some drawbacks and also challenges to address. Several are worth noting:

- Unequal access to the technology for all students. Some students in rural and urban areas have limited Internet broadband access or do not have the appropriate technology to be able to complete the work required outside of class. Suggestions to have content on DVDs or to have students access material at the public library do not solve the problem of equality.
- Especially in higher education, the need for faculty and student buy-in. Faculty will have to assign out-of-class material for instructional sessions and provide an assessment that requires students to complete assignments to prepare for in-class activities.
- Failure to complete work outside of class. If students do not view the videos, read articles, or listen to podcasts, they will come to class lacking preparation to interact with their peers to complete the in-class activities. Of course, often students do not do their homework in a traditionally structured class. Instructors must clearly state

expectations and penalties for not doing the pre-class work. For librarians who are working with faculty, there must be a combined effort to enforce that students complete the work. Some suggestions for motivating students include: not being able to participate in in-class activities until proof of completing pre-class tasks, and also grade incentives.

- More work and time involved. The amount of time to create pre-class high-quality materials or locate those created by others appropriate to the content may involve more time at the beginning. However, educators are more than eager to share, and with the increased knowledge of and usage of open educational resources (OER), work will decrease, especially after a repertoire of materials is created.
- What to teach during class. What activities should be taught during class time where in a traditional class the educator delivered content? Some teachers may have a million ideas; others may struggle to determine what in-class activities should be. The videos and other pre-class materials must be part of a larger framework of learning activities. Because of this fundamental shift in teaching style, professional development and institutional support for the model, particularly regarding the switch to a student-centered orientation, is deemed necessary.

A compilation of recent research (EmergingEdTech, 2016) indicates that students are more satisfied using the flipped class methodology, and that this satisfaction translates into higher achievement; thus the flipped classroom may have a positive impact on students' grades and other performance indicators.

Characteristics of Flipped Online Library Learning

The flipped online classroom is a model in which the transfer of information takes place online, where students can pace their own learning. Then the practice phase of learning takes place in the face-to-face or virtual classroom, where students have access to the subject area expert and a community of their peers with whom they can get support. Online flipped teaching and learning embodies the following attributes:

- Greater student control over the pace of instruction (e.g., pause or rewind videos, retake tutorials, and re-listen to podcasts on their own time)
- Class time devoted to application
- Instructor as coach or guide to offer just-in-time instruction
- Responsibility for learning placed on the students—no more passive attendees
- Learning achieved through hands-on activities in class
- Class goal to strengthen students' skills rather than transmit content

For example, for students who need to learn information literacy concepts, the librarian can create the content and faculty can insert the learning when students need it without waiting for a library class. Students can learn these concepts through diverse methods and materials (e.g., videos, worksheets, regular class discussions, library class activities) rather than just once or twice a year. It also enables a more efficient and effective use of library class time; that is, it can enable students to work on concepts that may require significant instruction and activities (e.g., narrowing a topic, thesis statements). Finally, it fosters a closer teacher-librarian-student relationship.

By making lecture materials available on demand, students can watch them whenever and wherever fits their needs. They can also review important or unclear details as often as needed until they're well understood. As a result, students come to class with a better grasp of the topic and can participate in discussions and activities that apply what they've learned using higher-level critical thinking (see figure 9.2).

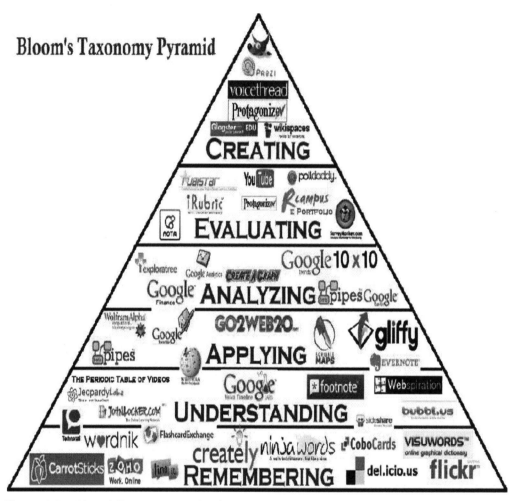

Figure 9.2. Bloom's Taxonomy. *Used with permission, Creative Commons*

Classroom activities may include group work, comprehension tests, presentations, and other applications of the subject matter. As individual questions arise, the teacher and fellow students can respond, providing each student with a more personalized learning experience.

Flipped Library Online Examples

Numerous examples of online flipped instruction in K–12, academic, and special libraries describe how educators are incorporating this learning model into their instruction.

Example 1—Mary Baldwin College Flipped Library Course

In 2012 at Mary Baldwin College, librarians (Datig and Ruswick, 2012) decided to try the method to flip instruction in their information literacy classes. This new strategy required that students actively participate and become more engaged with the learning. Information literacy instruction in course-integrated classes was an ideal starting point.

How It Works

Guides and tutorials had already been developed for other teaching, which decreased time spent to create pre-class materials. Instead of librarian demonstrations of information literacy skills, four activities—searching databases, selecting keywords, evaluating websites, and identifying source types—were targeted for flipped instruction. This also involved using a peer-to-peer learning model where students provided demonstrations with the librarian as a guide.

Pre-class Work

Before class students were assigned readings and video tutorials on the material to be covered in the next class session. They were also given an online research guide discussing search tools they would use in their assignments, as well as information on keyword searching and advanced search techniques.

In-Class Work

Students worked in groups, conducted searches, and then demonstrated the steps they used to find their information. In one activity, students learned to search for information in library databases. Each group searched a different database based on a class research project or a question assigned by the librarian and chose the best article from the retrieval. Next, they demonstrated their search before the class, sharing tips about searching their database and the appropriateness for their topic. The librarian was available to add information and clarify questions from either the presenters or class members. As part of this exercise, other search techniques, including keywords and Boolean operators, specialized databases, and source evaluation, were emphasized. Different subject matter could also be discussed.

Results

Both students and faculty enjoyed this interactive method of transmitting the content. Faculty and librarian collaboration prior to the in-class workshop was deemed important to make sure students had access to pre-class materials and that an assessment to ensure this work was completed prior to the workshop was in place. Review more details about the project at http://tinyurl.com/hjabc3l.

Example 2—Online Flipped Medical Library Instruction

Typical of library instruction over the years has been the "one-shot" session that the librarian is called upon by faculty members to either provide in their classes or when students are sent to the library. Times are changing, and now librarians are embedded to different degrees in classes or where blended learning takes place. Flipped teaching and learning is another possibility for students to improve their much-needed information literacy skills. An upper-level undergraduate health sciences class at the University of Maryland, College Park, implemented flipped learning with the goal to improve students' abilities to find, evaluate, and use information for their research assignments (Carroll, Tchangalova, and Harrington, 2016). An important part of the class was to incorporate peer instruction and active learning with the librarian facilitating in-class sessions.

How It Works

A week prior to the class, students were enrolled in the course LMS where they could access learning modules created by librarians. The Canvas LMS enables faculty to track assignments, quizzes, and student participation and performance, as well as to post videos and other materials for students. As co-instructors, librarians also had access to the LMS so they could view student progress. Modules, individualized for different courses, contained text, images, and streaming video, illustrating information literacy concepts.

Pre-class Work

A week before class started, teams of students were each assigned an online module. Each team was to read the module and synthesize the material in order to present the information to their peers. Additionally, all students had to complete all online modules and quizzes. Open-response quizzes indicated whether students read the pre-class modules.

In-Class Work

Each team received equipment and worked together to create an electronic five-minute presentation on their module. One requirement was that the presentation be more image based than text based. As a result, students had to find the images needed for the presentation online and create a presentation that was more engaging to their audience than a bulleted text one would have been.

Results

Student learning outcomes were assessed in several ways. They completed open-ended quizzes using rubrics. Other rubrics were used for peer evaluation of classmates' presentations. As a result of teaching their peers, students had to employ Bloom's higher-level thinking skills. A self-reflection required students to identify a concept or skill they had learned, as well as one that they were still unclear about. Following the librarian's part of the course, faculty also used a rubric to assess course assignments where students had to implement the skills they had learned in other research projects.

Another outcome of this pilot project was the stronger partnership built between disciplinary and library faculty. It also provided the opportunity for librarians to learn from one another as they planned the instruction. Read details of this study at http://tinyurl.com/hua49nx and view materials (e.g., rubrics, slides, questions) at http://tinyurl.com/zf7e6gh.

Example 3—K–12 Flipped Database Search Example

Having students search library databases has always been a goal of librarians in all types of libraries. With the advent of the Internet, searching library databases has dropped in academic libraries and especially at the K–12 level. Despite the need to know how to search these authoritative databases for quality information and to be ready for college research, according to the librarian, students did not see an immediate advantage and, therefore, found the whole process "boring." Would the popularity of databases increase if the librarian could conceive of an entertaining way to teach students how to search them? The librarian at Kutztown High School (Boyer, 2016) found just that method—a Search App Smackdown to teach database searching. This librarian created a fun, challenging game using a flipped format.

How It Works

The librarian selected databases that her ninth-grade students would be using in research projects for the next two years. Then she created short videos showing step-by-step instructions on how to search each database. Each video points out the importance of the database to current assignments, the type of information it contains, basic and advanced searches, and special features.

Pre-class Work

Students searched the database and used a printed chart to organize their notes so that they could watch for specific things in the videos. Questions on the organizer showed what to look for in the video, and then they used LibGuides and a search widget to look for additional features about the database not in the video. Two database explorations were required. This pre-class activity took approximately twenty to thirty minutes. Students could work at their own pace and review as often as necessary.

In-Class Work

Students worked in teams on the in-class activity. The librarian reviewed all students' organizers and scored them. The smackdown began with students working together to answer questions using the search apps (e.g., the new name given to databases). More than thirty questions ranged from basic to more complex. To answer many of the questions, students needed to know how to use a database's special features. Speed and accuracy was the name of the game.

The goal was for each team to answer the most questions during the activity. A member of each team reported answers to the librarian, and if right, received another question, with each correct response receiving one point. A second part of the competition required each team to come up with their own questions for another team to answer in the database. Questions on each of the four days of the tournament focused on a different subject area. Another goal of the exercise was to determine which database had the best information to complete all parts of the task.

Results

The activities provided formative assessment opportunities for student learning, as well as showed the value of these databases to students and administrators who pay the cost. For summative evaluation students reflected on what they learned and described how they'd used one app in class and how they could use it in the future in their daily lives (the application of the learning). The librarian and teacher reviewed these evaluations together. To review this engaging activity in detail, go to http://tinyurl.com/zgt7h24.

Example 4—Online Flipped Library University Psychology Classroom

Due to growing demand for library instruction and lack of librarians to teach the classes, the Georgia State University Library evaluated how, when, and why they delivered instruction and created instruction plans for each major (Madden and Martinez, 2015). The instruction plans helped identify which courses needed instruction and possible alternatives to deliver the content and instruction. An added need appeared to be for skills-based instructional sessions.

How It Works

Flipping the library classroom was determined to meet these needs of the psychology department. A required four-credit course in advanced research design and data analysis is required of all psychology majors. One of the course goals is for students to learn how to conduct research using the database PsycINFO, especially features such as the thesaurus and help menus. This information was not taught in the lecture part of the course.

Pre-class Work

Students were required to learn about search strategies outside of class by watching a series of seven video tutorials created by the librarian and compiled into a module called PORT. Links to the videos in a LibGuide were available in the LMS on course sites.

In-Class Work

During a lab session, the librarian guided students as they completed worksheet assignments, conducted searches as a group, discussed techniques and outcomes, and asked questions to clarify how to search the database. A graded quiz provided assessment on student learning outcomes. Results were reported to the psychology department chair and the library dean. Quiz results were important to help librarians modify any instruction for better results.

Students were required to complete a major research writing assignment for which students must use what they learned from the PORT module (see figure 9.3). The collaboration between the faculty member and librarian produced an effective flipped assignment to complete one of the most important course requirements. See http://tinyurl.com/j3jpbqm for more details of this case study and others.

Steps to Create an Online Flipped Teaching and Learning Course

Following a step-by-step plan enables you to organize your thoughts, collect and create needed materials, develop in-class and out-of-class strategies, and make sure assessment, objectives, and learner outcomes are aligned.

Psychology Online Research Tutorial (PORT): Menu

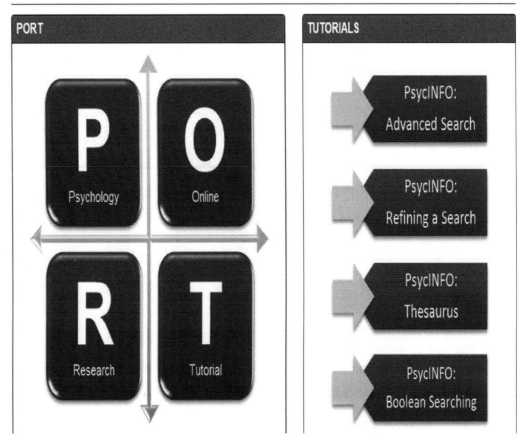

Figure 9.3. PORT Module. *Georgia State University Library. http://research.library.gsu.edu/port; Used with permission, Creative Commons*

Step 1: Getting Started

Just as with other online instruction, planning will take more preparation time, especially at the beginning, than your traditional in-class teaching.

Identify Your Tasks

First, ask yourself what you will and will not cover. With blended and online instruction, you are not bound by a traditional lecture format to deliver your instruction. Your materials may include short video presentations, podcasts, links to websites, and curated recordings, to name some. In the face-to-face or virtual class, time can now be used for experiments, activities, labs, demonstrations, and conversations in discussion forums or through social media when online. You will see some examples later in this section.

At the beginning, you may not know which activities students will find most engaging or even what topics to select for this format. Other considerations are how to pace the content, how to structure pre-class and in-class assessments, and which content you'll need to develop from scratch. As you develop your lessons, things will change, so keeping a journal of your flipped creations, such as what worked or activities to eliminate, new approaches for delivery, and content sources, will save you time in the long run.

Find Help

In higher education you may have faculty and teaching assistants who may help as you organize and create materials. Review the faculty role as discussed in chapter 8. You might be able to obtain help in recording videos or researching ones that have already been created on the topic. Also, having a tech guru to assist with integrating videos and other materials into the LMS and provide other technical support is useful. In high school libraries, you may be the main technology support or have a technology teacher that works with your school or the district to partner with you.

Prepare Your Students

This instructional approach may be totally new to your students; therefore, it is important to set clear expectations and communication methods for them. Remember they are familiar with the lecture format, so this new method may take them out of their comfort zone. During the first class, along with reviewing the syllabus or course outline, explain the reason for using the flipped approach and share examples of what they should expect in the online and in-class activities. Emphasize the advantage of repeated opportunities to review online content lectures and the engaging format of in-class activities. Explain how students can access the online materials. Point out how they will be held accountable for completing pre-class work; for example, if they fail to watch pre-class lecture recordings, they will not be able to participate in the interactive classroom activities. Note: For K–12 activities, make sure parents understand the benefits of flipped instruction and your expectations for students prior to the beginning of the class.

Anticipate the Most Common Questions

Prior to the first class, prepare a list of common questions you may have from students, parents, and/or administrators. You might want to create questions from the following and post them on the LMS.

- Students will not be struggling by themselves. On the contrary, the flipped class provides teachers with more time to cover content in more detail, foster discussion and collaboration, and spend time on individual student questions and needs.
- Because students will be working at their own pace, instruction can be more personalized to individuals' needs whether it's so students can spend more time if they don't understand a concept or can move ahead if they are more advanced.
- Students will work on traditional homework, including assignments, group work, and exercises, in class so that they can ask questions, learn from their peers, and actively apply the knowledge gained in pre-class work in a collaborative setting.
- The most valuable part of the flipped classroom is the opportunity for enhanced learning where students can consult individually with their instructor and learn from their peers. Activities might include problem solving, role play, demonstrations, peer instruction, and project-based learning.

- Assessment is integral to the learning situation. It may include in-class tests, online ungraded and graded assignments, peer reviews, and midterm and final exams. Evaluation could also be based on recorded video presentations created by students.
- Note: If you decide on your own to initiate flipped learning in your classroom, make sure that colleagues and the administration understand the concept to ensure success. It may be necessary to cite studies or articles from other educators and institutions to allay fears that student performance will suffer in a flipped classroom. Review information from the Flipped Learning Network at http://flippedlearning.org and table 9.2 later in this chapter.

Step 2: Determine Goals, Objectives, and Outcomes

Because there are two parts to flipped instruction, you must decide what to teach in each part based on what you want students to be able to do after pre-class work and also at the end of the instruction in class. Clearly write the learning objectives and outcomes that align with the activities students will do before, during, and after the instruction. Use active verbs—"construct," "write," "create"—and make sure outcomes encompass the levels of Bloom's Taxonomy, especially the higher levels of application, analysis, evaluation, and creation. Also, include affective, cognitive, and interpersonal outcomes.

Step 3: Decide On and Create the Online Pre-class Materials

Often online materials are videos of classroom lectures recorded by the instructor. The content presented forms the basis of knowledge needed throughout the course. While PowerPoint slides are most common and can be put together using screencasting software, other technology can add interaction to the videos. For example, Prezi presentation software; Powtoon, a storytelling technology; mind mapping tools; YouTube videos; and website content are available to engage learners. Based on the technology, you may be able to embed interactivity directly into videos you have found online or ones you have created. In a science class, for example, a video or simulation may provide a definition and examples of STEM (i.e., science, technology, engineering, and mathematics), and then in class the instructor might give a problem to solve and suggest different ways to do so. Virtual field trips, especially those in faraway places, can be captured on video, and interviews with experts or audio information on diverse subjects can be heard as podcasts and played on mobile devices.

Educators can often be overwhelmed by the notion of creating their own videos. Third-party free video academic recordings are also available on sites like Khan Academy. Video channels, such as YouTube, TeacherTube, and Vimeo, offer overviews and in-depth coverage of diverse subjects. And, recorded events, such as TED Talks, present free video presentations. Guest speakers are often recorded by universities and may be available through their websites or on Apple's iTunes University platform. Also try educational sources and khanacademy.org. Other sites, such as history.com, pbs.org, and national-geographic.com, contain documentaries, photos, interviews, demonstrations, biographies, articles, and much more in various formats. You don't have to reinvent the wheel; take advantage of the ready-to-use content that's already available.

A note about copyright, an important concern: Materials used for educational purposes are often available under fair use copyright, others under Creative Commons, and more through open educational resources (OER). Nonetheless, it is common courtesy to give credit to another's work (e.g., Source: Ball State University, 2011) and also avoid potential legal issues.

Another use of video is to provide feedback to students on their assignments. No one likes the "red pen" so familiar on student essays. Recording while reviewing a student's work provides a personalized approach where the instructor can highlight different sections of the assignment and provide audio comments.

As you create your pre-class materials, remember that variety is engaging. Simply recording the lesson in a monotone voice day after day will not encourage learners to review these materials. Make materials interesting and diverse, not only in format but also in who is presenting the material and how that person is interacting with the content.

Technology

Just viewing a video is not a lesson and does not require higher-level thinking skills. The video or other media must require that students do something with what they saw—online discussion, debate, or collaborative group work. For example, you might incorporate questions into the video—what in the content have they learned from the recorded lecture; what is the main idea; and can they take a position on an issue and support it with information and analysis?

Technologies offer different ways to build in communication, collaboration, and critical thinking:

- Creating and editing video. Basic editing equipment may be part of your software. Editing at the beginning and end of a video are often needed, and you may want to cut out portions and splice together more than one video.
- Incorporating interactivity. The higher-order thinking skills of application, analysis, evaluation, and creation are rarely engaged at home. However, there is an opportunity to get students thinking at a higher level at home if you combine content with extension activities that require students to think critically about what they just viewed. Embedded questions, comments, reflections, and notes provide students with something to do besides passively watching a video.

    Some technology programs enable you to add questions, comments, or quizzes into the screencast or video. Here are some programs to review to help you build flipped lessons:
    - **PlayPosit** (formerly eduCanon) (https://www.playposit.com/)—a free service (paid also available) to create and share interactive video, ideal to build interactive flipped lessons. You can select videos from the website, edit them, embed questions, and track student progress.
    - **VideoNot.es** (http://www.videonot.es/)—an open source application, enabling active learning through note taking while watching videos. Share notes with peers and teacher or save for review.
    - **Zaption** (https://www.zaption.com/)—a free service to turn online videos into interactive learning. Features include a list of videos in different subject areas; ability to customize with text, questions, and images; share or embed in LMS or website, and analytics to track student responses.
    - **EDpuzzle** (https://edpuzzle.com/)—a free tool to customize videos with questions, audio, comments, editing, quizzes, and analytics to provide formative

assessment and make sure pre-class work is completed. A list of videos is also available, or you can upload your own.

In the textbox on pages 190–192, review how to use EDpuzzle to find or modify a video, and see how easy it is to edit, add comments, quizzes, and audio to a video using EDpuzzle. This how-to serves as a model showing how to edit video on plagiarism in an activity in the sample module later in this chapter.

- Connecting students online outside of class. It is important for students to have a support network of peers to ask questions, bounce ideas around with, and learn from.
- Reviewing special features to include hosting and storing, searching, and analytics. Different technologies provide a range of options, some free and others part of a paid subscription.
  - Storing and sharing equipment. Host videos where they can be shared easily and securely accessed and played by students on their phones, tablets, and laptops.
  - Search features enable learners to search video content in your collection for the right one for an assignment or for review. Search is one of the most valuable tools for students who need to use your recordings as effective study aids. Without the ability to find the exact videos, users who want to study for a test, for example, can find it frustrating, and the videos will be mostly useless.
  - Analytics provide reports on such data as number of views, identity of user viewing, and more to show popular videos and ones that get little use or are hard to understand. This can be useful as you decide whether to revise or create new videos on a topic. The LMS helps here. Work together with your administration to determine the best way to manage your recording, sharing, and access to videos and other materials.
- When sharing, remember that your material should be accessible to learners with special needs as well. Closed-captioning for those with hearing disabilities, for example, provides text of the audio and is available on most LMSs.

To summarize, LMS video platforms provide recording software to capture video on any device, a secure location to store them, technology to ensure students watch the videos, editing software, video search capabilities, and analytics.

Step 4: Create In-Class Strategies and Materials

To generate a successful flipped learning environment, the in-class activities are most important. They do not regurgitate the recording; rather, the classroom is the place where interactivity takes place to solidify the learning. The pre-class material provides the impetus for the central in-class or virtual activities. These should be student centered and focus on getting students actively involved in the learning process when the subject expert is there to assist. Such activities as labs, experiments, collaborative research projects, debates, project-based learning, creative writing, online discussion boards, and more are all viable depending on the subject.

When the instructor is available, students are empowered with the content they need to generate discussion, ask intelligent questions, and apply what they've learned from the pre-class videos and other materials. The time spent in class is learner centered and should result in improved student participation, interaction, and performance. Often in

CREATING A VIDEO WITH EDPUZZLE

By using EDpuzzle or other similar easy-to-use applications to edit videos, you can select or create and edit videos for your flipped online lesson. Follow the steps below to serve as a model to create your own interactive video using EDpuzzle. This example is of a video on information literacy.

- Begin by logging in as "teacher" and follow the steps to customize the video for your class.
- Select from a list of EDpuzzle videos on different subjects; in this example click a video on information literacy to select it (see figure 9.4). Lengths of videos are short; approximately two to seven minutes is an adequate length. You can also upload your own video to customize.
- You can customize the video by clicking one of four icons on the timeline at the top of the screen.
- Trim the video by dragging bars to the beginning and ending points on the timeline under the video screen. For example, on this short video on information literacy, the beginning of the original video does not get to the point quickly enough. By cropping the video so that it begins at 0:43 and

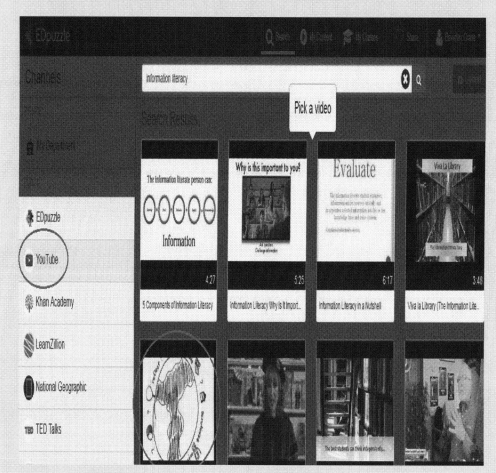

Figure 9.4.   EDpuzzle Videos. *Used with permission of EDpuzzle. https://edpuzzle.com*

Figure 9.5. Cropping a Video. *Used with permission of EDpuzzle. https://edpuzzle.com*

clipping it at 1:11, you see just the main points: recognize when information is needed, locate, evaluate, and use the information. When you have finished cropping, click another tool above the video screen to continue to personalize the video (see figure 9.5).

• Add an audio track to explain the video using your own words and language. From the timeline at the top of the screen, click the microphone to record an audio track or just record audio notes at different points in the video by clicking the megaphone. For example, click the megaphone on the video timeline to insert an introductory remark, add a comment to explain a point, and a remark at the end to let students know what they will do next.

• The question mark for quizzes on the timeline at the top of the screen has several options: embed open-ended, multiple-choice, or true/false questions that students complete while watching the video. Add comments to give directions or clarify a point. Add links to other sites for more information, or embed an image into the video. See figure 9.6 for interactivity features.

Figure 9.6. EDpuzzle Timeline. *Used with permission of EDpuzzle. https://edpuzzle.com*

When you have completed the changes to the video, click Finish to assign your video lesson to your class and invite students. Put the class name in the Add Class box and click Send.

At the top of the main EDpuzzle page, you see Search, My Content, My Classes, and Share. If you have created a video, it will appear in My Content. Check the checkbox and the Assign|Share button and then click Invite Your Students. A class code will be created that students can enter to get into EDpuzzle to see the video. You can also click the Create button to create a new folder and move the video to it, put it in a folder already set up, or upload the video. To upload your videos, drag and drop them, or click the Select Videos button and save to your own computer, a website, or use the created embed code to upload it to an LMS. Once you have shared your video with your students, you can start tracking their progress using the analytics that are part of EDpuzzle (see figure 9.7).

Figure 9.7. Sharing the Video. *Used with permission of EDpuzzle. https://edpuzzle.com*

Help Screens and Videos

To the right of the main video screen is a box that contains a question related to the image you clicked on the timeline (e.g., megaphone, question mark). For quizzes, a question displays and asks why you might want to add questions to the video, supplies a reason, and then gives a short video showing exactly how to create the quizzes.

Other easy-to-use features include:

- Using your Google ID and password to set up your EDpuzzle account
- Automatically saving work as you make changes, or you can click the Save button
- Setting restrictions, such as (1) checking a box to prevent students from skipping around in the video so they must watch from beginning to end; and (2) setting a due date and time to complete viewing the video so you know students have completed the assignment.

TIPS WHEN CREATING YOUR OWN VIDEOS

The following tips on creating videos will give you a head start as you create your own for your flipped classroom assignments. The technology is available and may be as simple as a microphone and camera. The equipment can be part of the institution's LMS system. Today's phones and laptops are usually equipped with a webcam for recording and include internal microphones. You can also record on a digital whiteboard including drawings, equations, and notes. Although not a camera, screen capture tools can record and create visual aids. You can be as sophisticated as you want by using more than one camera, filming from different angles, using tripods, and more. However, you are not expected to be a professional film producer, so simple and short videos are best. For example, showing the instructor's face helps engage the viewer. A good audio quality and ample lighting make viewing better, and if you appear in the video, engage your audience by making eye contact with your camera often.

Other things to consider when starting with video:

- Select content that can be delivered to students out of school.
- Create an online space for delivery of the instruction (e.g., LMS, Google Sites).
- Use software or an online program to create recordings (e.g., Snagit, Jing, Screenr, Screencast-O-Matic, Camtasia).
- Record video that can be easily uploaded to YouTube or your LMS.
- Use your LMS or website to scaffold the lesson and provide additional information. All resources should be on the course site.
- Collect any special equipment needed and find a suitable recording location. The recording location may depend on the content of the video; for example, a lab assignment may need specific equipment.
- Keep it short. Note that a number of videos mentioned in other chapters in this book range from two to four minutes; other longer ones run between five and fifteen minutes. A shorter video allows students to pay attention and remain engaged.
- Focus each video on a single subject. Effective micro-lectures are under seven minutes. If you need to combine several subjects in a single module, record and share two or three videos.

discussions of flipped instruction, the time spent in class is overshadowed by the hype of using videos. This in-class time will make or break the lesson and must be planned for to make the most of the newly structured class hours. In the flipped model, learners are no longer passive observers but part of a dynamic learning community whether online or in a classroom.

A variety of strategies can enhance the success of learning. Listed here are some that, if done well, focus on active learning and collaboration among peers and students, allowing for additional one-on-one time with their instructor.

- **Guided inquiry learning.** Similar to the flipped pre-class approach, students review materials before class. In-class activities are guided by questions from the instructor to encourage students to explore ideas, draw conclusions, and apply the concepts.
- **Discussion-based learning.** Materials such as TED Talks, YouTube videos, articles, and more are assigned in advance of class time, which is devoted to discussion and deeper exploration of the topic. This strategy works well in subjects like history or English where context of readings is the focus.
- **Team-based learning.** Students prepare before class and take a quiz at the beginning of class. Students receive immediate feedback, and the instructor then adapts the in-class lesson to address gaps in understanding. Following this review, students in teams conduct structured discussion or activities based on the content.
- **Demonstration-based learning.** Video demonstrations in the sciences and math require precise actions. Video demonstrations allow students to watch them multiple times and at their own pace and then apply what they learned in class activities.
- **Peer instruction.** Students prepare for class and comment on areas they found confusing. Class time uses mini-lectures and peer interaction, either in groups or as a whole class, to discuss questions and work together to obtain answers and achieve better understanding.
- **Virtual flipped classroom.** Some university courses use a totally flipped virtual model. Professors share videos for student viewing, assign, and collect work via the LMS, and require students to conduct peer reviews. Office hours are regularly scheduled and one-on-one help is based on each student's need.

Finally, teachers and librarians are not the only ones to create videos. Students can demonstrate and apply their knowledge by recording their own videos and posting them to the LMS for student review and instructor comment. Students can practice role-play activities to show their competency or even record themselves presenting a new concept or skill. These materials can then be discussed during class time. Teaching someone else is an excellent way to promote understanding of the content.

While all of these strategies are somewhat different, they all have commonalities: deeper exploration as a group based on information presented before class, students presenting and receiving feedback from their peers, time to work individually and in groups on assignments, and the opportunity to work more closely with their instructor. All strategies have the same goal: interactive, student-centered learning where learning is personalized to the individual student.

Step 5: Build In Assessment

Evaluation as mentioned in earlier chapters should be part of the initial design of the objectives, learning strategies, and content. In the early stages of developing your flipped learning instruction, you will want to assess outcomes you want students to achieve and also reflect on this new process and how it worked for you as the instructor. Also, using formative assessments throughout the course will give a better picture of how students adjust to this new learning format. Metrics from the LMS, such as online checks for understanding and participation in class, will also help in the evaluation process. Having students complete evaluations and a self-evaluation by the instructor will provide some qualitative data. The information in the "Flipped Library Online Learning" textbox could be used as a template to create your course.

FLIPPED LIBRARY ONLINE LEARNING

For your flipped learning experience to be successful, what you accomplish before, during, and after class must be in alignment. Use this sheet as an organizer to prepare your flipped learning.

1. Define content, learning objectives, and instructional strategies.
   - What is the scope of your topic? One main topic per module is usually sufficient. Map out your content in a mind map to see how topic/subtopics relate.
   - Create and communicate learning objectives to define what you want students to accomplish before, during, and after the module. Include cognitive, affective, and interpersonal domains. Using active verbs, describe what they will need to be able to do.
   - Which instructional approaches work best for the topic (e.g., peer collaboration, team-based approach, guided inquiry)?
2. Students use pre-class material to familiarize themselves with the topic. What materials will you use? Different types of resources can be more interesting.
3. In-class activities should deepen knowledge to attain higher-level thinking. What activities will be interesting, active, and engaging and provide collaboration? Match the activities with the objectives and outcomes.
4. Use a timeline or storyboard to show how objectives, strategies, activities, instructions, assessments, and other resources relate together visually.
5. What post-class activities will extend student learning and lead to the next module, if any, in a series? What additional practice will you provide for retention?
6. How will you evaluate users' learning? What formative and summative assessments will you include? Assess both pre- and in-class learning.
7. Review your template to make sure all components of your flipped plan are connected and coherent. Have a colleague review your plan and provide feedback. Make modifications based on remarks.

Factors to Consider When Building a Flipped Model

Although the flipped model is often associated with videos, that is just one small part of the process. Because there are two important parts to the flipped model, each portion needs to be addressed individually but with the emphasis that they are both equally important to the success of the whole model.

Pre-class Work

The work that precedes the activities in which students participate in class is important since it provides the content necessary to understand and collaborate in the tasks that occur in class. It is the information that is the focus, not the method of delivering it. When preparing the pre-class content, consider the following:

- Determine what content is appropriate for flipped instruction.
- Write objectives/outcomes for students to achieve from the pre-class materials.
- Decide on method of delivery (e.g., videos, LibGuides, infographics, podcasts, written material, websites).
- Collaborate, if necessary, with the teacher on an accountability measure for completing pre-word (e.g., set contracts, take off points, check notes).
- Write assessment to coordinate with objectives/outcomes.
- Select tasks that require learners to interact with the video or other material (e.g., questions, quizzes, comments).

In-Class Work

- Ask one question. What is the best use of face-to-face hands-on class time activities? (e.g., science—labs)
- Think about pedagogy and good teaching first not where technology fits into the lesson.
- Think of ways to engage learners in meaningful projects that result in authentic results and applications to real-world problems.
- Make sure collaborative interactivity builds higher-level critical thinking skills.

Building Your Sample Online Flipped Library Module

Knowing about copyright and plagiarism is an important topic for learners to understand to give them the skills they need to conduct research. Librarians have always been at the forefront in explaining these concepts to students in K–12 and academic libraries, to the public at their local library, and to professionals in special libraries. With the wealth of information in all mediums on the Internet, it is more important than ever to start teaching about copyright at an early age to students in K–12. Library lessons for all subjects can explain how to use copyrighted materials—what copyright means, when and how learners can use copyrighted materials, what permissions are needed, how to cite sources, types of copyright restrictions available, and more. This subject can be easily taught using flipped instruction in specific library courses or as part of a subject course in partnership with the instructor.

This sample lesson is the first in a unit focused on plagiarism and describes both the online pre-class and in-class portions of teaching Module I: Copyright versus Plagiarism. To understand plagiarism, students need a basic understanding of copyright.

Objectives

Objectives and outcomes here are only for the first lesson in this series of modules on plagiarism. You will already have identified what you want students to be able to do by the end of this course. Each module will have its own set of objectives and outcomes.

At the end of Module I, students will be able to:

- Explain the difference between copyright and plagiarism
- Describe types of plagiarism
- Collaborate in a team to answer questions about plagiarism in a game format
- Communicate in group discussions and class projects, demonstrating comprehension both oral and written

Pre-class Work

Begin by finding pre-class materials to explain the difference between copyright and plagiarism to the students. To determine what resources to use, ask yourself: Have I already created materials for my library that students can easily use at home? Are they at the students' level? Are they short enough to keep a student's interest? Can they be understood with little or no explanation? If they are media such as videos or podcasts, do students have the technology needed to use them? If so, review them and put together those that will form the basis for your in-class or virtual class lesson.

How It Works

For pre-class work, you want students to view four videos you found on the Internet that relate to copyright and plagiarism. This will give them a background so that they know the differences between copyright and plagiarism before in-class activities begin.

- Have students view Videos 1, 2, and 3 (rows 1, 2, and 3 in table 9.1). They are short and provide definitions, examples, and consequences of plagiarism. These sample videos are at different levels. Select additional videos based on your audience.
- Video 4 (row 4 in table 9.1) will be the last one of four videos that students will view before class. This video is twenty minutes long, normally longer than you want students to view at one sitting. Although all the information in the video is appropriate and useful, you may want to use EDpuzzle to edit Video 4 to only the content you want for this introductory lesson. Video 4 could be divided into at least four short videos: music examples, introduction to plagiarism, whether to cite sources to avoid plagiarism, and how to cite them. Here's how you might make edits:
  ○ The beginning of Video 4 shows a music example of two sets of different songs. Learners must decide if plagiarism exists after listening to both sets of songs. The exercise shows examples of plagiarized and non-plagiarized music clips. It also acts as formative evaluation to determine whether students understand the concepts about plagiarism from the first three videos they viewed and/or what their prior knowledge is about plagiarism.

- ○ Using EDpuzzle editing features, you could make Video 4 interactive by adding your voice comment at the beginning of the video to introduce the content students will see in the video (e.g., definition, examples, and consequences). At three points within the video you might add a comment, a multiple-choice quiz question, and an open-ended question at the end. Make other edits you consider necessary to provide content for your in-class activities. Note that these interruptions in the video require action by students to keep them engaged and assess their learning. The video in table 9.1, row 8, provides a tutorial on using EDpuzzle, created by a teacher. See also the "Technology" section earlier in this chapter for a model showing how to edit a video using EDpuzzle.
- After viewing the four videos, students will have an overview of plagiarism and the differences between copyright and plagiarism.
- Number the videos in the order you want students to view them and place them on the library website. The first four videos in table 9.1 are the ones students will view in the pre-class section of the lesson. Table 9.1 also contains other links to resources and materials you might wish to use for this module.

Table 9.1. Materials for Flipped Lesson

1	Video 1—differences between copyright and plagiarism. K–8	http://tinyurl.com/qh9hlbs
2	Video 2—5 tips to avoid plagiarism	https://www.youtube.com/watch?v=TcbTz2D3-ZY
3	Video 3—definition and types of plagiarism and how to avoid it, when to cite sources	http://tinyurl.com/nbms7vf
4	Video 4—"Avoiding Plagiarism—Classroom Workshop"—edit and use during pre-class	https://www.youtube.com/watch?v=G7gaRtYl9Kg
5	Video 5—quoting, paraphrasing and summarizing	https://www.youtube.com/watch?v=ssTKVakPvwQ
6	Plagiarism game to use in class	http://tinyurl.com/83abu42
7	Copyright basics at high school or higher education level	http://tinyurl.com/zc6mpkm
8	Video—detailed tutorial on EDpuzzle	http://tinyurl.com/hhz6tpd
9	EDpuzzle—create interactive video	https://edpuzzle.com/
10	Zaption—annotation tool to create/edit video—add narration, quiz questions, and comments; analytics	https://www.zaption.com/
11	Screencastify—video screen capture extension tool for Chrome, stores video in folder in Google Docs	http://tinyurl.com/p3qyp6r
12	Touchcast—create interactive video, can click active links in the video to view and manipulate; need to download software	http://tinyurl.com/gqjokaa

In-Class Work

This part of the lesson must engage the learners in active, collaborative activity with their peers. It should also have students delve deeper into the subject matter they learned from the pre-class videos.

- As a start-up activity to encourage immediate engagement, you can build a bridge to the pre-class videos. Have learners listen to another set of songs from Video 4. Ask learners to decide if plagiarism exists after listening to both songs. Using this example is engaging, and you have built-in accountability to determine if students have completed pre-class viewing as required.
- In pairs, have students select a topic or have the librarian provide one to access their knowledge of plagiarism and how to paraphrase a section of text and write a citation. Ask each pair to search for the topic online or in a library database and find three sources for the topic. Have them review Video 5 (table 9.1, row 5) on paraphrasing.
- Have each partner write a paragraph that makes use in some way of the information they gathered and to determine if a citation is needed, and if so, to write it. This activity draws from the information they reviewed in the pre-class videos.
- Have students post their writing for their partner to evaluate to the class discussion board under Module I. Each pair reads their partner's writing and evaluates it: how the sources are included, if the partner's writing is paraphrased and why, and whether a citation is needed. Partners should give reasons for their evaluations.
- Have each pair post their reviews and any comments on the discussion board under a section in Module I, titled Review Evaluations.
- Have students form teams of three and work on the plagiarism game (Broussard, 2016) in table 9.1 (row 6). This animated game has students move from room to room in a house answering questions related to plagiarism. The winner is the first team to successfully visit the first four rooms in the game by answering the plagiarism questions correctly.

Assessment

You incorporated formative assessment into the pre-class section of your flipped learning by embedding questions and a quiz into Video 4. You added an accountability measure, another formative assessment, at the beginning of the in-class session through the music plagiarism example.

Summative assessment includes the research problem in which each pair paraphrased a portion of text to illustrate their ability to avoid plagiarism. They also wrote a citation to demonstrate their knowledge of citation style. Finally, by playing the plagiarism game, students showed that they were able to answer questions on plagiarism. In these activities they demonstrated their collaboration and discussion abilities by working in pairs and teams.

⊚ Key Points

Flipped methodology is being explored and research done on the model in diverse subject areas, especially in K–12 and higher education.

- A flipped classroom inverts the traditional educational model so that the content is delivered outside of class, while class time is spent on activities normally considered homework. However, the major shift is from teacher-centered to learner-centered instruction.

Table 9.2. Additional Resources for Chapter 9

DESCRIPTION	URLS
Bergmann/Sams video on flipped classroom	http://tinyurl.com/atwo6x6
Animated video showing how a flipped classroom works	http://tinyurl.com/mphv6pe
A video beginner's guide to flipped teaching	http://tinyurl.com/hwf55lu
Flipped Classroom 101	http://tinyurl.com/zcfsp6l
How to create videos for flipped class	http://tinyurl.com/jsgg7kj
Infographic on flipped library instruction	http://tinyurl.com/j6trkj5
Infographic on active learning activities	http://tinyurl.com/zshytn9
Research on flipped learning	http://tiny.cc/gtcofy
Review of flipped learning	http://tiny.cc/bgcofy
Review of copyright	http://tinyurl.com/htcj259
Numerous flipped classroom models	http://tinyurl.com/h7u3b9g
Organizations that discuss aspects of flipped learning	flippedlearning.org, flipped-learning.com, flipped learning.eduvision.tv, flippedhighschool.com
Flipped classroom examples in different subjects	http://tinyurl.com/hf8tmke
Flipgrid—app to create questions in text/video for flipped instruction	http://flipgrid.com/info/
Infographic on flipped instruction	http://tinyurl.com/hg5vohf

- Examples illustrate how librarians are using flipped instruction in a university psychology class as well as using flipped instruction to teach information literacy and how to search databases.
- Two parts to the instruction include disseminating content knowledge in the pre-class session to prepare for interactive, collaborative work in class. If all instruction is online, the in-class activities and teamwork might be completed through discussion forums and social media.
- Videos, a part of the explaining and illustrating content, can be located from sources on the Internet or those already created by the librarian, or by creating new ones. Interactive programs offer editing features to make videos interactive and help with assessment.
- The interactive group work that occurs after learners receive content is the most important part of the flipped model. It allows for collaboration with peers, personalized time with the instructor, and time to apply what they learned.

Libraries that are exploring this strategy have exhibited success. Flipped instruction may be a strategy librarians want to include in their toolbox as online teaching and learning becomes a standard for library instruction. Chapter 10 discusses an additional model of online teaching and learning—massive open online courses (MOOCs).

⊚ Exercises

Reinforce your learning in chapter 9 by completing the following exercises to apply what you learned.

1. Think about the tips to create videos you learned in this chapter. Analyze the video at http://tinyurl.com/gn8xykp and determine the following:
   a. From 1 to 5 with 1 being the lowest score, rate the quality of this video. Give reasons for your rating.
   b. Who would be your audience for this video? Why?
   c. What changes would you make in the video, if you were using it in pre-class work of a flipped lesson? Why?
2. Practice creating your own flipped lesson at your library. Complete the following tasks:
   a. Select the audience (e.g., age, prior experience, education).
   b. Write at least two objectives indicating what students will be able to do after completing the lesson.
   c. Based on the audience, select the topic.
   d. Choose pre-class materials. What would you select and why? What are the criteria for your choices? How do they relate to the in-class activities you plan to use? How would your audience be involved with the materials? How would you formatively assess students?
   e. Create in-class activities. Involve interaction, collaborative group work, and application in your tasks.
   f. Assess to determine learner outcomes. What will students be able to do at the end of the lesson? What formative and summative evaluation will you incorporate into the lesson?
   g. Reflect on the flipped lesson. What went well? Did its being an online flipped lesson work better than a traditional one might have? Why? What would you change if you were planning other lessons in a series?

⊚ References

Benjes-Small, Candice, and Katelyn Tucker. 2013. "Keeping Up with . . . Flipped Classrooms." Association of College & Research Libraries. July 15. http://www.ala.org/acrl/publications/keeping_up_with/flipped_classrooms.

Bergmann, Jon. 2016. "Mastery Simplified: Five Tips to Make Mastery a Reality." *Flipped Learning Blog.* March 20. http://jonbergmann.com/mastery-simplified-five-tips-to-make-mastery-a-reality/.

Boyer, Brenda. 2016. "Goodbye, Boring Database Instruction. Hello, Search App Smackdown!" *School Library Journal,* March 1. http://www.slj.com/2016/03/technology/goodbye-boring-database-instruction-hello-search-app-smackdown/#.

Broussard, Mary. 2016. Plagiarism Game. Lycoming College. Williamsport, PA. http://www.lycoming.edu/library/instruction/tutorials/plagiarismGame.aspx.

Carroll, Alexander J., Nedelina Tchangalova, and Eileen G. Harrington. 2016. "Flipping One-Shot Library Instruction: Using Canvas and Pecha Kucha for Peer Teaching." *Journal of the Medical Library Association* 104, no. 2 (April): 125–30. http://www.ncbi.nlm.nih.gov/pmc/articles/PMC4816471/.

Datig, Ilka, and Claire Ruswick. 2012. "Four Quick Flips: Activities for the Information Literacy Classroom." *College & Research Libraries News* 74, no. 5: 249. http://crln.acrl.org/content/74/5/249.short.

EmergingEdTech. 2016. "10 Published Results Supporting the Benefits of Flipped Learning." Flippedclassroomworkshop.com. http://www.flippedclassroomworkshop.com/results-studies-supporting-benefits-of-flipped-classroom/.

Flip Learning. 2014. "Definition of Flipped Learning." March 12. http://flippedlearning.org/domain/46.

Hamdan, Noora, Patrick McKnight, Katherine McKnight, and Kari M. Arfstrom. 2013. "A White Paper Based on the Literature Review Titled *A Review of Flipped Learning*." George Mason University, Pearson, Flipped Learning Network. June. http://flippedlearning.org/wp-content/uploads/2016/07/WhitePaper_FlippedLearning.pdf.

Madden, Leslie M., and Ida T. Martinez. 2015. "The Flipped Library Classroom at Georgia State University: A Case Study." *Georgia Library Quarterly* 52, no. 1: Art. 9. http://digitalcommons.kennesaw.edu/cgi/viewcontent.cgi?article=1763&context=glq.

⑥ Further Reading

Yarbro, Jessica, Kari M. Arfstrom, Katherine McKnight, and Patrick McKnight. 2014. "Extension of a Review of Flipped Learning." Flipped Learning Network, Pearson, George Mason University. June. http://flippedlearning.org/wp-content/uploads/2016/07/Extension-of-FLipped-Learning-LIt-Review-June-2014.pdf.

CHAPTER 10

MOOCs: Raising the Library's Profile

IN THIS CHAPTER

▷ Defining a MOOC

▷ Comparing and contrasting different types of MOOCs

▷ Explaining the importance for librarians of knowing about MOOCs

▷ Identifying roles librarians might assume in a MOOC

▷ Differentiating between a MOOC for academics and the workplace

▷ Describing steps to create a MOOC

▷ Creating a micro-learning lesson for a MOOC

A DECADE AGO, ONLY A SMALL NUMBER of schools and universities had online programs, and they were not an integral part of their course offerings. As this book has discussed, online learning programs have experienced incremental growth as more students take classes in the digital arena. Key findings of the 2015 Online Report Card (Online Learning Consortium, 2015) show that the number of students learning online has increased to 3.9 percent, up from 3.7 percent in 2014. Moreover, in the last three years, the percentage of institutions offering a new type of instruction called massive open online courses, better known as MOOCS, has grown even more from 2.6 to 11.3 percent (Roscorla, 2016). MOOCs are one more way to deliver knowledge online to learners. How does this new online teaching and learning format affect libraries? Why do librarians need to know about MOOCs? This chapter deals with MOOCs as another way to raise the library's profile.

Because traditional libraries have always been looked upon as centers of information and as librarians become more deeply involved in online teaching and learning, they are ideally situated to deliver support to MOOCs on topics such as copyright, plagiarism, research, information literacy, and resources that have been the mainstay of librarians' responsibilities. Add to these traditional staples open educational resources (OER), collaborative spaces in learning commons, and their knowledge of technology, and the librarian can facilitate student engagement and manage the dissemination of knowledge of all kinds. MOOCs coupled with open educational resources are, therefore, a form of teaching and learning that the library must know about in order to make sure to play an integral role in MOOC team planning. This next section provides background on and insight into MOOCs as they become an educational teaching and learning platform.

What Are MOOCs?

MOOCs are courses, often free and easily accessible online, that offer large numbers of learners the opportunity to gain knowledge to further their careers or their own learning goals through high-quality online courses initially created by prestigious universities. The EDUCAUSE Library (2013) defines a MOOC as "a model for delivering learning content online to any person who wants to take a course, with no limits on attendance." A

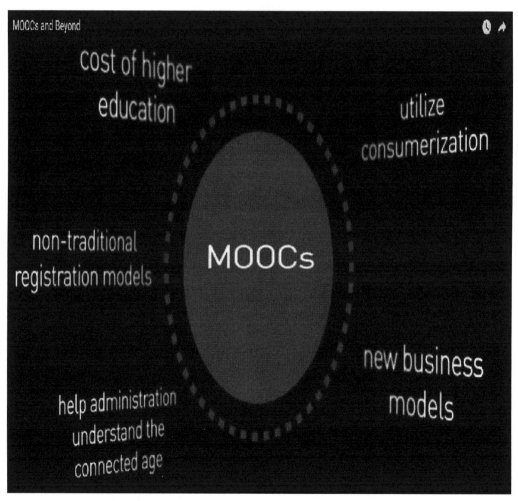

Figure 10.1. MOOCs and Beyond. *Permission through Creative Commons. EDUCAUSE Sprint 2013. Published on July 30, 2013. http://tinyurl.com/h84mlfc. Adapted from https://www.youtube.com/watch?v=XGMrzQ7YOfl&feature=youtu.be*

MOOC includes the whole learning experience—videos of recorded lectures, interactive exercises, and assignments that play a central role complementing the videos. A single MOOC can correspond to a course at a university. Most are non-credit courses. Many offer certificates at completion for a cost. Figure 10.1 shows a screen from a short video at http://tinyurl.com/h84mlfc. The video presents an interesting look at MOOCs as part of the connected age.

Two types of MOOCs have emerged—connectivist or cMOOCs, and xMOOCs (see figure 10.2).

- cMOOCs depend on active student learning and knowledge creation using wide-ranging, diverse tools. These tools, open educational resources (OER), are openly licensed and shared, used, and can be generated among students in the course.
- xMOOCs are more well known and similar to university courses. They rely on video lectures by professors, some student interaction, and online educational tools.

Although these are the first models for instruction, as MOOCs expand, there will be more types.

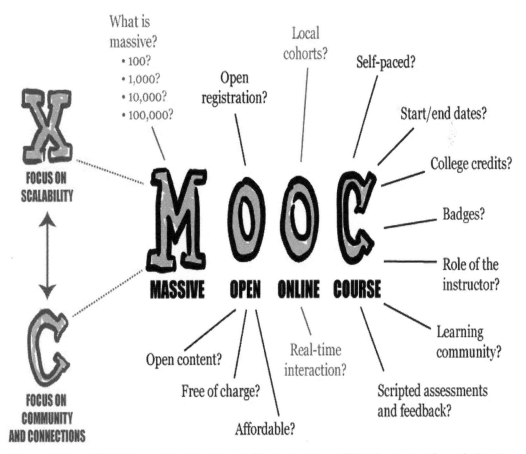

Figure 10.2. MOOC Types. *Mathieu Plourde (Mathplourde on Flickr). Permission through Creative Commons via Wikimedia Commons*

How Did They Get Started?

As early as 2008, online learning was growing, and traditional instruction was changing. Sophisticated multimedia tools had expanded the number of users able to communicate and collaborate widely. Pedagogy had begun to focus more on active student learning rather than lecture. Quality educational content and resources were also more openly available on the Internet to be used and adapted by institutions of higher education. With these trends the time was right to experiment with different types of learning like blended and flipped learning that you've already reviewed in previous chapters.

In 2011, MOOCs began as an experiment to offer openly available content through new technology to a large user base at no cost. With universities, such as Stanford, Massachusetts Institute of Technology (MIT), and Harvard, offering these courses, MOOCs gained credibility and public awareness. MOOC platforms (e.g., Coursera, EdX, and Udacity) now have grown to online course enrollments of nearly ten million (Wright, 2013). Having institutions of higher education collaborating also enables learning from one another and courses that are created based on sound pedagogy.

These major MOOC platforms have commonalities and some differences, but all are working on their business models to be sustainable.

- **EdX** (https://www.edx.org/). A non-profit company, EdX hosts online courses in sciences like computer programming and artificial intelligence or social science, depending on the higher education partner. Certificates of completion are awarded but not transcript credit at this time. Now in partnership with Google, EdX has expanded its open EdX platform outside of the sciences and will also be collaborating with Google on research on how students learn and how technology can transform learning.
- **Udacity** (https://www.udacity.com/). A for-profit company focused on the corporate marketplace, Udacity also provides courses in the sciences, including computer science, physics, and statistics, to name some. Certificates of completion are awarded upon completion, and learners can have their résumés distributed to Silicon Valley companies who are looking for qualified job candidates. Georgia Tech, AT&T, and Udacity have now teamed up to offer the first MOOC format degree program, a master of science in computer science from Georgia Tech.
- **Coursera** (https://www.coursera.org/). A for-profit company, Coursera has a diverse range of more than two hundred courses, including humanities, medicine, biology, mathematics, business, social sciences, and computer science. These MOOCs are an institutional-level effort because faculty members from more than thirty universities create the courses. These courses have a designated time frame and a structure that includes student collaboration and peer reviews. Certificates of completion are also awarded but not transcript credit.

Course format, including videos, quizzes, exercises, assignments, links to resources, and perhaps interactivity among students, is much the same from all providers. Other companies, including Khan Academy, MOOC Factory, and Udemy, are offering MOOCs for higher education, K–12, and professional development.

How Do They Work?

Just as with a traditional course, most MOOCs start and end on specified dates, extend for a number of weeks, and may be offered more than once at different times during a year. Students sign up for a MOOC online even if the course is offered at no cost. A syllabus or outline of the course is available online so students know what to expect. Content is often delivered through video lectures and online demonstrations. Interactivity built into some videos helps to keep students engaged, and analytics track student progress. Assessment in MOOCs frequently includes computer-scored quizzes and tests, as well as peer-assessed written assignments.

Some courses have assigned instructors that students may see in online videos and also communicate with. Most interaction, however, occurs through online discussion boards, blogs, wikis, and social networking sites, such as Twitter, Facebook, and Google Hangouts. Support usually comes from the online learning community rather than academic staff, and activities and assignments emphasize collaboration and communication among class members. Using Google Hangouts or Skype, some courses may have online interactive sessions weekly to answer questions, provide guest lectures, and discuss assignments. Students are encouraged to be independent and self-motivated throughout the MOOC.

Characteristics of MOOCs

Because of many factors—large number of students, no prerequisite requirements, and no boundaries of location or time, learners exhibit some different characteristics than the traditional learner. Some of those characteristics include:

- More diverse learners. Student knowledge, financial status, and age are varied.
- Learners external to the institution. Students do not register at an institution and can be located worldwide.
- High attrition rate. No entry requirements, non-credit, and no accountability increases dropout rate.
- Enjoyment, not degree, is often the goal. Learners are not necessarily aiming to complete a course but still want to enjoy the experience they have in the course.
- Diverse expectations. Career, personal, self-improvement, and professional development are all possible goals of taking a MOOC.

Different dynamics of MOOCs affect learners' motivation, perseverance, and goal setting throughout the course. For example, massiveness of the MOOC, the degree of diversity of participants, the types of multimedia used, the various forms of communication and collaboration, the degree of learner autonomy, and the amount of reflection built in—all can affect learner outcomes, how well they will enjoy the course, or even whether they will stick with the course to the end. These variables are part of the planning, delivery, and evaluation that must take place for the MOOC to be successful.

An engaging virtual classroom experience with a collaborative environment must be accessible for all learners despite learning style or special needs. In addition, the MOOC delivery system needs capabilities to meet the organization's or institution's goals whether they are to transfer knowledge, retain students or employees, or even in the corporate world to improve the bottom line.

⊚ Changes in Librarian Roles Resulting from MOOCs

In earlier chapters you've reviewed different roles librarians are assuming—that of embedded librarian and assisting in blended and flipped teaching and learning models. Although MOOCs are relatively new, they can also provide opportunities for libraries and expand their roles. New problems librarians must face also present themselves.

Copyright and Intellectual Property Issues

With thousands of students for one course, the question of who owns materials and other resources used during the MOOC can cause massive copyright and other intellectual property problems. Librarians' forte and part of their current role is dealing with copyright, fair use, plagiarism, licensing, and other intellectual property issues. Thus, as MOOCs evolve, one role librarians may have to assume is how to provide access to copyrighted and licensed electronic resources for MOOC learners around the world. Librarians already guide faculty on the proper scope of fair use for copyrighted materials in totally online, blended, and flipped instruction. Understanding intellectual property issues in MOOCs may also be added to the librarian's role, as well as developing MOOC-specific copyright policies, or even working on a collaborative team to draw up a new licensing model that would provide a large national and international market access to library resources.

Other new problems involving copyright may also present themselves. For example, how is copyright handled for faculty members' writings? Who receives royalties and for how much? How will database companies, publishers, and aggregators control access to their licensed databases, and what revenues will they receive? Dealing with these groups has always been the job of the librarian, but with thousands of users accessing data, librarians may require new strategies for on-campus and off-campus users.

Technology Assistance

Librarians continue to help patrons, students, employees, and other users with technology. Currently, they demonstrate, explain, and create instructional materials for technology from Web 2.0 tools to social media to information literacy. For MOOCs, they may be called upon to assist huge numbers of students with technology both inside and outside organizations or universities. However, because MOOCs use their own technology systems, librarians will need to work together with faculty teaching the courses to create and/or provide links to resources needed as part of the class, as well as with organizational technology. These tasks are time consuming for librarians who already have countless responsibilities.

Instructional Support

Librarians who are now assuming more instructional roles may also be called upon to help faculty members teaching MOOC courses, as well as to provide resources for thousands of students. Another possibility is for libraries to offer MOOCs on research skills, such as how to navigate databases, evaluate content and websites, or locate and assess open educational resources (OER).

An additional role might include instructional support for faculty, such as assisting in explaining how a new MOOC platform works, creating and providing access to new training resources (e.g., tutorials, videos, LibGuides, research guides), and locating additional instructional materials, especially OER. Moreover, considering the massive number of students worldwide, librarians, at a minimum, will need to rethink how students outside of a university, for example, can gain access to sections of the affiliated library's website and provide links to resources.

Data Storage and Control

An emerging role for libraries may be as "big data" repositories and analysts in many fields. Except for companies such as Coursera and EdX, no one is keeping track of data for MOOCs. Another opportunity for academic librarians at MOOC-providing institutions is to design a structure to preserve MOOC content before the amount of content is too overwhelming to handle.

Open Educational Resources (OER)

Discussing copyright with faculty gives librarians the opportunity to advocate for the use of open educational resources (OER) that broaden students' understanding of a topic without problems of copyright restrictions. OER are freely accessible, openly licensed documents and media that are useful for teaching, learning, and research. They are available under a Creative Commons license. OER can include entire courses or portions of them, materials, modules, videos, software, music, and any materials used for educational purposes. Using OER is a definite benefit for students who are faced with high costs for textbooks and other educational materials. The resources can also be shared and modified for special use.

Sometimes it's difficult to find resources you can rely on. Peer-Reviewed Instructional Materials Online Database (PRIMO) at http://primodb.org provides these materials created by librarians to teach information literacy skills. Multimedia Education Resource for Learning and Online Teaching (MERLOT) at https://www.merlot.org/merlot/index.htm also provides tutorials and diverse material types that can supplement course resources. See table 10.1 for a list of some aggregators of OER.

Table 10.1. Aggregators of Open Educational Resources (OER)

DESCRIPTION	URLS
OER Commons—a searchable library for K–12 and higher ed. resources, video how-tos	https://www.oercommons.org/
EDUCAUSE Library of more than 24,000 resources	http://tiny.cc/r9hofy
Open Course Library	http://opencourselibrary.org/
WikiEducator—plan, develop, build OER	http://tinyurl.com/amttea
FREE—OER from the federal government	http://free.ed.gov/
Google University Learning—OER and open courseware	http://tinyurl.com/jn6cle4
OpenCourseWare Consortium—higher ed OER worldwide	http://ocwconsortium.org
Khan Academy—OER strong in science	https://khanacademy.org

All these challenges and the opportunities that MOOCs can provide as they relate to intellectual property, fair use, licensing, instructional support for instructors and courses, open source content and materials, and support for students' acquisition of research and information literacy skills are possible roles that librarians might be asked to perform. However, the most important thing is for librarians to be represented at the start of any MOOC process.

◎ Examples of MOOCs

Institutions offering MOOCs have been increasing at a rapid rate in just a few short years, especially in academic settings. Courses include diverse subject areas in higher education. Despite the fact that most courses are not taken for credit, learners of all ages register for MOOCs for professional development to enhance skills for a current job or gain techniques for a new position. Moreover, those seeking lifelong learning sign up because the courses are online, and they provide learners with the flexibility they need for anytime, anyplace learning at their own pace. MOOCs have been created for the corporate world, for academic K–12 and higher education environments, for government organizations, and for non-profits like public libraries.

Possibilities for librarian participation in the growing area of MOOCs are many. For example, one librarian related a story of a group of librarians at the University of California, Berkeley, who had discussed the possibility of developing a research skills MOOC that would help users as they begin to search for open resources and then show how to use them (Dalton, 2013). Other ideas center around supporting MOOC faculty and helping them build a MOOC, similar to how embedded librarians help faculty members with their online courses. The following examples show how some libraries are participating in MOOCs.

Example 1—MOOC Experiments at San Jose State University and the School of Information

San Jose State University (SJSU) has undertaken several experiments with MOOCs with mixed results. In a first endeavor, a MOOC for math and statistics offered in 2013 produced lower passing results than the face-to-face class held on campus. The course was suspended, and a review was undertaken to determine why the results were poorer. During the 2013 summer session, a psychology MOOC course was initiated with a different mix of students. Results from this course produced student outcomes that greatly surpassed pass rates of the face-to-face sections held during the same session. In another experiment at SJSU, three introductory electrical engineering courses, one flipped and the other two face-to-face, produced very different results. A large percentage of the flipped class students passed, while in the two traditional sections students performed poorer. This has prompted SJSU officials to consider blended courses for the future. SJSU continues to review MOOC courses and the makeup of students to try and determine what works best (*EDUCAUSE Review*, 2013). Read more at http://er.educause.edu/articles/2013/11/libraries-in-the-time-of-moocs.

In 2013, the SJSU School of Information offered a course, titled Hyperlinked Library MOOC. The course described various theories of library service, the impact of emerging technologies, and how the changes affect libraries and information work in the digital age. In the interactive course, students explored diverse materials, OER, and online videos with their peers. Assignments included creating an emerging technologies plan, a social media policy, and strategies for serving library members. The course was non-credit with a certificate upon successful completion. It followed the pattern of some of the courses discussed in earlier chapters in that students are encouraged to participate in online discussions, collaborate with other students on assignments, and comment on each other's work. Students could also earn badges as formative assessment on assignments. See more at https://ischool.sjsu.edu/programs/moocs/hyperlinked-library-mooc.

Example 2—Public Library MOOC Roles

For would-be MOOC students who don't have broadband and the fairly new computers necessary to use the courseware at home, the public library is where they'll go to take a MOOC class. The library has to provide headphones or speakers in a private space, perhaps a learning commons. Computers need to be reserved for longer periods of time than some libraries currently allow. Participants also need help operating the technology.

The County of Los Angeles Public Library is incorporating MOOCs into the Center for Learning initiative as part of its new strategic plan for instruction in the library. A future plan would have the library as a meeting place for people enrolled in different MOOCs. The library sees the MOOC as a way to increase the library's adult lifelong learning offerings at little expense. From the MOOC perspective, it exposes the courses to a new audience, potentially drawing in students who wouldn't have signed up to take a MOOC in isolation, as well as providing support to those who might otherwise have dropped out of one. It also provides ongoing professional development. Technology as an increasing part of librarianship means that updated training is needed every few years as well (Chant, 2013). Read more at http://lj.libraryjournal.com/2013/05/library-services/massive-open-opportunity-supporting-moocs/#.

Example 3—Georgia Tech, AT&T, and Udacity MOOC Partnership

In 2013, Udacity, a for-profit MOOC provider, formed an alliance with Georgia Tech and AT&T to develop the first MOOC-based master's degree in computer science. This two-year course is not free but costs much less than an on-campus degree. Higher numbers of applications for the course were received than for the same courses on campus. This course offers students worldwide a more accessible, affordable degree. Courses were developed using the Udacity model and now include such courses as Advanced Operating Systems, Computer Networks, Software Development Process, Machine Learning, and AI for Robotics. Thus far, continued registration for the program and results seem positive. Read more at http://www.news.gatech.edu/2014/01/15/georgia-tech-launches-worlds-first-massive-online-degree-program.

Example 4—Library-Based Copyright and Permissions Service for MOOCs at Duke University

One area in which librarians are frequently the source of advice and assistance is in providing copyright education and obtaining permissions to use copyrighted material. This is an important area for MOOCs to address. As Duke University began to develop MOOCs, the Office for Copyright and Scholarly Communication at Duke University

Libraries began working with faculty early on in Duke's foray into MOOCs to address copyright-related challenges in course development. The library handled copyright by negotiating with rights holders on behalf of instructors to gain permission needed for specific materials for the MOOC. The biggest problem, however, was timing. Some permissions were not given until the last minute, and sometimes lectures had to be redone. The library also provided assistance in finding alternate material in the public domain or made available through a Creative Commons or open license (Fowler, 2013). Read more at http://www.dlib.org/dlib/july13/fowler/07fowler.html.

Example 5—Syracuse University Library School MOOC

Syracuse University's School of Information Studies (SUiSchool) experimented with other MOOC formats. SUiSchool helped to develop and teach a MOOC, titled New Librarianship Master Class, to test how MOOCs could supplement or perhaps replace standard online courses. The course was split into two sections: (1) an on-demand course students could take at their own pace and on their own schedule; (2) the second for-credit course, a more guided MOOC where students received more attention from faculty involved. To receive credit for the guided class, there was a cost. This pilot was offered to explore different ways of supporting MOOCs and also varied business models (Chant, 2013). Learn more about this experiment at http://lj.libraryjournal.com/2013/12/digital-content/opening-up/.

Example 6—New York Public Library (NYPL) MOOC

A large collection of research and scholarship on the history of China developed by a librarian for the New York Public Library was perceived to be ideal content for lifelong learners. Based on a flipped classroom model, a MOOC, titled Sinology 101, was created that included two parts: (1) an on-demand course students could take at their own pace and explore Chinese history that most interested them; and (2) a face-to-face research workshop where instructors could spend more time engaging students in practical exercises to improve skills (Chant, 2013). Read more at http://lj.libraryjournal.com/2013/12/digital-content/opening-up/.

Example 7—K–12 MOOCs

MOOCs have been created for a number of uses in the K–12 arena, such as pre-college courses for high school credit, SAT study courses, and more. At the Andover Massachusetts Public Schools, several students enrolled in three MOOCs, offered by the non-profit EdX group. Students take a course for no grade so it does not affect their GPA, yet they receive high school credit for completing all the requirements of the course. In addition, some teachers take portions of the course to include as mini-units in their science classes or perhaps as an after-school project (Jackson, 2013).

The University of Miami's Global Academy, a virtual high school, developed their first MOOC, a three-week course for students in their last year of high school. The course content was a way to prepare students for the SAT test in biology. This popular MOOC was attended by almost one thousand students (Jackson, 2013). Read more at https://www.districtadministration.com/article/moocs-go-k12-higher-ed-trend-expands-high-schools.

Example 8—Law Library MOOCs

The University of Florida Levin College of Law (UF Law) launched its first MOOC on the Coursera platform in 2014. The MOOC, titled The Global Student's Introduction to U.S. Law, was designed by a team of faculty members and librarians and included one instructional designer. Law faculty looked upon the MOOC as a way to recruit law students for its Comparative Law Program. More than nineteen thousand students worldwide participated in the initial launch. A second session in 2015 added more than six thousand students. Two types of certificates were given, depending on scores and projects completed. Other university law schools (e.g., Boston University, Stanford, Northwestern) are also offering MOOCs on topics, such as Legal Risk Management, Law and the Entrepreneur, Copyright, and more. Read more at https://www.law.ufl.edu/law-news/uf-law-offers-first-free-massive-open-online-course.

MOOCs are changing, but they aren't going away anytime soon. Statistics from an article "By The Numbers: MOOCs in 2015" from Class Central, an aggregator of MOOC courses, show more people signing up for MOOCs in 2015 than in the first three years of the MOOC movement. For example, the number of students who signed up for at least one course is more than thirty-five million, up from approximately sixteen to eighteen million from 2014, and more than five hundred universities offer more than four thousand courses (Shah, 2015). Others, including medical, law, and corporate organizations, are also participating either by creating their own MOOCs or collaborating with other organizations.

Since librarians already manage many of the resources that MOOCs use to support learning and are involved in creating and presenting online teaching, they can take the lead by recommending alternatives to faculty so students have access to the information they need in a MOOC. To successfully serve these new communities of learners, librarians must apply existing best practices established by librarians teaching online to develop new skills and approaches. Signing up for a MOOC of interest is one way to understand how they work and see how the library fits into the model. MOOCs represent an opportunity for librarians to actively participate in developing and designing MOOCs for the benefit of their organizations, the library profession, and their professional development.

Creating MOOCs in the Workplace

Thus far in this chapter you've reviewed different types of MOOCs and how libraries are using them. Special libraries have the opportunity to get involved on the ground floor as well. Before creating a MOOC as part of a team or individually, it's important to note several things that will affect special libraries discussed in the next section of this chapter.

What Makes a Workplace MOOC Different?

Although a MOOC is an online course, there are a number of differences between MOOCs and elearning courses, as well as differences between the general academic types of MOOCs discussed earlier in this chapter and the MOOC designed to meet the needs of the corporate, organizational, or governmental environment. Here are some:

- Audience attendance is limited to employees and prospective workers within an organization, partner organizations, and/or customers, depending on the goal of the MOOC. It is not available to the general public worldwide unless expanded by the group that has initiated the MOOC.

- While communicating mainly through online forums, the MOOC may have off-line sessions depending on the location of participants.
- Course content, timing, and length may differ and include shorter sessions. Resources may still include videos, links to blogs and articles, podcasts, books, and content contributed or created by the organization.
- Corporate MOOCs are not for-credit courses.

Depending on how an online course is taught, however, there are a number of similarities:

- Content in a MOOC can be replaced/updated quickly because a well-designed MOOC can be based on the principles of micro-learning with no learning piece ideally exceeding a maximum of ten to twelve minutes unless the topic calls for a longer chunk of learning for it to be meaningful. More on micro-learning later in this chapter.
- MOOCs require online collaboration and facilitation skills. Participating in a MOOC is a two-way process—participants are consumers as well as creators.
- MOOCs can be synchronous and/or asynchronous, with learners connecting and collaborating with others in the MOOC.
- The power of a MOOC is that learning is in the hands of the participants.

Although much is made of the poor retention rate in a MOOC, they are still popular and those signing up may not finish the course but may take just what they need from it.

Why Should Special Libraries Be Involved with MOOCs?

Online learning has been beneficial to organizations, especially those with sites worldwide that span time zones. It also makes transmitting content and skills or compliance training to an organization easy, less expensive, and uniform so all employees receive the same information. MOOCs, on the other hand, take online teaching and learning one step further. They offer opportunities for users to generate content, share ideas and experiences when it suits, and as a plus for the organization, it takes advantage of employee expertise and encourages innovation within the organization.

MOOCs can be valuable to populations serviced by special libraries. Numerous organizations complain that new employees do not come with requisite skills for their jobs; others worry about keeping pace with changing technology and updating employees, especially those at a distance, on new services and products. There is also an increasing need for organizations to build and facilitate an environment of continuous learning. MOOCs can play a critical role in achieving these goals as they can be customized to represent an organization's goals, values, and brand.

MOOCs can be used to:

- Provide workplace and on-the-job training
- Encourage self-directed development and continuous learning
- Spark collaboration and innovation through discussion forums and content generated by participants to solve problems of the organization

- Build bridges among colleagues and new employees. Experts within an organization can be recognized widely, thus motivating employees.
- Train customers and partner organizations

The MOOC format provides scope for bringing together diverse learning forms—formal, informal, and social, and different modalities—elearning modules, videos, podcasts, book excerpts, articles, and links to blogs, communities, and more. Communication is an important aspect of learning, and MOOCs support conversation. Moreover, providing MOOCs on mobile devices further improves interaction and networking, thus increasing the participation level.

Librarians have been trained to teach their patrons to find information. Often, however, they have not been trained in adult learning theory (i.e., andragogy) or instructional design. They must now improve their skills in these areas to assume the teaching role in the corporate, legal, and medical environments, to name some. See parts 1 and 2 for more on these subjects. Creating a course that is personalized to learners' needs using discussion and containing practical applications must be a part of the tools of today's special librarian so that ultimately companies see the librarian's enhanced role as a benefit to the organization and its employees. In a MOOC, special librarians have the unique opportunity to prove their value by playing a greater role in their organizations.

Special Libraries and Workplace MOOCs

Special libraries encompass a host of different types from corporate to health to legal libraries as the most common. These librarians need both specialized and broad-based content knowledge. They must also be able to impart their information literacy skills to their colleagues or clients. For example, legal librarians must have the background to search a variety of sources, such as case studies in legal databases from LexisNexis, but must also be able to find medical information if they are working on a malpractice case or patent data to deal with copyright issues. News sources may also be important to get the latest information for a client searching a trademark.

The following example provides a step-by-step outline that special librarians can use as a model to create a MOOC or an online course for their own organization. Each step describes one aspect that needs to be considered when creating an online course for a non-student audience.

Step 1: Getting Started

A MOOC is usually only as good as the team that creates it, so initiating one in isolation is a staggering task. Just as a MOOC functions as a community in operation, it also needs a team to launch it. MOOCs require content curators, subject-matter experts (SMEs) on the MOOC topics, and one or more facilitators to drive discussion and build community in the course. The designer is also important to structure the MOOC with the goal to make participants the center of learning. Interaction, discussion, and idea initiation will make or break a MOOC.

Needs Assessment

Start with a needs assessment to determine your training needs. Assess employee performance and any hindrances to performance. Based on the organization's mission and objectives, identify areas that need improvement and what content is needed and how to deliver it to the audience.

Audience Analysis

Ask yourself questions, such as who is your audience—is it colleagues in the company, a certain department, other librarians, or customers? Knowing your audience will enable you to develop an online training strategy that offers certain necessary skills and caters to individual employees.

- Conduct a short survey of your learners' knowledge base and skills to determine their prior knowledge. What is their educational background and experience in your industry? You can also do a pre-test of existing knowledge and skills. Your goal is to expand your audience's knowledge base in a way engaging to the learners.
- Observe learners on the job, if possible. Interview them and their supervisor to determine what skills they feel need improvement.
- Find out what audience expectations for the course are. What kinds of tasks do they like? Are learners interested in the topics that are planned for the course? By creating a short video or brief module that might provide insight, you can point out the benefits of the course. Including real-world applications in the content is also important to motivate your audience.
- Analyze learners' technical abilities and how they will be accessing the course. Are they tech savvy? Have they taken a MOOC or an online training using an LMS before? Have they worked with groups online? What are their technical limitations? Will they be accessing the course from a phone, tablet, laptop? Is access to the Internet limited? Answers to these questions will determine the structure of the MOOC and the technology you plan to use.
- Check on your audience's learning preferences. Do they learn best from videos or visual maps or from their peers? This will enable you to tailor your modules to meet their learning needs.
- Assess learners' performance before the course starts and what they should achieve by the end of the course. Is their current performance high or low? Were they hired with skills necessary to perform daily tasks? If they have taken training, do they have current knowledge of the organization's products and services to perform successfully at the level required? Considering answers to these questions will help you determine areas of training to focus on.
- Determine your learners' weaknesses and areas they need to improve. Identify why some areas are weak so that you can create training and include resources to meet those needs. Have they been provided with content necessary to perform their jobs? Is current training focused on improving the right skills?
- Decide what you want your audience to achieve. Do they need to improve their information literacy skills, for example, or do they need to research the Internet for a project they are doing or search specialized databases like MEDLINE or U.S. Patents? Have they created a new invention and need to find out if it's something

that has already been patented? Once you know what outcomes your audience needs to achieve, you are ready to write objectives and build an effective online training strategy to attain learner outcomes.

- Look for any obstacles that might be preventing your learners from performing as required. Is the problem an organizational one? Missing qualifications? Can the problem be solved with training or some other method, yet to be determined?
- Consider your organization's objectives so you can create an employee development plan in line with company objectives.

Identifying and organizing specific characteristics of the audience would be an ideal way to use a mind map. For example, what is their experience with the type of work they are doing, how long have they been employed with the organization, do they work alone or in groups on their projects, what is the audience's average age? Is the organization locally based or does it contain offices in widespread locations? All of these factors can affect performance, attitude, and collegiality. Figure 10.3 provides guidelines to use to create a mind map of audience characteristics. The graphic would let the learner visually see how the topic is narrowed using branching, color, and hierarchy. The visual quickly shows the learner how to narrow a topic so the number of results will be more focused on a specific topic. This is especially important when searching the Internet where results number in the millions.

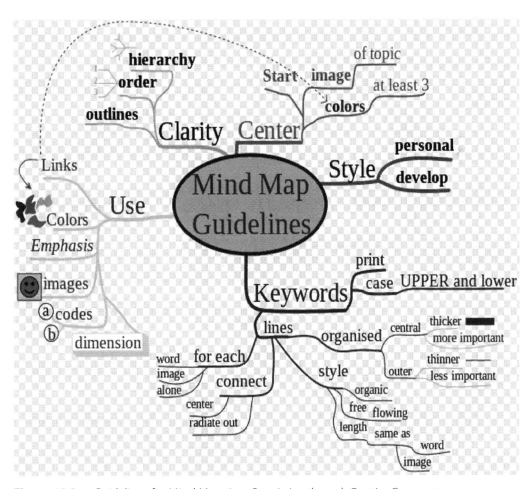

Figure 10.3. Guidelines for Mind Mapping. *Permission through Creative Commons*

Step 2: Write Concise, Clear Goals, Objectives, and Learner Outcomes

Much has been said in earlier chapters about the importance of deciding upon goals, objectives, and learner outcomes. What are the outcomes you want the audience to achieve? Is it a new skill? Knowledge of a product or service? A refresher to keep up to date? An interest to pursue lifelong learning? Review chapter 3 before you write them for your MOOC.

Remember to write clear objectives that contain criteria for evaluation and have the outcomes consistent with the goals of the course. Course assessments also need to be considered at the same time you write the goals, objectives, and outcomes.

Step 3: Design the MOOC

The organizational MOOC should be designed to facilitate workplace performance, just-in-time learning at the point of need, and collaboration. Think about design of a MOOC in the following ways:

- **Micro-learning.** No component of a MOOC should be more than ten to fifteen minutes. Because learners often access the MOOC on a mobile device in a free moment during lunch, in transit, or waiting for an appointment, they must absorb what they are viewing or hearing quickly. Librarians are used to conducting quick demonstrations for their patrons. A two- to three-minute video on how to find an article on the latest research for a health topic, locate a patent or trademark, or find information on a competitor's product would supplement content in a MOOC.
- **Social learning.** Key to a MOOC is discussion and collaboration with participants on group projects or peer review. Collaborative learning is a need of today's organizations in a rapidly changing world. Special librarians are service oriented and work together with employees to solve problems on a regular basis.
- **Facilitation.** Encouraging and engaging participants through discussion forums or social media are part of any MOOC. Librarians have public presence. They work as a team in the organization and teach the skills employees require to locate needed library resources; thus, they are an important part of the process.
- **Collaborative learning.** Through collaborative learning, users learn as much from others as from the content. Librarians are especially adept at locating appropriate OER for specific organizational projects and bringing together diverse groups to problem solve.
- **Connected learning.** In the twenty-first century, learning occurs in a networked world. The librarian is often the mainstay for technology and content in an organization, and thus a vital team member.

Step 4: Develop the MOOC

Identify the components from the following list as you develop the MOOC:

- **Content.** There are three types of content to include: (1) Based on the audience and purpose for the MOOC, create custom content, such as video or elearning modules in a micro-learning format; (2) Gather curated content (e.g., Creative

Commons–licensed materials, OER, or permissions from creators of content); and (3) Add user-created content that evolves from original content.

- **Asynchronous learning.** Learning takes place on demand using video, LibGuides, tutorials, case studies, and infographics, to name some, and can be reused in multiple MOOCs, thus cutting down on overall development time. Synchronous learning, for example, through live video lectures with questions and answers or case studies, can be taped and then edited and tailored to a webinar audience.
  - Divide material into small segments for each week. Decide where exercises should be included.
  - Create videos by writing a script, practicing it, and recording segments.
  - Edit and enhance the video and put in visuals, graphics, and animation for clarity and engagement.
  - Obtain permissions for necessary resources or locate OER.
  - Add closed-captioning for special-needs participants.
- **Discussion forums and facilitators.** Discussion is an important part of the MOOC. Reasons for having discussion forums and clear instructions on how to use them are vital to keep the MOOC going. The interactivity among participants through discussion creates community. Facilitators enable conversations, questions, observations, and personal experience to stimulate discussions around a topic. Monitoring and commenting on the discussion forums should take place regularly.
- **Program outline and objectives.** An overview of the course with objectives and various strategies for learning is needed. Develop the syllabus, including which topics to cover and how long each will take.
- **Strategies.** Select strategies to transmit content and create interaction. Teach in short blocks. Select the big messages and omit everything else. Determine how to deliver the main point in a limited time frame to an audience you can't see. More on micro-learning strategies next.
- **User guide.** A user guide supplies a blueprint for those who have never taken a MOOC so they can anticipate what to expect in the course.
- **Mobile access.** On-the-go accessibility is necessary for employees who are learning when and where they are available with colleagues who have the same restrictions and interests.

Step 5: Decide on Forms of Formative and Summative Assessment

Evaluation on content, collaboration and communication, product, and retention are necessary. Compile summative evaluation that assesses each of the learner outcomes of the course.

- **Formative assessment.** Intersperse formative assessment throughout the course using different formats. Because of the numbers of participants, objective quizzes throughout are usually best, leaving the facilitator free to communicate via discussion forums. For example, create more than one quiz for formative evaluation so that participants can retake them until they attain mastery of the content.
- **Summative assessment.** An evaluation of content knowledge or skill achievement as well as participation in discussions should be used at a minimum. A course evaluation is also important to assess participants' thoughts on the overall value of the instruction and how it meets the needs of the learners.

A team approach to course design and implementation often works best as team members assume specific roles and also collaborate together. There are many elements to the MOOC environment that require expertise unique to the online delivery method.

⊚ Putting It All Together in a Micro-learning Lesson

As has been discussed, on-the-job training is very important as the need for technical training increases, and hiring managers are not finding the right combination of skills in those seeking positions. Workplace learning has become a must in today's society. Because of limited time available for training, micro-learning provides organizations with short lessons that they can access cost effectively at any time and location.

Micro-learning—learning through short, focused, easy-to-understand, well-designed lessons or modules—fits the criteria. Companies offer micro-learning lessons searchable on platforms such as Grovo (https://www.grovo.com/) and Coursmos (https://coursmos. com/), or you can create your own content based on the needs of your attendees. Video is a primary content delivery mode as it appeals especially to today's younger workers. A lesson on video allows the learner to focus on small chunks of information and review it as often as necessary. Because it is short and modular, content can be easily updated to meet an organization's needs. In addition, the shortened time frame for a lesson or course costs the company less, and if the librarian is creating the instruction, it can be done amid other responsibilities.

General steps for creating the blueprint or storyboard for workplace training MOOCs are outlined above. The following example on information literacy uses content that librarians in any library are often called upon to create and teach. The lesson you will see contains a video that can be a part of an entire course or used as the introduction, explaining what the course will contain. Several screenshots show one aspect of a course on information literacy that could be expanded into a complete MOOC offered by a special library and customized to the organization's audience and need.

Review your current training, including types, frequency, mode, and format. Personalize your modules to include only the information relevant to individuals in your audience. For example, if the module refers to searching authoritative databases, you don't need to show them how to do a basic search on the Internet. Avoid information overload by including only the most relevant material illustrated in a concise way.

Step 1: Outline Objectives/Outcomes

After completing this short micro-learning exercise as an introduction to information literacy, the objective is that learners will be able to identify specific topics related to information literacy. As the outcome, the audience will have information to decide whether the MOOC course will provide the components to meet their information literacy needs. It is designed so that the librarian creating the course can incorporate the components that are needed by the designated audience after a needs and audience assessment is completed as shown in "Step 1: Getting Started" earlier in this chapter.

Step 2: Create a Short Micro-learning Lesson

Create a short micro-learning lesson that uses a video or screencast to describe the content in an upcoming MOOC—what skills are required to be information literate and why they are important. For those who are not familiar with the topic, it provides a definition and explains reasons it is meaningful for the audience.

Another screenshot identifies whom they can turn to for help and point out the important role the special librarian plays in learning about information literacy.

There are five components that encompass information literacy in this MOOC. This is the main content of the course, and each lesson in the MOOC will delve into one of the components. Although lessons are designed to be taken in order, one or more can be skipped if a participant already has knowledge on that topic. Each screenshot on a topic can also be used at the beginning of the lesson for that topic (e.g., evaluating databases). See figure 10.4, "Information Literacy Components."

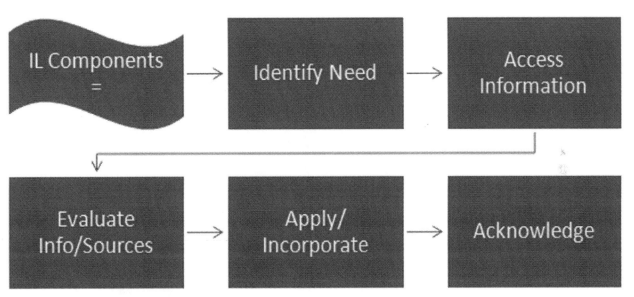

Figure 10.4. Information Literacy Components. *Seminole State Library video. https://www.youtube.com/watch?v=1ron p6lue9w; used with permission, Creative Commons*

Each screenshot in the screencast would visually depict one topic you want to discuss in the MOOC. For example, figure 10.5 illustrates the different types of sources a researcher might be looking for.

Figure 10.6 provides five general questions to ask when evaluating sources for credibility. Questions include who is the author, what's the point of the information, are the questions answered, when was the information written or updated, and where does the information come from? Note that rather than read intense text, visuals provide the same information quickly and also engage the viewer.

Step 3: Develop the Lesson

You have the content you need to develop the micro-lesson.

- Use Screen-O-Matic or a video recording program like Vimeo to create the screencast or video.
- Write a script and record it for each screen. Keep an eye on the timing as the finished product should be two to three minutes at most.

Figure 10.5. Information Sources. *Created by author online*

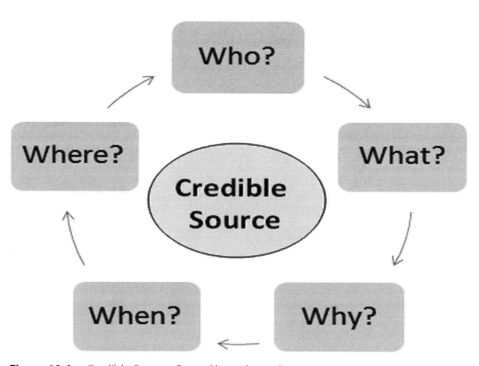

Figure 10.6. Credible Source. *Created by author online*

- Review and edit the final draft. Have a human resources employee or one from the department who will receive the training also review the final product before using it in the MOOC.
- Add interaction such as a question to spark comments in the discussion forum.
- Build in a formative assessment to the lesson. It could be a short objective quiz on the different components or questions about particular components like citing sources.

Whether this micro-lesson is designed as Lesson 1 to introduce the content in the MOOC or as publicity to draw participants in, it can be completed in less than ten minutes—even while having lunch! Once you have created one lesson, the next one you develop is that much easier.

TIPS FOR BUILDING A MOOC

Not only are these tips for building a MOOC, but some should also be considered when creating an online course.

- Design an online training course that includes content that can be viewed on a mobile device. Employees must be able to acquire new information at any time in any place.
- Consider not only how to deliver the information, but also how the employee will be absorbing that new information.
- Write clear guidelines and detailed instructions for assignments, activities, group work, and especially for interactive discussion forums. For example, a group needs to know why they are joining together and how to sign up, how to submit assignments, and how to work together.
- Set specific deadlines for completing each task or assignment. Identify how, when, and where they submit work and in what format.
- Consider their learning environment, which platform they will be using, and when and where they will be accessing the online training course or module.
- Before training, ask questions to encourage learners to think about the topic.
- Set expectations that prepare the learner for an engaging but challenging experience.
- Chunk the information delivered so learners can absorb some content thoroughly before proceeding.
- Leave time between sessions so everything is not crammed into one session.
- Assess during and after a session to promote retention; for example, have participants write out what they learned.
- Test the course on the platform you will use before the course starts to make sure the technology works as you expect. For example, if you have participants link to outside websites at the same time, the site may be overwhelmed and crash.
- Make sure copyright is cleared for materials you plan to use in the course.

This is just one example of a screencast that could be used for information literacy instruction for any content. There are numerous YouTube videos and others on the web that you could use in your own MOOC to save you from having to create your own. You may already have some of your own materials that could be turned into a short micro-lesson.

With the number of diverse tasks librarians are called upon to complete and with the changing technology and roles just discussed, they too need training. Luckily, there are online opportunities that today's librarians can take advantage of. Most of the resources are free and can be used in their own libraries or to help them create materials for their students, colleagues, or patrons. See table 10.2 for synchronous and asynchronous training possibilities.

Table 10.2. Additional Resources for Chapter 10

DESCRIPTION	URLS
Presentation from law librarians on legal research for law librarians	http://tinyurl.com/zbxycqy
Library of Congress: • Primary sources in the classroom, information on citing sources and copyright • Primary sources analysis tool • Self-paced, interactive modules for professional development	http://tinyurl.com/72swu4b http://tinyurl.com/ktsjuj http://tinyurl.com/yfxs8op
Internet Library for Librarians—Internet tools, libraries, ready reference	http://tinyurl.com/z78xgb7
Colorado libraries offer free training to suit all types of libraries on many subjects	http://tinyurl.com/ha8yt4u
Free and fee-based online courses through WebJunction	http://www.webjunction.org/
Virtual Web 2.0 Library	http://www.webology.org/2006/v3n2/a25.html
State of the MOOC 2016 report	http://tinyurl.com/jhlo2hv
Screencasting to engage learners and information about flipped classroom	http://tinyurl.com/zefxomw
Building a learning community	http://tinyurl.com/hnf5fss
Using social media to develop community in an online class	http://tinyurl.com/hgzyguy
"MOOCs and Beyond" video	https://vimeo.com/70811271

Key Points

As online teaching and learning continues to expand, new types of instruction will be introduced. MOOCs offer opportunities for librarians in all types of libraries.

- MOOCs, or massive open online courses, often free, provide instruction on diverse subjects to thousands of participants who do not have to have prerequisite knowledge.
- MOOCs were initially created by some of the most prestigious universities using special platforms for delivery. There are now hundreds of courses offered by many universities, K–12 schools, public libraries, and corporate entities.

- Three major MOOC platforms—EdX, Udacity, and Coursera—host MOOCs in academic, K–12, public, and special libraries.
- MOOC learners are diverse, external to an institution, and may have multiple goals (e.g., career, personal, self-improvement, and professional development).
- MOOCs have the potential to expand librarian roles in areas, such as copyright, technology assistance, instructional support, data storage and control, and open educational resources (OER).
- Open educational resources (OER), available without copyright restriction, are useful for online teaching, learning, and research.
- MOOCs benefit organizations, especially those with sites worldwide in different time zones.
- MOOCs for the workplace can be used for on-the-job training, to encourage learning, build bridges among colleagues, and encourage collaboration and innovation.

In chapters 1 to 10 you have reviewed and analyzed different forms of online teaching and learning. Chapter 11 offers a look at future trends and how librarians not only fit into the picture but can also become leaders in online teaching and learning.

⊚ Exercises

In chapter 10 you have reviewed another type of online teaching and learning, strategies, and especially materials, and applied them to create a portion of a MOOC. It's time to explore some of these new resources. Complete the following activities.

1. Explore at least three OER websites (e.g., OER Commons at https://www.oer commons.org/; Open Educational Consortium at http://www.oeconsortium.org/; and Open Source.com at https://opensource.com/education/15/12/best-educa tion-2015).
   a. At http://tinyurl.com/hbg4b35, complete the self-paced module Why OER? to get started using and creating OER. You should have an OER Commons account set up by the end of this first module.
   b. At http://tinyurl.com/hbg4b35, select several OER materials you can include in an online learning module in your subject area/grade level/workplace train-ing.
   c. What was a surprising find as you searched for materials?
   d. What frustrations have you encountered while searching for materials?
2. Read the article about MOOCs and libraries at http://tinyurl.com/zkfa4jd.
3. You have learned more about OER. Using a micro-lesson, create an introduction to a MOOC to teach researchers in an organization about OER.

⊚ References

Chant, Ian. 2013. "Opening Up: Next Steps for MOOCs and Libraries." *Library Journal*. Decem-ber 10. http://lj.libraryjournal.com/2013/12/digital-content/opening-up/#_.

Dalton, Michelle. 2013. "MOOCs and Libraries: The Good, the Bad and the Ugly." Libfocus. July 17. http://www.libfocus.com/2013/07/moocs-and-libraries-good-bad-and-ugly.html.

EDUCAUSE Library. 2013. "Massive Open Online Course (MOOC)." https://library.educause.edu/topics/teaching-and-learning/massive-open-online-course-mooc.

EDUCAUSE Review. 2013. "Libraries in the Time of MOOCs." November 4. http://er.educause.edu/articles/2013/11/libraries-in-the-time-of-moocs.

Fowler, Lauren. 2013. "Drawing the Blueprint as We Build: Setting Up a Library-based Copyright and Permission Service for MOOCs." *D-Lib Magazine* 19, no. 7–8 (July/August). http://www.dlib.org/dlib/july13/fowler/07fowler.html.

Jackson, Nancy Mann. 2013. "MOOCs Go to K12: Higher Ed Trend Expands to High Schools." *District Administration*. August. http://www.districtadministration.com/article/moocs-go-k12-higher-ed-trend-expands-high-schools.

Online Learning Consortium. 2015. "Online Report Card—Tracking Online Education in the United States, 2015." http://onlinelearningconsortium.org/read/online-report-card-track ing-online-education-united-states-2015/.

Roscorla, Tanya. 2016. "Online Learning Report Takes Snapshot of Student Enrollments." Center for Digital Education. February 9. http://www.centerdigitaled.com/higher-ed/Online-Learn ing-Report-Takes-Snapshot-of-Student-Enrollments.html.

Shah, Dhawal. 2015. "By the Numbers: MOOCs in 2015." Class Central. https://www.class-cen tral.com/report/moocs-2015-stats/.

Wright, Forrest. 2013. "What Do Librarians Need to Know about MOOCs?" *D-Lib Magazine*. 19, no. 3/4 (March/April). http://dlib.org/dlib/march13/wright/03wright.html.

⦿ Further Reading

Empson, Rip. 2013. "Georgia Tech Teams Up with Udacity, AT&T to Offer $6K Master's Degree in Computer Science, Entirely Online." TechCrunch.com. May 15. http://techcrunch.com/2013/05/15/top-10-engineering-college-teams-up-with-udacity-att-to-offer-6k-online-masters-degree-in-computer-science/.

Koller, Daphne. 2012. "MOOCs on the Move: How Coursera Is Disrupting the Traditional Classroom." *Knowledge@Wharton*. November 7. http://knowledge.wharton.upenn.edu/article/moocs-on-the-move-how-coursera-is-disrupting-the-traditional-classroom/.

New Media Consortium and EDUCAUSE Learning Initiative (ELI). 2015. *NMC Horizon Report > 2015 Higher Education Edition*. http://cdn.nmc.org/media/2015-nmc-horizon-report-HE-EN.pdf.

———. 2016. *NMC Horizon Report > 2016 Higher Education Edition*. http://www.nmc.org/publication/nmc-horizon-report-2016-higher-education-edition/.

Turner, Loren. 2015. "Case Point: How to Make a MOOC." *Computers in Libraries* 35, no. 7 (September). https://www.questia.com/magazine/1G1-429736745/case-in-point-how-to-make-a-mooc.

CHAPTER 11

What's Ahead in Online Teaching and Learning for Librarians?

> **IN THIS CHAPTER**

> ▷ Explaining some of the challenges for online teaching and learning

> ▷ Describing future trends for online teaching and learning and librarian roles

> ▷ Identifying possible actions librarians can take to prepare for the future of online teaching and learning

MANY OF THE CHAPTERS IN THIS BOOK have discussed current directions in online teaching and learning. They have also described new roles and responsibilities that librarians in academic, public, K–12, and special libraries have undertaken. Librarians' involvement with embedded librarianship, blended and flipped learning, on-demand instruction, OER, and asynchronous learning materials will no doubt continue in the foreseeable future. With higher education seeing funding decreases and as more students need to find ways to obtain degrees in more flexible ways, online teaching and learning will continue to grow.

What then will online teaching and learning look like ten years from now? What directions will it take? What challenges does it face? How does the library fit in and what can librarians do to prepare for future changes? This chapter looks first at a few challenges and then provides possible trends that will extend what's happening today and offer new directions for online teaching and learning.

⊚ Challenges Facing Online Teaching and Learning

Despite online teaching and learning becoming one of their core missions, institutions of higher education face a number of challenges ranging from financial issues to accreditation to compliance related to learners with special needs.

- With state funding decreasing, colleges and universities are facing financial problems. Moreover, universities now encounter greater competition because students have more online choices and methods to obtain a college degree. Institutions of higher education are looking to offer unique features to attract students and differentiate themselves from other programs.
- Federal authorization: Policy makers at the federal level are still skeptical about the benefits and value of an online education as compared to the traditional brick-and-mortar degree. Universities and companies that want to teach in more than one state must obtain authorization. The State Authorization Reciprocity Act (SARA, 2016) (http://www.nc-sara.org/state-actions/state-actions-regarding-sara) may smooth this process by enabling authorization in other states once the institution is approved in one state; however, not all states accept this authorization. Therefore, faculty must prove them wrong by continuing to show benefits that students obtain from their online coursework.
- The Americans with Disabilities Act of 1990 requires that online courses must be accessible to all students. This means videos, for example, require captions to meet the problems some students with special needs have. Again, this requires more time, effort, and funds.
- Another issue is authenticating student identity so students who register for courses are actually the ones who do the work and receive appropriate credit.
- Attitude is also a problem. Faculty resistance to change, as well as the need to educate them on new technology and methodology for online teaching, is one issue. Another relates to acceptance of online degrees by employers. Educating faculty and employers is necessary to meet this challenge.
- Technology is another challenge—education on new technology and also providing infrastructure and learning management system support and training is ongoing.

⊚ Trends in Online Teaching and Learning for Libraries

In the future, libraries will continue their teaching roles whether they are totally online courses, blended sessions, on demand, or a huge MOOC. Librarians may see some of the following trends as they take their place as partners in online teaching and learning. Some suggestions describe actions librarians can take to prepare to play an active role in the evolution of online teaching and learning:

1. **Trend:** Growing reliance on mobile as the "go-to" technology for content and social interaction will only increase with perhaps improved features, making it an integral part of online teaching and learning.

Action: When librarians create online learning modules or lessons, all forms of delivery should be included, ensuring that the content is accessible especially on mobile devices. Millennium-age users are bound to their phones and use it for communication, collaboration, and access to information. It is integral to all parts of their lives.

2. **Trend:** Video as a learning tool is also growing, and more educators are now able to create their own videos. Moreover, the visual millennium generation of students depends on video.

   Action: Whether creating instructional modules on information literacy topics, collaborating with faculty in a subject area, or training employees at a distance, librarians must analyze audience needs, characteristics, and purpose. They can then create videos personalized to that audience: (a) compile a list of videos already prepared, (b) learn how to use a video or screencasting tool, and (c) practice creating short one- to two-minute screencasts or videos to add to their personal libraries.

3. **Trend:** K–12 initiatives are incorporating online learning from totally online schools to online courses to online lessons or modules as part of face-to-face courses. Online courses are currently a mandated part of graduation requirements in many states.

   Action: To be prepared for K–12 online learning, librarians should review some of the research to see how other educators are incorporating online teaching and learning. They can take the lead at their own schools; talk to teachers about the curriculum, especially about topics where research is an important part; and suggest ways the library can support online learning through direct teaching and/or online learning materials.

4. **Trend:** With access to the Internet at any time from any place, lifelong learning is now easier to achieve. Whether it is a hobby like learning to paint, a career goal to obtain a promotion, finding tax help, or learning about a medical condition, everyone is using different devices to look for some kind of information.

   Action: Public libraries especially will be tasked with fulfilling these needs. Creating online learning objects—LibGuides, tutorials, and research guides, to name some that are accessible from home—will be important to this audience, especially the elderly and those with special needs. Special libraries who service employees worldwide will be called upon to create materials, such as how-to pieces, videos, and infographics, to train employees at their location and at their own pace. Reviewing current materials and learning about the latest technology and instructional design principles as outlined in this book will ready librarians for these new instructional tasks.

5. **Trend:** Blended and flipped online teaching and learning are becoming more popular in all academic venues. There will also be a need for part-time online learning to supplement the core brick-and-mortar instruction.

   Action: By collaborating with higher education faculty and K–12 teachers, librarians can become an integral part of blended teaching teams. To do so, they must get to know the curriculum, and approach educators they think will be receptive to a library partnership that can serve as a model to increase library instruction on the campus.

6. **Trend:** Student-centered, personalized, competency-based learning seems to be the wave of the future. Team collaboration is often necessary to create an online course focused on students' needs.

Action: Academic librarians must gain a deeper understanding of the academic courses they serve in order to become equal partners with faculty. Often faculty members have not been trained to teach; rather, they know their subject matter, and lecture is the standard. Creating online courses with a student-centered approach takes knowledge of pedagogy, instructional design, new technology, and collaboration and communication in the online environment. Teamwork is necessary. Librarians need to team up with faculty and other members, such as instructional designers and tech experts. They will then know the courses where they can create assignments that include aspects of information literacy and where students might need assistance with materials or micro-learning lessons.

7. **Trend:** MOOCs have provided an online teaching and learning alternative, and, despite problems to work out, the numbers of courses and students are still increasing. While these free, massive, open courses may change, the concept is still a viable one to involve librarians.

   Action: Librarians have skills they can offer and roles to play in all aspects of MOOCs from creating MOOCs to teach information literacy skills, to sorting out issues related to copyright, to assisting faculty who create MOOCs in their online forums, to supplying learning commons where participants can gather. Librarians must, however, be prepared to participate at the beginning in MOOCs on campus so they can provide leadership to faculty and administration. They must become knowledgeable about MOOCs, keep up with ongoing developments, and promote them within their communities. Taking a MOOC themselves is a first step.

8. **Trend:** In order to engage learners, interactive teaching and learning is more important online than in a face-to-face classroom.

   Action: Currently, librarians work closely face-to-face with their clientele—students, employees, and patrons—to improve their skills, teach content, and facilitate learning. They are accustomed to collaborating with learners in groups and one-on-one. Who better to facilitate discussion in online discussion forums or through social media as part of online classes? They also understand the technology so they can help users who struggle at the start of a course, and provide instruction on topics including plagiarism, copyright, OER, and evaluating websites or sources, to name a few benefits. Engaging as a team at the beginning of the process to map out instructional strategies for online teaching and learning is a good place to begin.

9. **Trend:** Open access (OA) and open educational resources (OER) are increasingly available worldwide. This trend seems one that will only proliferate in the future. Because dealing with copyright is already an important part of the librarian's role, duties related to open access is a natural step for librarians.

   Action: Open educational resources will expand the duties of librarians as they relate to online teaching and learning. Although OER provide many benefits, there will be challenges. Librarians may be called upon to work with faculty, students, and administrators to sort out how to deal with copyright in print and multimedia sources, find authoritative OER sources for student and faculty research, deal with database publishers, and even compile OER for libraries. They must be prepared to recommend these alternative sources, perhaps help to modify them for specific audiences, show students how to evaluate them, and more.

10. **Trend:** Data analytics are being used more and more to inform teaching and learning and other administrative decisions. They are a part of LMS, programs, on the web, and more.

    Action: Programs for collecting and analyzing data are becoming more sophisticated. It is up to librarians to become familiar with the programs to be able to use the data to enhance teaching and learning. By reviewing data, they can personalize and adapt content and teaching practices and better allocate resources to the learner. Libraries can also store and curate the data just as they have other library materials over the years.

11. **Trend:** New types of learning spaces are expanding in libraries. These learning commons offer a center for teaching and learning for online users.

    Action: As more and more facility changes occur in libraries, it is up to librarians to set up learning commons to accommodate the learning needs of online students who need comfortable places to learn with a team of classmates on online projects, explore asynchronous materials, or meet with the facilitator of an online course. Librarians who work together to create this new space have opportunities to foster conditions for online learning. In public libraries, for example, online learners may access their instruction in the library, so the learning commons becomes an integral part of the online course.

Online learning has become almost mainstream (Roscorla, 2015). More institutions are offering a mixture of face-to-face, blended, and online classes to students who live on campus or on the other side of the world. Special libraries train employees, customers, and colleagues online. K–12 librarians work with teachers in flipped classes to teach information literacy skills to their students. And, public libraries create asynchronous learning materials for their patrons to access outside the library or in the library's learning commons. Even face-to-face classes have online components so that libraries have opportunities to provide outreach and instruction to students wherever they are and for whatever the purpose. Table 11.1 provides additional resources to keep librarians abreast of new innovations as they plan for the future of online teaching and learning.

Table 11.1. Additional Resources for Chapter 11

DESCRIPTION	URLS
Faculty Focus—free resources and current articles on teaching and learning in higher ed	http://www.facultyfocus.com/ http://www.facultyfocus.com/topic/articles/online-education/
Education Dive—focused on happenings in K–12, including online	http://www.educationdive.com/
Learning Revolution Project—free online conferences, articles, communities for classroom 2.0, library 2.0, and more about education	http://learningrevolution.com/
Free TED Talks—more than 2,000 talks	https://www.ted.com/talks
Center for the Future of Libraries	https://americanlibrariesmagazine.org/tag/center-for-the-future-of-libraries/
eLMS with enhanced teaching and learning features	https://elearningindustry.com/lms-old-news-enter-era-elms
Online Learning Insights blog	https://onlinelearninginsights.wordpress.com/

⊚ Key Points

Online learning has yet to reach its full potential. Librarians must embrace the important changes taking place in online teaching and learning. They may need to expand their skills, embrace pedagogy, increase their technological knowledge, learn more about instructional design, and reach out to colleagues, employees, and patrons who have information needs. It may require that they, too, participate as learners in online learning. Figure 11.1 illustrates what Jane Birks and Liz Oesleby (2003) state in their article "Mere Mortals Need Not Apply": "What seems superhuman to you is normal to us."

Figure 11.1. Superheroes. *Supergirl by Jessie St. Amand, Flickr. Used with permission, Creative Commons*

Whatever is necessary, however, librarians have always been up to the task. The next ten years will see librarians, no matter what library clientele they serve, become pillars of online teaching and learning.

⊚ References

Birks, Jane, and Liz Oesleby. 2003. "Mere Mortals Need Not Apply." In *Expectations of Librarians in the 21st Century*, edited by Karl Bridges, 33–36. Westport, CT: Greenwood.

Roscorla, Tanya. 2015. "Despite Challenges, Online Learning Is on a Continuous Vertical Climb." Center for Digital Education. November 15. http://www.centerdigitaled.com/higher-ed/De spite-Challenges-Online-Learning-Is-on-a-Continuous-Vertical-Climb.html.

SARA (State Authorization Reciprocity Agreement). 2016. State Authorization Reciprocity Agreement. Accessed June 15. http://www.mhec.org/sara.

Index

elearning, 39. *See also* embedded online course

embedded librarian, 24, 88, 123, 147; characteristics, 127; roles, 128; skills, 127; tips, 134–35. *See also* embedded librarianship

embedded librarianship, 124–26. *See also* embedded librarian; embedded online course

embedded online course, 135–47. *See also* embedded librarianship

evaluation, 20, 111, 146, 162, 170, 172, 194, 219. *See also* instructional design, evaluation step, implementation

experientialist, 4, 13

Facebook. *See* social media

face-to-face learning, 12

fair use, 94–95, 187, 208. *See also* self-paced materials

flipped instruction, 88, 175–77, 180–81, 186–87, 193, 196, 200, 208

flipped learning, 8–9, 24, 88, 156, 175–202, 206, 208, 210, 212, 229, 231, 233; benefits, 177–78; challenges, 178; characteristics, 179; factors, 195; instruction, 175. *See also* flipped instruction

Gagné, Robert, 14, 17, 19, 20–23, 31, 52, 56, 59, 66–68, 155

Giesecki, Joan, 154

goals, 39, 41–43, 46–47, 101, 103, 114, 138, 161, 187, 218

Google, 162, 165, 169–71

Google Hangouts, 11. *See also* social media

Google Scholar, 95, 142, 160, 162, 170–72

graphic organizers, 78–79. *See also* mind map

graphics, 60–65

humanist, 4, 13

implementation. *See* instructional design

infographics, 61

information literacy, 1, 24, 30, 33–34, 43, 52, 94–95, 123–24, 128–29, 133, 136, 138–39, 142–46, 152–56, 159–63, 179, 181–82, 200, 202, 204, 208–10, 220–23, 230–32; components, 221; sources, 222

instructional design, 84, 152; best practices, 25–26; checklist, 59; definitions, 17; elements, 60–65; evaluation step, implementation, 70; interaction, 65; principles, 65; skills, 24–25; steps, 26–27, 218; theories. *See* ADDIE; Gagné, Robert; tips, 166. *See also* design plan

interactivity or interactive learning, 139, 143, 147, 164, 176, 181–82, 188, 207, 211, 232

Internet searching. *See* evaluation

Ithaka S+R Survey, 152

job search (example), 97–98, 101–2, 112, 119–20

K–12 libraries, 10, 24, 30–31, 72, 83, 87, 91, 119, 130–34, 147, 151–57, 160, 175, 180, 183–84, 196, 199, 206, 212, 231, 233, 235

keywords, 43, 56, 95, 128, 138, 144–46, 165, 181

Khan Academy, 175

Kirkpatrick, Donald, 20, 28, 30. *See also* evaluation

Knowles, Malcolm, 4, 5, 13

Kolb, David, 4

Krathwohl, David, 22, 67. *See also* Bloom's Taxonomy

learning commons, 157, 174, 204, 211, 232

learning content management system (LCMS). *See* management systems

learning management systems (LMS), 8, 11, 70–71, 138–40, 182, 184, 189

learning strategies, 176, 193–94, 219, 226

LMS. *See* learning management systems

Mager, Robert, 40, 49

management systems, 70–73; examples, 72; features, 71–72, 83; LMS, 111, 138–39, 155, 158, 166

massive open online course (MOOC), 9, 88, 200, 203, 213–15, 224, 226; characteristics, 207; cMOOC (connectivist), 205; definition, 204–5; history, 206; roles, 208; tips, 223; types, 206, 209, 211–13, 225, 227; xMOOC, 205

micro-learning lessons, 143–44, 214, 218, 220–23

mind map, 13, 22, 64, 187, 195, 217. *See also* concept map

Mitre Corporation, 134

mobile, 219, 230

Moodle, 25, 58, 70, 72, 90, 138. *See also* learning management systems

multimedia, 55, 58–60, 90, 117, 140, 149, 155–56, 161, 206–7, 209, 232

Multimedia Educational Resource for Learning and Online Teaching (MERLOT), 156. *See also* technology

needs analysis, 36–37, 98, 136–37, 216. *See also* assessment

netiquette, 139, 141, 143

objectives, 39–47, 101, 103–4, 114–15, 138, 161, 163, 165, 167, 171, 187, 196, 218–20

online instruction. *See* online learning

online learning, 9–12, 214; audience traits, 10–11; learner traits, 11. *See also* elearning

online resources, 8

online teaching, 87; asynchronous, 87, 90; challenges, 1–3, 6, 10, 12–13, 22, 85, 88, 157, 177–78, 210, 212, 229–30, 232, 234; on-demand, 90; self-paced, 90; synchronous, 87, 89–90

open educational resources (OER or OA), 9, 55, 65–66, 156, 179, 187, 205, 209, 218–19, 232

outcomes, 39, 42, 43, 45–47, 101, 138, 161, 187, 196–97, 218, 220

paraphrasing, 158

pedagogy, 4–5, 13

peer review, 165

personalized learning, 10, 133, 177–80, 213

Pew Internet study, 161–62, 165

Piaget, Jean, 4

plagiarism, 42, 126, 130, 189, 196–201, 232. *See also* copyright

planning, 39, 42

posting, 139–41, 146–47, 165, 199. *See also* interactivity; discussion forum

PowerPoint, 155, 187

presentation tools, 155, 187

public libraries, 23–32, 212

reflection, 82–83, 146, 182, 184

resumes, 98–111; chronological, 107; cover letter, 98–99, 101, 108, 112–16, 118–19; electronic, 116; formatting, 103, 110; functional, 107

Rogers, 4

rubrics, 77–78, 80–81, 108–9, 114, 117, 182

Schumaker, David, 124–25. *See also* embedded librarianship

screencasts, 94–95, 224

screenshot, 221

search terms, 128–29, 143–46, 160–62, 164–66, 169, 170–71. *See* keywords

self-paced materials, 93–94

Shank, John, 152

Sinclair, Bryan, 157

Skinner, B. F., 4

Skype. *See* social media

social interaction, 8

social media, 8, 11, 57–58, 97, 107, 127, 140, 155, 207, 218

special libraries, 129, 134, 213–14, 231

Special Libraries Association (SLA), 124

staff development, 92. *See also* asynchronous learning

state libraries, 93; Baltimore County Public Library, 92, 211. *See also* asynchronous learning; Public Library Association, 92; Turning the Page, 91–92. *See also* online courses, on-demand

storyboards, 100, 102, 112, 137, 139, 220

Talley, Mary, 124, 125. *See also* embedded librarianship

technology, 25, 155–56, 187–89, 208–9. *See also* LMS; CMS; Web 2.0

Technology Integration Matrix (TIM), 156

Udacity. *See* MOOC

University of Central Florida (UCF) library, 130, 131

videos, 156, 175, 184–85, 187, 197, 198, 220–22, 232; interactive, 188–93. *See also* screencasts

warm-up exercises, 163

Web 2.0, 22, 155

About the Author

Beverley E. Crane has an EdD in instructional technology/design, providing a background, both theoretical and practical, in designing instructional materials of all kinds and using technology as a part of learning—both important to online learning. Her BA and MEd are in education, forming the basis of her training to develop and write instructional materials. She has also taught both face-to-face and online courses at three universities as well as middle school and high school to students, other educators, and librarians in all types of libraries.

In addition, working for Dialog and ProQuest, Beverley spent more than twenty years designing face-to-face and online webinars, as well as online materials, including one-page how-to guides, short instructional videos, and other information to deliver concise training using images, figures, and text to librarians, educators, and the business community.

Her six books—*Teaching with the Internet, Internet Workshops: 10 Ready-to-Go Workshops for K–12 Educators, Using Web 2.0 Tools in the K–12 Classroom, Using Web 2.0 and Social Networking Tools in the K–12 Classroom, How to Teach: A Practical Guide for Librarians* (Rowman & Littlefield, 2013), and *Infographics: A Practical Guide for Librarians* (Rowman & Littlefield, 2015)—are written to present similar information to educators and librarians as well. A focus of her books has been to illustrate ways to use technology to enhance teaching and learning.